Strategy and Structure

Strategy and Structure

SHORT READINGS FOR COMPOSITION

Second Edition

William J. Kelly

Bristol Community College

Allyn and Bacon

Boston   London   Toronto   Sydney   Tokyo   Singapore

Vice President, Humanities: Joseph Opiela
Series Editorial Assistant: Rebecca Ritchey
Executive Marketing Manager: Lisa Kimball
Composition and Prepress Buyer: Linda Cox
Editorial-Production Service: Omegatype Typography, Inc.
Manufacturing Buyer: Suzanne Lareau
Cover Administrator: Jenny Hart
Production Editor: Christopher H. Rawlings
Electronic Composition: Omegatype Typography, Inc.

Copyright © 1999, 1996 by Allyn & Bacon
A Viacom Company
160 Gould Street
Needham Heights, Mass. 02194

Internet: www.abacon.com
America Online: Keyword: College Online

Library of Congress Cataloging-in-Publication Data
Strategy and structure: short readings for composition / [edited by]
William J. Kelly. — 2nd ed.
    p.   cm.
    Includes index.
    ISBN 0-205-28602-X
    1. College readers.   2. English language — Rhetoric.   I. Kelly,
William J. (William Jude)
PE1417.S7685   1999
808'.0427 — dc21   98-3727
                                                         CIP

Credits start on page 379, which constitutes an extension of the copyright page.

Printed in the United States of America
10 9 8 7 6 5 4 3 2 1   03 02 01 00 99 98

To my children,
Nicole Catherine Kelly and Jacqueline Michelle Kelly:
Your gifts—your intelligence, your compassion, your humor,
your capacity for life and love—day after day amaze and delight
me. I couldn't love you more.

Contents

Thematic Contents

Ethics

Family and Childhood

Health, Medicine, and Genetics

Human Behavior

Humor

Women and Men

Preface

If you want to write better, read more.

This idea is certainly not original; American statesman Benjamin Franklin, among others, acknowledged that what he had read in his youth influenced the style of his own writing. In fact, if people did nothing more then derive pleasure from an essay and imitate the writer in their own writings, their essays would no doubt be better.

But effectively learning from reading goes far beyond mere appreciation of the quality of the writing and imitation of the writer's mastery in expressing the message. Improving writing through reading means recognizing the significance of an essay and then responding in some way to it. *Strategy and Structure* is designed to help your students develop these skills. It presents a wide range of outstanding writing to be enjoyed, discussed, and analyzed, and it provides guidelines that will help your students use what they've discovered to achieve their own mastery of writing.

The Arrangement of Text

Strategy and Structure is arranged to make it easier to master writing. The first two chapters focus on critical reading and the writing process. Chapter 1, "Writer as Reader," shows students how to recognize the strategies and techniques a writer has used so that they will be prepared to use these strategies and techniques themselves. It also features an annotated essay that demonstrates the process that should be followed. Then Chapter 2, "Working through the Writing Process," walks students through the various stages of the writing process. Both chapters also introduce the concept of meeting the needs of the reader by recognizing the important relationships between *aim* (the purpose) and *form* (the rhetorical modes) in an essay.

The remaining nine chapters contain thirty-six writings, arranged on the basis of the modes and covering a wide variety of subjects, many embodying multicultural experiences. The collection contains works by such outstanding writers as Ellen Goodman, Langston Hughes, Joan Didion, and Richard Rodriguez, among others. This collection ensures that your students will face challenging, stimulating readings chapter after chapter.

The chapters themselves are laid out so that your students begin the course by writing from their own background and experiences, and then they gradually proceed to writing about different aspects of the world around them. Your students will thus face different writing challenges throughout the semester.

An important feature of *Strategy and Structure* is that the subject of Chapter 11, argument, is presented not as a mode but as an *aim*. This method of presentation makes perfect sense. Depending on the subject and situation, writers use a variety of modes to persuade the reader of the validity of their standpoints.

The Presentation of the Readings

Chapters 3–10 all follow the same pattern. First the mode is briefly discussed and explained, and then four essays dominated by that mode are presented. The first essay in each chapter is annotated to show how the writer has taken advantage of the mode.

The remaining three essays in each chapter are followed by four sets of questions, each focusing on a different aspect of the piece of writing. The questions are generally open-ended to allow a range of answers, always a great lead-in to spirited class discussions. *Understanding the Significance* deals with basic comprehension of the selection. *Discovering the Writer's Purpose* concentrates on the writer's message. *Examining the Writer's Method* covers matters of structure and arrangement. And *Considering Style and Language* emphasizes particular stylistic devices used and examines the meanings of key words from the selections.

Each essay is also followed by a section titled *Your Turn: Responding to the Subject,* consisting of two possible writing assignments stemming from or reacting to the essay. Then, at the end of each chapter, fifteen additional topics for development are presented. Chapter 11 follows the same pattern as Chapters 3–10 except that in the final chapter, *aim* rather than *mode* is the focus. Thus, chapter after chapter your students will find ample opportunities to analyze successful writing and face a broad range of possibilities for creating successful writing of their own.

New in this Edition

The second edition of *Strategy and Structure* features a number of significant changes. For example, the prewriting examples as well a number of the sample paragraphs are new. In addition, several new essays have been added, including works on rating television shows by *New York Times* columnist Frank Rich; on children and natural ability by syndicated columnist Thomas Sowell; on the real significance and effect of homelessness by Pulitzer-Prize winning writer Anna Quindlen; on accuracy in the media by Steven A. Holmes; on shoes and the stories they have to tell by Diane Riva; on the process responsible for fall's dazzling display of color by Diane Ackerman; on prejudice and police brutality by Paul F. Fletcher; and on different perceptions people have about the opposite sex by Steven Doloff.

Besides these new essays, an exciting, innovative feature called *Practical Application* has been added to Chapters 3–11. These entertaining and engaging assignments feature writing scenarios grounded in real-world writing. Each calls for a specific application of the writing technique discussed in that particular chapter, with guidelines provided about *approach* and *format.* In some cases, a memorandum or op-ed piece is called for and in others, a short report or position paper. Each assignment also includes a model prepared by a student writer in response to a similar scenario with similar guidelines. Therefore, each of these chapters contains two distinctively different possibilities to practice and apply the principles addressed in that chapter, which translates into many interesting opportunities to develop a mastery of writing.

ACKNOWLEDGMENTS

I would like to thank a number of people for their assistance and support as I revised *Strategy and Structure*. First, I'd like to thank John M. Lannon, University of Massachusetts, Dartmouth, and Robert A. Schwegler, University of Rhode Island. I'm grateful for the expertise they've shared with me, but I'm even more grateful for their friendship. The following skilled professionals who reviewed *Strategy and Structure* deserve thanks as well; their comments and suggestions helped me shape this second edition: Linda Eanes Jefferson, Richard Bland College of the College of William and Mary; Joseph McSweeney, Rhode Island College; and Greta Stroope, Delta College.

I would also like to thank a number of my colleagues at Bristol Community College for their continued encouragement and support, especially Dan Avedikian, Raymond Butts, David Feeney, Paul F. Fletcher, Peter Griffin, Cynthia Hahn, Deborah Lawton, and Jerry LePage. Their kind words and interest in my work mean a great deal to me. Special thanks are due Ruth Sullivan and Paula Bartolo of BCC's Learning Resources Center for their help with several readings.

I would also like to thank the talented students who created the models for the various *Practical Application* assignments. They include Edward Angell, Christine Baker, Allen E. Brickhill, Jessica A. Fletcher, Steven M. Haugh, and Therese C. MacKinnon, Bristol Community College; Timothy Matos, University of Massachusetts, Amherst; and Nicole C. Kelly, Rhode Island College. Thanks also to Lyn Metivier, Bristol Community College, whose essay, "The Reading Disorder," is featured in the first chapter.

A number of people at Allyn and Bacon deserve my thanks as well. Rebecca Ritchey, Editorial Assistant, Humanities, shepherded the text through the initial stages of production. She then placed it in the capable hands of Kathy Olson at Omegatype Typography, who made the finished product look so good, and Executive Marketing Manager Lisa Kimball, who used her considerable talents to make people aware of the text's unique features. But most of all, I'd like to thank Joseph Opiela, Vice President, Editor in Chief, Humanities. He is a true professional, and his vision and enthusiasm continue to influence me. I am delighted to have had this chance to work under his direction again.

As always, I owe the most to my family. I'd like to thank my parents, Mary Kelly and the late Edward F. Kelly, for their unfailing love and support. They provided me with a foundation to build the rest of my life on, and that's a debt I could never repay. I would also like to thank my in-laws, Flo and Leo Nadeau, who welcomed me into their home and made me a part of their family. Their love and their interest in my work means so much to me.

I would also like to offer special thanks to my children, Jacqueline and Nicole. They are what every parent dreams of— bright, talented, compassionate, beautiful, funny. Day after day they inspire me to be just like them when I grow up.

But nobody deserves my thanks more than my wife, Michelle Nadeau Kelly. More than twenty-seven years after we first met, I'm still dazzled by her, by her intelligence and beauty, by her enthusiasm for life and learning, by her dedication to her family and her profession, by her brilliant insight into people. My life is rich, and my work possible, because of her.

Strategy and Structure

1

Writer as Reader

Developing Your Abilities

The best way to improve your writing is to write. There is no substitute for sitting down and developing, shaping, and refining an idea. No class can teach you what it is to write. You simply have to do it.

But there are a number of strategies that can help you as you hone your writing skills. Taking a writing class is of course one of them. And another is examining how other writers have successfully developed an essay. The rationale behind this method is simple: by analyzing how another writer has handled a topic, you will be prepared to follow a similar strategy should the situation arise. The more writing strategies you become familiar with, the better prepared you'll be to approach a topic in a variety of ways.

In short, you need to develop your *critical reading skills,* that is, your ability to note not just what the writers say but what they mean and how they've expressed it. You accomplish all of this by

- identifying *the writer's purpose;*
- involving yourself in *active reading;* and
- focusing on *the writer's approach.*

1

THE WRITER'S PURPOSE

What's the point here? That's the implied question that all readers have. The answer, in general terms, is that every piece of writing fulfills some purpose or aim: to inform, entertain, or persuade. Although a piece of writing may fulfill more than one of these purposes, chances are that one aim will dominate.

For example, with an essay maintaining that the ever-increasing number of patients seeking cosmetic surgery is proof that American society is too concerned with personal appearance, the primary purpose would be to persuade. But if the paper focused on another aspect of the same subject, such as describing one of these surgical procedures, the primary intent would be to inform. And if the essay discussed the dramatic improvement in self-esteem enjoyed by one of the patients, the primary intent would be to entertain.

Generally speaking, the writer's purpose will appear in the first few paragraphs; the title often gives a hint, too. Therefore, as you begin reading, pay close attention to the opening. After reading through the first few paragraphs, stop and write a brief note to yourself in the margin or on a separate sheet of paper identifying the main idea. If, as you continue to read, you come across examples or details that show that your original interpretation was incorrect, simply go back to the beginning and reread so that you can gain a full and accurate sense of the writer's purpose.

ACTIVE READING

What's going on between the lines? When you read strictly for pleasure, you generally move quickly, focusing on the overall effect of the piece. You don't necessarily consider the writer's motives, choice of language, construction, and so forth. Your goal is to take pleasure from the writing without investigating it.

Active reading is different. Active reading, as the name suggests, means reacting to and interacting with the writing; it means reading the piece several times, examining it in detail each time through. As a result, you will still derive pleasure, but you will also understand why the essay has that overall effect.

Active reading involves establishing a context, identifying the structure, focusing on key ideas, and responding to the material.

Establishing a context.   What's going on? Who is involved? When did it happen? Where? How? Why? These are the questions that news stories generally answer in their opening sentence. The answers to these questions establish a *context,* a setting or grounding, for the reader. As you read, use these kinds of questions to identify those details and examples that represent the context of the essay.

Identifying the structure.   How is the writing set up? In most cases, the essays you examine will be composed of three parts: *introduction, body,* and *conclusion.* The introduction, often a single paragraph, sets forth the main idea and provides direction for the reader; the body is the series of paragraphs that contains the story or concept the writer is presenting; and the conclusion, also often a single paragraph, brings the paper to some logical close through a restatement of the main idea or an explanation of the significance of what you have just read.

As you read, note where one section begins and the next ends. Then, look at each part separately. In the introduction, identify the *thesis,* the writer's main idea. In the body, highlight the examples of details that best support or explain that idea. And, in the conclusion, note any restatement of the main point or emphasis of some other point of view expressed in the body.

Focusing on key ideas.   What support does the writer offer? To understand a writer's point fully, you need to focus on the *key ideas* used to make that point. Therefore, as you read, look for cue words such as *important, vital, crucial,* and so forth, as well as specific names, dates, distances, amounts, conditions, statistics, and concrete details. Also try to identify the main or *topic sentences* of the various paragraphs in the essay. Generally speaking, a topic sentence represents the primary or dominant idea of the paragraph. The other sentences provide details and examples intended to illustrate or support this idea.

Responding to the material. What do you think of the piece? Why? Your answer to these two questions will help you greatly in understanding the writing you are evaluating. Writing is an extension of thinking. As you articulate your reaction to the piece, you will also be making sense of it. You might even write two reactions, one after you complete your first reading and the other after your more thorough readings. You'll no doubt discover some elements or aspects in the second critique that you missed in the first. Overall, you will gain a greater understanding of the piece.

THE WRITER'S APPROACH

How did the writer do that? In addition to figuring out what the writer means, it's also important to figure out what techniques and strategies the writer has used to make that point. How has the writer begun the paper? Developed it? Brought it to a close?

This book focuses on writing from the standpoint of types or patterns of writing known as the *rhetorical modes: narration* (Chapter 3); *description* (Chapter 4); *example* (Chapter 5); *process* (Chapter 6); *definition* (Chapter 7); *comparison and contrast* (Chapter 8); *cause and effect* (Chapter 9); and *division and classification* (Chapter 10). When you examine a piece of writing, note how the writer has combined these types or patterns in the essay.

But more than anything else, ask yourself this question: what stands out — what element or aspect catches your eye, causes you to stop, makes you connect with the point being made? Perhaps it's the way the writer opens the essay — or closes it. Perhaps it's the writer's humor or reverence or passion. Perhaps it's a striking image or a poignant scene. Regardless of what it is, that particular element or aspect helped to make that writing successful, so it is worth your effort to figure out what it was so that you will be able to use a similar approach in your own writing.

Remember as you read that a good piece of writing touches the reader. When you read, identify what the writer has done to make this happen. The better able you are to find out how a writer has reached you, the better prepared you'll be to reach your own reader.

The Process Illustrated

In the following writing, "The Reading Disorder," student Lyn Metivier discusses how her love of reading has affected her life. The selection has been annotated to show you how to make the critical reading process work for you.

The Reading Disorder

Purpose: She explains, in a lighthearted way, her reading "problem" — her great love of reading.

Introduction: Her use of personal anecdote draws the reader in.

Key ideas: These are emotions she associates with reading.

1 As I turn the last few pages of *Memnoch the Devil*, the final book in Anne Rice's *Vampire Chronicles*, I am both <u>saddened and relieved</u>. I know that when <u>I finish</u> this book, all the characters I have thought about constantly over the last few weeks will be dead to me. Lestat, with whom I have fallen in love will no longer exist, and <u>that familiar feeling of melancholy</u> will come over me once again.

2 At the same time, however, I am also <u>relieved</u>. The constant haze I have <u>been in</u> since first starting these books will lift, and I can get back to my daily routine and real life. After the <u>mild depression</u> passes, I will have a <u>surge of</u> energy as I emerge back into reality. I will wait several months before attempting another book.

Thesis: The use of anecdote sets the reader up for her "disorder."

I am an obsessive, compulsive 3 reader. I don't know that there has ever been any documentation of such a disorder, nor have I looked. I have simply given myself this name because of the irrational way I behave when I am involved in a book.

Key detail: This backs up her point about her "obsession."

For days *Memnoch The Devil*, the 4 hardcover because I could not wait for the paperback, had been sitting on the nightstand next to my bed. It taunted me like an unopened bottle of vodka within the grasp of a recovering alcoholic. I dared not open it yet; preparations had to be made.

Note tone: She pokes fun at herself.

Body: These episodes all illustrate or support her main idea, that she has a "disorder" that affects her life.

Understand that when I read a 5 book, I read it cover to cover in as few sittings as are physically possible. This is not a conscious decision. Once I open a book and begin reading, my disorder takes over, and I become so involved in the story that everything else around me ceases to exist. The laundry piles up, the beds don't get made, and the dirty dishes are left to pile up in the sink. Suppers usually consist of something delivered from a local fast food or Chinese restaurant. Finishing the book is my only priority.

Context: The details demonstrate how her "disorder" affects her life.

Great details, key ideas: All are showing the effects of her "illness."

I didn't know it then, but this dis- 6 ruptive way of reading started with the very first novel I ever picked up. I was eleven years old and complaining to my mother that I was "booored." She suggested, as she always did, that I go read a book. For some reason, after giving her the usual "yeah right, Ma" face, I took her advice and went upstairs. Then I began looking through her collection of best-sellers and hardcover

Nice tone!

She uses narration and cause and effect to explain the origin of disorder.

classics. My mother's taste in books always amazed me; she could go from a Stephen King novel to *The History of England,* without missing a beat. Every other week, something new was arriving from the Doubleday Book Club.

Then I found it. *Rich Man Poor Man* was wedged between *Lady Chatterly's Lover* and a well-worn copy of *The Exorcist.* After standing there for a few minutes skimming the first chapter, I shut myself in the room I shared with two of my sisters and started to read.

I emerged two days later, unshowered, tired, and completely oblivious to anything that may have occurred that weekend. I had only stopped reading to eat, sleep, or perform bodily functions; I slept only because my eyes refused to stay open. I was beaming with excitement at my discovery. So this is what my mother was talking about. I couldn't wait to open my next book.

When I was a teenager, this method of reading was far from a problem. Spending an entire weekend in my room, with a book, I was a teenager's parent's dream. I had no desire to go to the mall or the movies, and even a phone call from my best friend was an unwelcome interruption. I was deep in the world of *Little Women* and *The Diary of Anne Frank.* At this point, only my already weak social life was suffering.

However, after I got married and started my family, this was no longer the case. Forgetting the ramifications of my little habit, I would often pick up a book whenever I had a free hour in the morning. Lying across my bed

The specific book titles are good details.

Body continues.

Key ideas: Her details emphasize how affected she is by her disorder.

Good use of narration to show the extent of her "disability."

Key ideas: She shows the effect of the disability by using specific titles.

Nice use of narration to show how her "problem" resurfaces.

7

8

9

10

or curled up on the couch, I would tell myself that I had only one hour.

The next thing I knew, it was supper **11** time and I was still in the clothes I had worn to bed the night before. Swollen remnants of Lucky Charms would be stuck to the morning's cereal bowls, and the shopping list was untouched and still stuck to the refrigerator door, under the rubber chocolate chip cookie magnet. A beautiful day would have flown by, and I hadn't even noticed. My mind was inside that book.

Because of my habit, the times **12** when I did have to stop reading, either to pick the kids up from school, get ready for work, or just be a mom, I was almost always cranky and intolerant. I would sometimes snap at the kids if they took too long eating their dinner or taking a bath, and I would often skip pages when reading them a bedtime story. I rushed impatiently through tasks with an irrational feeling that I was missing something while the book was closed.

Once, I even went so far as to call **13** in sick to work because I was so close to finishing the book I was reading that I couldn't bear to work for the next eight hours not knowing how it was going to end. I was out of control. It had never occurred to me that this innocent passion of mine would turn out to be such a disruption to my life.

At first, realizing that I could no **14** longer function this way, I just decided to stop reading altogether. The daily newspaper was the only thing I allowed myself. I avoided the library, the

Nice transition

Great description with good specific details!

Wonderful phrase

Key ideas: This shows the effects when she didn't "feed her habit" — same playful tone, comparing her love of reading to a real addiction.

Body continues

Excellent specific example!

Key idea: She is "powerless."

Key Idea: Desperation leads her to avoid her "drug" completely.

bookstores, and the paperback section of the supermarket, hoping this would curb my cravings for a new book. I wouldn't discuss the latest books with my mother or brother, and I asked them to stop giving me the ones they had just finished. This method worked somewhat; I didn't pick up any new books. I just reread everything I already had at home.

Finally, I decided to come up with some kind of compromise. I loved reading and didn't want to give it up, but I hated myself and the way I behaved as a result. I needed to figure out a way to balance my everyday life with my favorite pastime.

Unfortunately, and every obsessed person would agree, this was easier said than done. As soon as I picked up the next book, the compulsion started again. I read it completely, with little regard for any of my other responsibilities. My revelation of the problem hadn't, however, solved the problem.

Then one day it dawned on me. I was finishing Stephen King's *The Stand* for the third time when I realized something: the only time I do have control is when I'm not actually in the middle of reading something. Once I finish a book, I can take as much time as I want before picking up another one. With this in mind, I was ready for "recovery."

Now, I no longer just pick up a book and begin reading. I have some specific guidelines set for when I find something that beckons me. I found that summertime works the best. My

Marginal notes:

Body continues

Key idea: Like an addict, she finds a way to get a "fix" — repeats main idea.

She uses good technique to connect with her reader.

Good: Reiteration of main idea

Key idea: She recognizes the root cause and the solution.

Body continues

Paragraph numbers: 15, 16, 17, 18

schedule is less demanding then, and the longer days give me more time to work with.

My routine usually starts with getting up early in the morning, immediately doing the dishes and laundry, and quickly cleaning the house. I go to the grocery store to make sure there is enough food for the next few days and I'll often make dinners in the crockpot, because the average meal cooked this way takes eight hours and requires no supervision. Then I find something to keep the kids busy for a while. I'll either pick up a movie or video game or plan a project they can do without my help. I am not a beach person, but because it means being able to read without feeling guilty, I'm out the door with sunscreen in hand at the mere mention of the word.   19

Now, I realize I'm not completely cured and probably never will be, but at least I'm no longer dysfunctionally literate. And, although my "to read" list grows daily, the temptation to relinquish all my friends, family, and worldly goods in exchange for residence in a well-lit, book-lined cave no longer tortures me — not much, anyway.   20

She uses process well to explain how she now deals with her "disability."

She makes good use of specific details concerning her "management" of her "problem."

Conclusion: She restates her main point.

Good tone: She ends on a light note.

Response: I like this essay! She does a wonderful job explaining how reading makes her feel. Her tone is great — she is "addicted" to reading; I like how she calls herself an "obsessive, compulsive reader." I also like how she talks about what happens when she reads (laundry and dishes pile up, take-out food instead of the supper she had planned, calling in sick to work) and how she feels when she doesn't read ("cranky and intolerant," "snap at the kids," etc.). I love to read, so I know exactly what she means!

Exercises

1. Clearly, Lyn Metivier's primary purpose in "The Reading Disorder" is to entertain. Does her writing also inform and persuade? Explain.
2. What is your overall impression of this selection? Briefly articulate what you think of the piece and why.
3. In your judgment, what feature or element in Metivier's essay stands out above everything else? Why? Explain.
4. Now it's your turn to put the critical reading process to work. Choose one of the essays from Chapter 11 and answer the following questions:
    a. The primary purpose of this essay is to persuade, but what specific point is the writer advocating?
    b. What is the context of the essay?
    c. What is your reaction to it?
    d. What specific writing techniques or patterns of writing has the writer used?
    e. What specific feature or element stands out above other aspects of the essay? Why?

2

Working through the Writing Process

Examining the Writing Process

You've probably heard it said, and you might even have thought it yourself: "Good writers are born, not made. Some people can create successful essays and some can't. It's as simple as that." Don't be fooled, however; it's not that simple at all. In fact, if you can think and you can speak, you can write. Of course, as with anything in life — music, mathematics, athletics, drawing, and so on — some people have more natural writing talent than others, and for these individuals, success comes more easily.

But success in writing is indeed attainable for the rest of us. What's required is a willingness to work at it, to take the time to master the writing process. To develop a successful essay, you must first identify a focus and generate material to support or explain that focus, then mold that information into a working draft, and finally polish it, often revisiting these other stages until the paper is finished. Understanding these stages, called *prewriting, composing,* and *revising,* is your first step toward success in writing.

Whenever you write, your goal is the same: to communicate your ideas on a subject to someone else. This figure, called the communications or rhetorical triangle, shows this relationship:

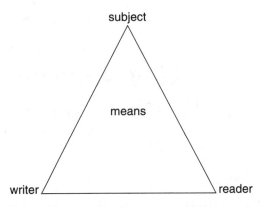

When you write, you as the *writer* use the written word — the *means* — to communicate your ideas about your *subject* to your *reader.* Success in writing comes when you meet the needs of your reader. The point you must remember about this figure is that you and your reader are different, and to overcome the gap between writer and reader you must explain your ideas in complete detail, which in writing is called *amplifying.*

PREWRITING

It's the rare athlete that can make the big hit or make the record-setting leap without warming up. The same is true of writing. The reason many people find writing initially difficult is that they don't devote enough time to warming up, or *prewriting.* In prewriting, you develop a focus and the seeds of information that you'll cultivate into a full paper.

Basically, prewriting includes all the work you do prior to putting ideas in the more complete form that they will take in the various drafts you will produce. Any technique you use to slow yourself down and force yourself to examine a topic can be a good prewriting technique, but if you haven't yet developed a system that works for you, there are a number of methods that other writers have found effective.

Perhaps the best known of these techniques is *freewriting*. In freewriting, you take your subject, set aside a period of time — usually ten minutes or so — and write everything that comes to mind without stopping. It doesn't make any difference if you drift from one subject to the next, repeat some ideas, or end up with some material that isn't even connected to the topic you began with. You don't worry about correct spelling or sentence structure, either; nobody but you will ever see these preliminary ideas. Your goal is to overcome the inhibitions that most people have about making mistakes and to unleash your creativity, developing as many details and examples as possible from which to choose. A brief piece of freewriting on the Internet might look like this:

Just started using the Internet — I can't believe all the stuff I am able to do — click on Netscape and I can go anywhere — I like Yahoo! the best of all the search engines they have at school, it's really easy to use — just type in a name and click on and you're there. I had to make a five-minute presentation for my intro to marketing course about stereotypes in advertising — in fifteen minutes I had visited fifteen different sites about this subject, and I was able to print up a bunch of information that I was able to base my presentation on. My professor said I was lucky because not all the material out there on the Internet is reliable — have to check all sources carefully. You can read so many newspapers and magazines right on-line — just type in the address and up the stuff pops on the screen — shopping, people can order just about everything right over the Internet, airline tickets, clothes, you name it. One of the guys I work with went on vacation last year, he did the whole thing, picking the place to stay, setting up airline tickets, renting a car, all on the Internet and all for less money than it would have cost him to go through a travel agent. I wonder how safe it is — you're giving out your credit card number and everything — I guess it's the same risk you take anytime you buy something by phone or by mail with a credit card. Being able to contact and communicate with so many people is great — there's e-mail — so easy and quick to use, you can also search the Internet to try and find someone who you've lost contact with — even contact celebrities. The entertainment page of the paper lists the times movie or television or music stars — even politicians during election time — are going to be on-line and you can

*contact them. A lot of them also have home pages or pages set up
about them by fans — it's like you're meeting them personally.*

As you can see, while there is some occasional drifting away
from the subject, this freewriting does contain a number of
possibilities for development: for example, the power and influence of the Internet. In addition, there are several details
here that could be developed to support the idea that the Internet has greatly influenced our world. (See the next sections
on composing and revising for ways to develop supporting
material.)

Another effective freewriting method is *brainstorming*.
When you brainstorm, instead of listing everything in your
mind, you list only those bits of information that are directly
connected to your subject. A brainstorming piece on the Internet would look like this:

Power of the Internet
    get information from all over the world in a second
    *research for school projects — easier and faster than a
        traditional library*
    *needed information for my aunt on diabetes because she's just been
        diagnosed — got it in an hour*
Communications
    e-mail can put you in touch with anyone who is also on-line
    search for people you've lost track of or for family genealogies
    actually contact politicians, celebrities, and so on
Consumer Stuff
    *shopping on-line, get prices, actually purchase items — clothing,
        computers, vacation packages*
    changing the way businesses operate?
    most major companies plus a lot of small ones have Web pages
    cheap advertising?
Potential Problems
    *anyone can publish anything on the Internet, not like traditional
        publishing — is information reliable? verifiable?*
    *how about scams — can your credit card numbers be stolen more
        easily?*
    perfect way for someone to distribute a computer virus?

As you can see, because you are deliberately choosing which details to include, brainstorming produces fewer pieces of information, so you have less flexibility as far as your ultimate focus is concerned. The advantage with brainstorming, however, is that you don't tend to drift from your subject. As a result, all the material you end up with is more closely connected to your topic.

Another useful prewriting technique is *clustering,* a technique that involves listing ideas and drawing lines between connected ideas. An added advantage here is that the connection between ideas is graphically indicated. A clustering on the same subject would look like the sample diagram on page 18.

Clustering, like brainstorming, results in fewer ideas, but the material you develop is all directly connected. If you are the type of person who reacts best when the connections between ideas are actually drawn out, clustering may well be the solution for you.

A variation of clustering is *branching,* in which you also graphically connect related ideas. The main difference is that rather than starting in the middle of a page and then moving in any direction with the next piece of related information, you begin on the left side of a piece of paper and move out to the right, with one related idea connected to the next by a horizontal line, spreading out much in the way the branches of a tree would if you turned the tree on its side.

All of these techniques have proven to be effective. Try them all and choose the one that best suits you. Or you can use a combination of methods or adapt one to suit your own style. Remember that prewriting lays the foundation for a successful paper. Therefore, whatever method enables you to feel comfortable planning your paper is the proper choice.

MAINTAINING A JOURNAL

Another way to develop ideas from which to develop papers is to maintain a *journal,* a notebook that you devote to writing. Think of it as an idea book, a place where you can, for

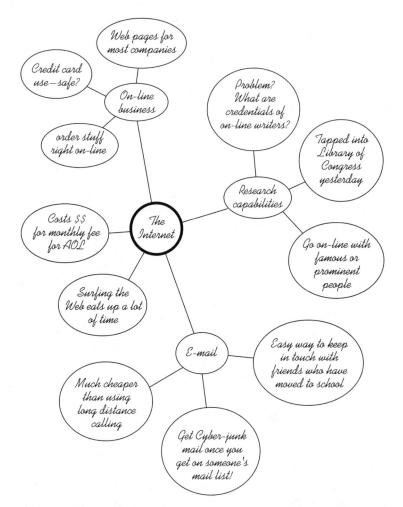

instance, list your thoughts, incidents that interest or disturb you, or questions about the world that have troubled you. You can also use it as a way to respond to a classroom lecture, a performance of some kind, and so on. Good writing develops from good ideas, and writing in a journal on a regular basis — at least two or three times a week in addition to the other writing you are working on — is a great way to develop good ideas. The practice alone is worthwhile, but an added advantage to maintaining a journal is that some of those great ideas may actually lead you to great papers.

COMPOSING: DEVELOPING AN EFFECTIVE DRAFT

Once you have worked through the prewriting stage, you are ready to begin turning those ideas into related sentences and paragraphs constituting an effective essay. From a structural standpoint, an effective essay can be roughly divided into three parts: the *introduction, body,* and *conclusion.*

The *introduction* of your essay is usually a single paragraph that contains the thesis. This part of the essay plays an important role in your paper. An effective introduction not only provides a clear direction for the reader, but it also makes the reader want to continue reading. As the readings in the next 10 chapters show, writers employ a number of devices or techniques to achieve these ends. Sometimes the introduction includes an *anecdote,* a brief, entertaining story that emphasizes the overall point of the essay. Other times, an introduction includes relevant statistics or facts, famous sayings or quotations, leading questions, and so on. No single technique is always appropriate; the requirements of a particular essay will help shape your introduction. Remember that whatever enables you to fulfill your reader's needs — to be directed and to be encouraged to read more — is the proper choice.

The *body* of an essay is the series of paragraphs through which you develop the thesis and provide support for it. There is no set number of paragraphs that make up an effective body; the length will differ depending on the subject and focus of your paper. Remember, however, that the paragraphs of the body must be *amplified* — that is, fully detailed and specific, unified, and organized. (See "Amplifying to meet the needs of your reader," p. 24.)

The *conclusion* of an essay is the part of your paper — usually a paragraph — that brings your paper to a logical, pleasing, or appropriate end. Often the conclusion is a restatement of the *significance* of your essay, that is, the overall message expressed by the thesis and the supporting information. In most cases, you don't introduce any completely new ideas in a conclusion. As with an introduction, however, you may occasionally bring your paper to a close by using a relevant quotation, raising a question, telling an anecdote, and so on. Remember — whatever technique helps you bring your paper to an effective close is the right choice for that particular essay.

The thesis: the bridge from prewriting to composing. With prewriting, your goal is to develop a specific focus on a subject and information to support that focus. Once you have prepared this preliminary work, your next step is to create the bridge between prewriting and composing: the *thesis,* the encapsulation in sentence form of the focus you've selected. In other words, the thesis is the part of your paper that provides a clear direction for your reader, setting up your reader's expectation of the paper that follows. Although sometimes the thesis is expressed in a single sentence, other times it will be spread out over several sentences. As long as your thesis gives your reader insight into what is to come in the rest of your essay, it makes no difference whether that thesis is one sentence or more than one.

Of course, as with other aspects of the preliminary stages of writing, the thesis you create for your first draft is tentative. Writing is an act of discovery, and as you complete that first draft, you may find your original focus shifting a bit. There's no problem with this. If your focus has shifted and the paper itself is good, simply adjust the thesis in a later draft.

Developing an effective thesis.   An effective thesis is generally composed of two parts: a topic and the writer's attitude, or opinion about, or reaction to that topic. The prewriting material presented earlier on the Internet and its influence might generate a thesis such as the following:

> In the last few years, no technological advance has had more impact on the way people communicate, pursue information, and conduct business than the Internet.

In this example, the topic is the Internet, and the opinion is that it has been a major influence on various aspects of people's lives.

As long as the material that follows the thesis in the draft provides plenty of support and illustration for this idea, your paper will be a success.

Another way to understand what an effective thesis is, is to note what it *isn't.* For example, an effective thesis isn't an announcement:

> I plan to show that over the last 10 years the Internet has greatly influenced our world.

In most cases, restating the thesis so that you eliminate such expressions as *I plan, I intend, This paper concerns,* and so on, will help you change an announcement into a thesis, as long as the remaining sentence provides a clear direction for your reader.

A thesis is also not a statement of fact:

> The Internet is easily accessible through a Web browser such as Netscape.

Because a fact is merely a verifiable truth, it doesn't by itself present much room for discussion. Effective writing develops from your *opinion,* your reasoning based on facts. To turn a fact into an effective thesis, you need to take that fact and add your reaction or attitude.

Nor is a thesis a title:

> The Internet: The Doorway to the Entire World

For one thing, a title is often not a complete sentence. Also, a title is designed to provide a broad hint of your paper's subject matter and to encourage your reader to begin reading. It generally doesn't specify your focus on that subject, however. A good title can be a valuable addition to a completed paper, but you must not depend on the title to direct your reader. That's the job of your thesis. If the title is good, keep it, but provide an effective thesis, too.

Placing the thesis effectively. Because your reader depends on the thesis to provide direction, where you place it is important. If you are responding to a statement or an essay question or taking a specific stand on an issue, making the thesis the first sentence of the introduction (shown here underlined) is obviously the most direct way to bring your idea across to the reader:

> <u>In the last few years, no technological advance has had more impact on the way people communicate, pursue information, and conduct business than the Internet.</u> With a few clicks of the computer mouse, people can contact anyone from a friend in the next house to a perfect stranger on the other side of the globe. They can search for information in major on-line libraries and from a wide variety of other sources. They also have the opportunity to communicate with nationally and internationally recognized experts, just by hitting a few keys on the keyboard. For both corporation and consumer, the Internet has forever changed the way business is conducted. Today everything from clothing to computers to vacation packages is available on-line, making the shopping experience simpler and cheaper for the companies and the customers.

Sometimes, depending on the subject you are writing about, you might find it more effective to place the thesis (shown here underlined, with the transitional word *however* added) later in the introduction so that you can ease your reader into your stance:

> As the twenty-first century begins, people enjoy lives made increasingly better by advances in technology. <u>In the last few years, however, no technological advance has had more impact on the way people communicate, pursue information, and conduct business than the Internet.</u> For those on-line, contacting and conferring with people anywhere in the world start with a few simple clicks of a computer mouse. The availability of the Internet also means that both beginning students and serious scholars now have at their fingertips vast repositories of information. Thanks to the Internet, businesses can set up "virtual stores," and consumers can do their shopping in front of their glowing computer screens rather than in some crowded mall.

Often, however, you may feel that the thesis would make a fine bridge between the introduction and the body of your paper. In such cases, you would place your thesis (shown here underlined, with the transitional phrase *In fact* added) at the end of your introduction:

> The number of technological changes witnessed at the end of the twentieth century is amazing. For example, in the 1980s most people had never heard of the Internet. Personal computers had become commonplace by the early 1980s, enabling people to perform a variety of tasks more quickly and effectively, but for the average PC user that was the end of the computer's use. By the early 1990s, however, all of this changed with the advent of the Internet. Once their computers were on-line, people were suddenly able to do things that before they could only dream of. <u>In fact, in the last few years, no technological advance has had greater impact on the way people communicate, pursue information, and conduct business than the Internet.</u>

The final decision about where to place your thesis should be based on which location best serves your reader. The secret to writing a successful paper is to be flexible as you work through the process. Therefore, try the thesis in more than one location in the introduction, and then choose the spot that best communicates your ideas to your reader.

Recognizing weaknesses in content and form. The composing stage marks the point at which you begin to focus more attention on the development of effective *content* — the information you choose to include in your paper. When you prewrite, you don't need to worry if your initial material makes sense to anyone else. Nobody but you will see this material. Prewriting material is *writer-centered;* it makes sense to you as the writer but not necessarily to anyone else.

But in composing, your goal is to produce a writing that is *reader-centered,* that is, a paper that makes sense to somebody else. To achieve this, you must make sure to *amplify* (to provide plenty of specific details and examples); to keep that material unified, organized, and coherent; and to provide clear transitions throughout.

The composing stage also marks the point at which you begin to focus on matters of *form* — spelling, grammar, usage, punctuation, and so on. When you prewrite, you don't need to worry about mistakes in form because only you will see this material. In the composing stage, you take the ideas you've generated and develop a competent first draft, a paper that must communicate your ideas simply, directly, and correctly to your reader.

Amplifying to meet the needs of your reader.   The composing stage of writing is the stage at which you begin to focus your attention on your reader. In prewriting, your goal is to generate the rough material from which you will develop your essay, so it isn't especially important that this initial material make sense to anyone but you. With composing, however, you must make sure that the information you write communicates your ideas to someone else, that it meets your reader's needs.

One problem in trying to meet the needs of your reader is this: because you know a great deal about most of the subjects that you will write about, it's easy to conclude that your reader has the same knowledge. This is an assumption that you shouldn't make. The secret to meeting the needs of your reader is to think of yourself before you learned about the subject and ask yourself this question: what did I need to know in order to understand what I am writing about?

Assessing the needs of your reader.   That you understand what you mean when you write is no surprise. The ideas are coming from your head, after all. But the measure of a successful paper is if somebody else will understand it, a person who may lack your overall background and knowledge.

Think of your point of view on a topic, such as mandatory HIV testing for medical professionals. You are now dead set against mandatory testing, but you didn't always feel this way.

In fact, it wasn't until you had an extended conversation with a close relative who is a health care worker that you began to develop this opinion.

She explained to you that the tests currently available are simply not that reliable; they can register a false-positive reading and thus conceivably ruin the career of an uninfected person and cause patients unnecessary panic. Also, since the HIV virus can be latent for anywhere from six weeks to two years — or longer — after it is contracted, the tests have the added danger of false-negative results, providing a false sense of security for practitioner and patients alike. Furthermore, she noted, health care workers are actually at a far greater risk of contracting the infection from their patients than they are of giving the infection to others, yet patients aren't required to submit to testing. Therefore, not only is mandatory HIV testing for medical professionals dramatically flawed, it is discriminatory as well.

Certainly, you can assume that your reader will know what HIV is and even how it is spread. But not everyone understands the built-in liabilities of HIV testing the way you do now.

Originally, like many other people across the country, you thought that mandatory testing of health care professionals would be a good idea. After all, you thought, finding out which medical professionals have HIV would greatly reduce spread of the virus. It wasn't until you spoke with your relative, who explained the consequences that could result from unreliable testing and the fundamental unfairness that such testing would represent, that you began to rethink your position. Then, with your interest raised, you read several articles dealing with this controversial issue, which helped to cement your position against testing.

Your reader is likely to think as you did before you learned more. In order to fill this gap of knowledge separating you and your reader, you must *amplify*. In other words, you must supply specific details and examples that enabled you to understand the subject. In this case, the information on the lack of reliability of the tests, the potential for panic, the inherent unfairness of this type of testing, as well as the bits of information you gained from your reading, are all aspects that should be explained and illustrated in full detail and in simple, direct, correct terms, just as your relative and your research explained and illustrated the subject for you. When you amplify, you create a more complete picture for your reader, and as a result, you meet your reader's needs.

Keeping your writing unified and organized.   In addition to making sure you amplify so that your reader gains a full understanding of what you have to say, you must also ensure that you express those ideas in such a way that they are directly connected to your subject and that they are effectively arranged. In other words, you need to make sure to maintain *unity* and provide *organization*.

When a paper is unified, all the information you provide directly supports or illustrates your main idea. With the paper against HIV testing, for example, you might be tempted to provide a paragraph like this one:

> The Reagan administration must take the major blame for the AIDS crisis here in the United States. The Reagan White House provided little attention and funding for AIDS research at the beginning of the crisis because at that time AIDS was thought to be merely a disease affecting gay men. It wasn't until HIV had spread into the heterosexual population through contaminated blood, prostitution, IV drug use, and bisexual activity that Reagan acted. By then, the crisis was out of control.

Including such a paragraph, however, would disrupt the unity of the paper. True, it does concern the spread of HIV in the United States, which is of course connected to the matter of mandatory testing; without an AIDS crisis there would be no reason for testing. But this information about the Reagan administration's lack of action (unlike the information about the potential flaws in HIV testing, the discriminatory nature of the testing, the potential and needless psychological harm for unaffected medical personnel and patients — and unwarranted comfort for those affected — and so on) isn't *directly* connected to the idea that mandatory testing would be a bad idea for all concerned. Therefore, to preserve the unity of your paper, you would either eliminate such a paragraph or, if the material is truly interesting and compelling, you might change the focus of your thesis and develop new material that is directly connected to how a political administration contributed to the AIDS epidemic.

In the composing stage of writing, you also focus your attention on how to present the material in the most effective way possible. The most common methods to arrange an essay are *chronological order, linear order, spatial order,* and *emphatic order.*

Chronological order is the order in which the various episodes making up a situation or an occurrence actually took place in time. Whenever you recall a series of events in order, as you would, for example, if you were writing about the time that you witnessed an assault on the street, you would use chronological order. In this way, you would *first* talk about coming on the scene, and *then* about noticing a man holding a woman by the throat with one hand and slapping her in a doorway, and *next* about hearing her scream out, and *then* about yelling at the man to stop, and *finally* about having them both yell back, "Mind your own #*@!!! business." Chronological order makes the story easier to understand because the sequence is clear.

Sometimes, you deliberately break up chronological order by using a *flashback,* an episode presented out of sequence to help emphasize or explain some point. If you were writing an essay about the assault in the doorway and you had just read an article about the unwillingness of people to become involved with stopping crime, you might insert information from the article after you write about encountering the couple, because it would help explain why you were willing to speak up this time.

Linear order is a variation of chronological order. You use linear order when you provide steps or procedures that must be presented in a specific order. A recipe, for instance, and a set of instructions for assembling a toy wagon feature linear order.

Spatial order is the arrangement you use whenever you need to explain where one thing exists in relation to other objects. If you were describing an accident scene involving several cars and a school bus, spatial order would make it easier for your reader to visualize where the cars were in relation to each other — for instance, that the small sports car had been traveling *in front of* the school bus and was *behind* a car that suddenly stopped, causing the bus to crash *on top of* the sports car and the three cars *following* the bus to slam into each other. As the italicized words show, spatial order enables the reader to make sense of the chaotic accident scene. The key is to make the presentation sensible so that your reader can logically follow the description or explanation.

Emphatic order involves ranking your supporting examples or illustrations, presenting them from strong to stronger to strongest. In a paper that advocates banning all smoking in restaurants, for example, you would be likely to use as supporting elements the fact that cigarette smoking causes serious health hazards for the smokers themselves; that carelessly disposed-of smoking materials can cause serious property damage; that secondhand smoke has been shown to cause serious health problems for nonsmokers; that smoking areas have proven to be ineffective in keeping smoke away from nonsmokers; and that smoke and odor from cigarettes add an unpleasant element to the dining experience of nonsmokers and smokers alike.

But listing the supporting information this way would not be nearly as effective as using emphatic order to arrange the essay. Clearly the point that cigarette smoking, which has been definitely linked to lung cancer and serious respiratory illnesses for smokers and those around them, is more serious than the point that cigarette smoking is unappetizing and aesthetically unacceptable. If you applied emphatic order to this material, you would probably begin by discussing the unpleasant element smoking adds to a dining experience, then present the material about the ineffectiveness of nonsmoking areas, and then add the material about potential property damage from carelessly disposed-of smoking material. Finally, you would follow up with the material about the detrimental effects on smokers themselves and finish with the material concerning the effects of cigarette smoke on innocent nonsmokers. By following such an order, you continue to feed your reader's interest, following strong or significant points or examples with even stronger ones, while saving your best for last.

Maintaining coherence. In addition to keeping your essay unified and arranging it effectively, you must also make sure that the resulting paper is *coherent,* that all the elements are clearly connected. To maintain coherence in your writing, you need to provide that connection, which in writing is called *transition*. One way that writers provide transition is to repeat key words (or their synonyms), phrases, and ideas. In addition, writers often use these common transitional expressions:

To add or restate		*To compare or contrast*	
again	in conclusion	although	in spite of
also	in other words	and	likewise
and	moreover	as	nevertheless
besides	next	at the same time	on the other
finally	too	but	hand
further	to sum up	despite	regardless
in addition		even though	still
		however	though
		in contrast	yet

To illustrate or specify		*To show time or place*	
accordingly	indeed	after	once
after all	in fact	as soon as	presently
as a result	of course	below	since
because	particularly	currently	soon
consequently	specifically	earlier	then
for example	therefore	here	there
for instance	thus	immediately	until
		lately	when
		later	where
		now	

Using transition ensures that each idea flows smoothly to the next. The result is an essay that is coherent. Consider the italicized and underlined words in the following paragraph:

> *Computerized listings of holdings* have made college libraries everywhere more accessible to *students*. The unwieldy card catalog has <u>now</u> been replaced with electronic files, and other valuable reference tools are on CD-ROM databases. <u>Because of</u> *these innovations, people* find it easier to locate the information *they* need *to write research papers.* <u>As a result</u>, *students* are less intimidated by the thought of *doing this kind of library work.*

As you can see, transistion holds this paragraph together. For example, *these innovations* renames *electronic files* and *CD-ROM databases,* so it functions as a transition. *People* and *they* rename *students,* and *doing this kind of library work* refers back to *to write research papers.* In addition, *now, because of,* and *as a result* are transitional expressions; *now* relates two ideas in time, and *because of* and *as a result* signal a cause-and-effect relationship between ideas.

In the simplest of terms, the foundation for an effective essay is composed of numerous specific ideas, details, and examples. With this foundation in place, you develop the essay by making sure that all the information you choose to include is unified and logically and appropriately arranged, with plenty of transition to emphasize the connections between ideas for your reader.

Completing multiple drafts.   Once you have completed a draft of an essay, your real work has begun. While there is no rule indicating what number of drafts a writer should create before completing that final draft, it is nevertheless unrealistic to expect that you will write the best paper you are capable of on the first try. Athletes and musicians warm up, actors rehearse, artists paint and repaint, and so on — in any field you can name, you'll find that professionals don't expect to do their jobs correctly in one continuous movement.

Even when the best among us *appear* to be completing something effortlessly the first time around, they are often actually making adjustments in their actions as they go along, moving back to retrace small parts of a step just completed as the situation calls for it. A skilled surgeon, for instance, cuts slowly and deliberately, adapting her movements in whatever way necessary to complete the operation successfully; a star professional baseball pitcher pays as much attention to the mechanics of his throwing as he does to the speed, changing this movement or that to place the ball where he wants it.

As a writer, you will find that your papers improve if you complete multiple drafts. Sometimes you will rework your essay paragraph by paragraph to develop your second or third draft. In other cases, you may find that your initial drafts have some sections that are already solid. With these more acceptable drafts, you keep the strong material while reworking or eliminating the weaker material. Even with drafts that are initially strong, though, you will probably find that both your introductions and conclusions need reworking draft by draft.

Keep in mind that most first drafts show some degree of promise. Don't shortchange your reader or yourself. Fulfill your promise by carefully and deliberately reworking your initial draft.

REVISING

As you begin reworking your initial draft, you enter into the *revising* stage of writing. When you revise, your goal is to reexamine and improve the draft that you've created in the composing stage. Think of revising as a three-step process. First you *reassess,* noting as objectively as possible what works in your paper and what doesn't. Next you *redraft,* generating and shaping additional information to correct the weaknesses you've noted. Finally, you *edit,* tightening your paper and proofreading for any errors in spelling, diction, usage, and so on.

Reassessing. To reassess your draft effectively, you first need to create distance by allowing some time between composing your first or second draft and revising it. By allowing some time — at least a full day — before turning a solid draft into a final draft, you will be better able to see any weaknesses that remain in your content.

Such distancing is necessary because after struggling through several hours to complete a solid draft, you are in no position to evaluate it fairly. You are tired, your mind saturated. You no doubt honestly feel at this point that your paper is as good as you can make it. To continue working on it when you've reached such a point is fruitless. By now what you intended to express and what you have actually written are all jumbled together, and the whole piece is so familiar and understandable to you that you may incorrectly assume that it will be just as familiar and understandable for your reader.

Imagine, for instance, that you have decided to write an essay about the necessity for Americans to manage their trash better. While in high school, you were an active member in your school's environmental affairs club. During your senior year, the focus of the meetings and the group project was the effect on the environment of the millions of tons of trash that Americans create each day. You learned disturbing facts: disposable diapers don't break down for more than two hundred years; the amount of energy lost when we don't recycle glass products could fuel entire cities; many of this country's landfills are rapidly reaching their limits with far fewer replacement sites available, and potentially dangerous substances can contaminate the surrounding areas; deep-water dumping of trash from major municipalities such as New York City is polluting our oceans; and so on. By the end of your senior year, you had developed a broad background concerning America's serious trash-management problems.

Because of your involvement in the environmental affairs club, your own reading on the subject, and your resulting strong background in this area, an essay on this subject was a natural choice for you. Your strong background, however, may actually be a drawback. Because the information seems so familiar and matter-of-fact to you, you may mistakenly assume that your reader possesses a similar background. As a result, you may occasionally find yourself writing paragraphs such as this:

Many of the things we use every day are adding to the growing environmental problems in our country. What we are currently doing doesn't affect us for just today, either. Even if we were to start acting responsibly now, the problems would take hundreds of years to clean up.

If you were to reassess your draft immediately after you completed it, you would probably assume that such a paragraph is acceptable because the ideas it *suggests* are so obvious to you. When you compose and revise, however, you must write so that someone else will understand what you are saying.

A day or more later, though, with your mind rested, you are better able to discover any parts of your paper that don't express your ideas the way you intended them to be expressed. In other words, a little distance between drafts will enable you to recognize the need to provide the specific examples you were thinking of when you originally wrote the passage.

Although feedback is helpful throughout the entire writing process, the evaluation by an objective reader — a classmate, friend, or family member who you know will be honest and fair about your work, a former instructor whose opinion you respect, a more experienced student, and so on — is especially useful during the reassessing stage. Another reader is obviously far more objective than you could ever be about your writing, so sharing your paper and asking your reader to indicate any remaining problems is a sure way to develop a successful final draft.

Redrafting. Once you have reassessed and identified the problem areas, you need to move back through the writing process to generate and develop information to substitute for or supplement the ineffective material. In the paragraph from the paper on environmental issues, the examples are not reader-centered. *What,* for example, are some of the everyday items that add to the environmental mess, *how* are today's actions going to affect us in the future, *what* responsible steps should we take, and *why* will the problems remain with us so long?

Once specific examples are provided that answer these questions, the formerly writer-centered passage becomes this reader-centered one:

> Many of the things we use every day are adding to the growing environmental problems in our country. <u>For example, without active recycling programs in place, many plastic and glass items that are used one time only end up taking valuable space in landfills.</u> What we are currently doing doesn't affect us for just today. <u>Many people still don't realize that items such as disposable diapers take more than two hundred years to break down and that some styrofoam packaging and cups will last almost forever. Even if we were to start acting responsibly now by recycling and severely limiting our use of plastics, the problems would take hundreds of years to clean up. Many landfills across the country are environmental time bombs, gradually spilling hazardous waste into our water supply.</u>

This redrafted material, shown here underlined, makes the passage effective because it fulfills the reader's needs.

Editing. Once you have eliminated the weaknesses in your draft, you're ready for the final aspect of the revising stage, *editing*. If your goal with the rest of the writing process is to develop an effective draft, then your goal with the editing step is to polish that draft to ensure that all the promise of the paper appears without any minor flaws to distract the reader. To do so, you need to *tighten* your writing by eliminating any unnecessary words and then *proofread* for any remaining errors in spelling, usage, punctuation, and so on.

Tightening your writing. One way to eliminate some unnecessary words is to favor the active voice over the passive voice. In the active voice, the subject is the doer of the action; in the passive voice, the subject is acted upon. In most cases, the active voice is more efficient because you generally need fewer words to make your point than with the passive voice. Look at these examples:

> *Active voice:*   I recently played the part of Lennie in a production of *Of Mice and Men.*
>
> *Passive voice:*   The part of Lennie was recently played by me in a production of *Of Mice and Men.*

The active-voice version is shorter than the passive-voice version — in these sentences, fifteen words versus seventeen. More important, the active voice is more direct. In the active-voice sentence, your reader knows right from the start who did what, while in the passive-voice version, your reader doesn't know until the end who played the part.

In some cases, however, the passive voice is a better choice. If the actual doer of the action is not known or is less important than some other aspect of the sentence, the passive voice would probably be a better choice, as these examples show:

> *Passive voice:*   A twelve-year-old girl was shot last week outside my church.
>
> *Active voice:*   Someone shot a twelve-year-old girl last week outside my church.
>
> *Passive voice:*   Last weekend, the $100,000 experimental solar car was displayed at the mall.
>
> *Active voice:*   Last weekend, the mall displayed the $100,000 experimental solar car.

With the first pair of sentences, the passive voice is the better choice because the assailant is unknown and the focus of the sentence should be the victim. In the second pair of sentences, the passive voice is better because the unique and expensive automobile is clearly more important than where the car was displayed. In most cases, however, you'll probably find that the active voice better communicates your ideas to the reader.

Another way to keep your writing streamlined is to eliminate any deadwood. Words like *very* and *really* are examples of deadwood, since they rarely help you clarify a point. What exactly is the difference, for instance, between a person who is *attractive* and one who is *very attractive?* In most cases, you should eliminate *very* or *really;* if the modified word itself isn't specific enough, choose a stronger, more specific word rather than try to make another word strengthen a weak word. Other similar nonspecific expressions include *a lot, definitely, quite, extremely,* and *somewhat.* Make sure that if you use such words, they actually help you make your point. Otherwise, eliminate them.

Another way to make sure your writing is streamlined is to eliminate or alter phrasing that doesn't make its point as succinctly as it could. For instance, *the majority of* is far less efficient than *most; has the ability to* is far less direct than *can.* Here are some other common phrases, along with superior alternative versions:

Deadwood	*Alternative*
due to the fact that	because
a large number	many (or the actual or estimated number)
in the near future	soon
prior to	before
completely eliminate	eliminate
come to the realization of	realize
with the exception of	except for
in order that	so
at the present time	now
take action	act
the month of October	October
give a summary of	summarize
mutual cooperation	cooperation
make an assumption	assume

Proofreading.   The final step in any essay is to *proofread.* Your job is to eliminate any weaknesses that have escaped your scrutiny as you worked through the rest of the writing process. Once you have completed a couple of papers and received some feedback from a reader, you will probably discover a few specific problems that trouble you. With this information, you will be able to develop your own proofreading system that focuses on those problems. Then, rather than trying to find all your errors in one reading, you should proofread your paper more than once, each time looking for one particular error.

Until you know what problems you are most prone to make, use the following list of six common weaknesses as your proofreading guide:

1. Have you eliminated all ambiguity and awkwardness? Effective writing communicates one specific message to a reader. In other words, effective writing is unambiguous. To eliminate ambiguity, you need to make sure that each passage you write makes one point only. The sentence, "I can't speak too highly of my high-school English teacher," is ambiguous; it could mean that you give your highest endorsement, but it could also mean that you can't offer much of a recommendation. The sentence, "Once John and Joe finished talking, he walked out of the office," is ambiguous because the reader isn't sure who walked out of the office. Eliminating the ambiguity in the first sentence is a simple matter of restating it so that proper praise — or complaint — comes across clearly:

Improved: I have nothing but praise for my high-school English teacher.

or

Improved: I have little good to say about my high-school English teacher.

And eliminating the ambiguity in the second sentence is merely a matter of specifying who left the office:

Improved: Once John and Joe finished talking, Joe walked out of the office.

Misplaced, dangling, and *squinting modifiers* are also instances of ambiguous writing. The sentence, "As a youngster, my grandmother often took me grocery shopping with her," is ambiguous because the modifier *As a youngster* is *misplaced.* It modifies *my grandmother,* which is logically impossible since a grandmother cannot also be a child; the phrase belongs with *me.*

Correcting such a sentence means restating part of the sentence so that the proper word is modified, as these versions show:

Improved: When I was a youngster, my grandmother often took me grocery shopping with her.

or

Improved: As a youngster, I often went grocery shopping with my grandmother.

The sentence, "Listening to the orchestra, the music was a mixture of classical and New Age," is ambiguous because there is nothing in the sentence for *Listening to the orchestra* to modify; it is a *dangling* modifier. Correcting such a sentence involves either restating the sentence to eliminate the dangling modifier or making sure there is something in the sentence for *Listening to the orchestra* to modify, as these examples show:

Improved: The music the orchestra played was a mixture of classical and New Age.

or

Improved: Listening to the orchestra, I realized the music was a mixture of classical and New Age.

The sentence, "Edie indicated as she awoke she had smelled smoke in the living room," is ambiguous because *as she awoke* could indicate when Edie made the statement or when she smelled the smoke; it is a *squinting* modifier. To eliminate this ambiguity, you need to move the modifier so that the sentence sends the proper message:

Improved: As she awoke, Edie indicated that she had smelled smoke in the living room.

or

Improved: Edie indicated that she had smelled smoke in the living room as she awoke.

In addition to eliminating any ambiguity, you must also eliminate any *awkwardness* in your writing. Awkward writing isn't necessarily incorrect; rather, it is writing that doesn't express ideas as simply, directly, and clearly as it could. The sentence, "One seldom encounters distressing situations worse than the extremely painful glare from children under temporary state care who have been informed of another imminent move," while grammatically correct, is too formal and indirect to be fully effective. By retaining the same idea but expressing it in simple, direct, and correct terms, you end up with this version, which does a far better job of making the same point:

> *Improved:* Few things are as sad as the eyes of foster children who have been told that they are being moved to yet another foster home.

2. Have you made any sentence errors? The very least your reader expects from you is effective ideas arranged in complete sentence form, that is, in groups of words that contain a subject and verb and express a complete thought within the context of your essay. Therefore, as you proofread you need to recheck your work to make sure you have eliminated the three most serious sentence errors: *fragments, comma splices,* and *run-on sentences.*

A *fragment* is an incomplete sentence, recognizable because it does not make sense by itself. You correct a sentence fragment by supplying whatever words are necessary for it to express a complete thought. Look at this brief passage, with the fragment underlined:

> *Incorrect:* Year after year, electric and other utility rates continue to rise. <u>A condition that often affects those people who can least afford to pay.</u> Fortunately, at least in this state it is against the law for utilities to shut off services to customers for nonpayment during cold-weather months.

To correct this fragment, you either add this fragment to the sentence immediately before it or turn it into a complete sentence by adding to or restating it, as these versions show:

> *Correct:* Year after year, electric and other utility rates continue to rise, a condition that often affects

those people who can least afford to pay. Fortunately, at least in this state it is against the law for utilities to shut off services to customers for nonpayment during cold-weather months.

or

Correct: Year after year, electric and other utility rates continue to rise. Often this situation affects those people who can least afford to pay. Fortunately, at least in this state it is against the law for utilities to shut off services to customers for nonpayment during cold-weather months.

The second serious sentence error is the *comma splice,* an error in which whole sentences are mistakenly connected with a comma. But commas can't connect — they do the opposite, separating elements within a sentence. Here is an example of a comma splice:

Incorrect: It's still hard for many Americans to imagine that it was once legal for one human being to own another human being on the basis of skin color, society is still suffering from slavery's effects more than a century after its abolition.

To identify a comma splice, you need to examine each comma you have used; if a comma appears between complete sentences, as it does in this example, you must either properly connect or correctly separate the sentences. You may connect the sentences by using a *semicolon,* the mark of punctuation that does enable you to connect complete sentences, or a comma plus a conjunction, as these versions show:

Correct: It's still hard for many Americans to imagine that it was once legal for one human being to own another human being on the basis of skin color; society is still suffering from slavery's effects more than a century after its abolition.

or

Correct: It's still hard for many Americans to imagine that it was once legal for one human being to own another human being on the basis of skin color, and society is still suffering from slavery's effects more than a century after its abolition.

To separate the sentences properly, you can of course use a period (or, when it's appropriate, a question mark or an exclamation point) at the end of one sentence and begin the next sentence with a capital letter:

Correct: It's still hard for many Americans to imagine that it was once legal for one human being to own another human being on the basis of skin color. Society is still suffering from slavery's effects more than a century after its abolition.

The third major sentence error is the *run-on sentence,* a mistake in which one sentence appears immediately after the next, with nothing to connect or separate them properly. It is therefore like a comma splice without the comma. Here is an example of a run-on sentence:

Incorrect: Over the last decade, the way voters view the major political parties has changed many Americans no longer consider themselves members of either the Democratic or Republican parties.

An excellent way to identify run-on sentences is to read your work aloud; an even better method is to have another reader read your work aloud to you. Whoever is reading is likely to stumble at the point where one sentence should end and the next should begin. Once you have identified the break between sentences, you correct the error the same way you correct a comma splice. That is, you either properly connect the sentences with a semicolon or a comma and a conjunction, or you separate them with an appropriate mark of end punctuation, as these versions show:

Correct: Over the last decade, the way voters view the major political parties has changed; many Americans no longer consider themselves members of either the Democratic or Republican parties.

or

Correct: Over the last decade, the way voters view the major political parties has changed, and many Americans no longer consider themselves members of either the Democratic or Republican parties.

or

Correct: Over the last decade, the way voters view the major political parties has changed. Many Americans no longer consider themselves members of either the Democratic or Republican parties.

3. Have you made any spelling errors?   The mistakes that are most easily recognized by readers are spelling errors. However incorrect an assumption it is, many readers will judge your overall intelligence and writing ability on the basis of your spelling. This isn't fair, but it is reality. Therefore, you need to focus on eliminating all spelling errors.

Actually, unless you suffer from a learning disability such as dyslexia, which can impair your ability to read and write, you can improve your spelling by first identifying your own personal spelling problems. For instance, many people have a few words that they use on a regular basis that they consistently spell wrong. Sometimes it's because of a silent letter, as in *psychosis* and *readily.* In other cases, the word is an exception to a rule that you've learned, such as *leisure* and *neither,* which are exceptions to the "*i* before *e* except after *c*" rule you learned in elementary school. Others may have trouble when the word is one of a pair or group of *homophones,* words that sound the same, such as *principal* and *principle.* Among the most troublesome of this group of words are possessive pronouns and contractions involving forms of the same pronoun — *your/you're, their/they're/there, its/it's, whose/who's* — and pairs or groups of commonly confused words, such as *affect* and *effect.*

The best way to eliminate these spelling errors from your writing is to keep your own alphabetized list of troublesome words. Each time you come across a word that you or another reader has identified as misspelled, add it to the list. Then, whenever you've completed a draft, run through your own spelling list, checking your paper to ensure that you've properly spelled all of your own personal spelling demons.

Incidentally, when you proofread for spelling, try this method: read your essay backwards, from last word to first. When you check for spelling errors in the conventional way, you are often distracted from focusing exclusively on spelling by what you are reading. When you scan the essay backwards, however, there is no story to distract you; you are better able to focus on individual words and thus are more likely to find previously overlooked spelling errors.

4. Have you maintained consistency in verb tense? In writing, *tense* refers to the point of time, *past, present,* or *future,* indicated by the verb. Actually, each verb in the English language has a total of twelve tenses, a variety that enables writers to translate the actions and conditions of the world to words. The danger with such a wide variety is that a writer may inadvertently shift from one tense to another, thus distracting and potentially confusing the reader.

Many shifts in tense within an essay are of course justified. For example, if you included in your writing a childhood episode to explain some attitude or opinion you have today, it would make sense to shift from the present to the past and then back again. When you proofread, simply make sure you haven't accidentally shifted tenses, especially in the middle of a sentence or paragraph. Look at this example, with the verb shifts underlined:

Incorrect: Suddenly, a small pickup track crashed through the plate-glass window at the front of the cafeteria. The man driving <u>climbs</u> out of the truck, <u>pulls</u> out an automatic rifle, and began firing. By the time he had finished firing and turned the gun on himself, more than fifty people were dead or severely wounded.

Except for the two underlined present-tense verbs, this episode is written in the past tense. Correcting this problem is simply a matter of changing the underlined present-tense verbs to past tense, as this version shows:

> *Correct:*   Suddenly, a small pickup track crashed through the plate-glass window at the front of the cafeteria. The man driving climbed out of the truck, pulled out an automatic rifle, and began firing. By the time he had finished firing and turned the gun on himself, more than fifty people were dead or severely wounded.

5. Have you maintained agreement throughout?   As you proofread, you need to check for errors in both kinds of agreement: *subject–verb agreement* and *pronoun–antecedent agreement*. To identify and correct any errors in subject–verb agreement, locate each verb and its subject, making sure that singular subjects have singular verbs and plural subjects have plural verbs. Look at this example, with the faulty subject–verb agreement underlined:

> *Incorrect:*   The books on the best-seller list remains on sale through Saturday.

The subject, *books,* is plural; the proper verb choice therefore is *remain,* as this version shows:

> *Correct:*   The books on the best-seller list remain on sale through Saturday.

Other problems with subject–verb agreement include sentences in which the verb comes before the subject, as with most sentences beginning with *there* or *here,* and sentences with compound subjects or collective nouns such as *committee* or *audience* used as subjects.

You must also make sure that all pronouns agree with their *antecedents,* the words they refer to or replace. Singular antecedents call for singular pronouns, and plural antecedents require plural pronouns. To correct errors in pronoun–antecedent agreement, check each pronoun, making sure it agrees in number with the word it refers to or replaces; many of these errors involve the use of singular indefinite pronouns such as *everyone* with the plural pronoun *their*, as this example shows:

> *Incorrect:* When it comes to giving to charity, <u>everyone</u> must be able to satisfy <u>their</u> own conscience.

To eliminate this weakness, you must change one of the pronouns so that they match. You might make both singular by changing the sentence this way:

> *Correct:* When it comes to giving to charity, <u>everyone</u> must be able to satisfy <u>her or his</u> [or <u>his or her</u>] own conscience.

As you can see, when referring to a singular pronoun such as *everyone*, you must include both the feminine and masculine personal pronouns to avoid any sexism. Other singular indefinite pronouns that pose the same potential problem include *everybody, nobody, no one, somebody, someone, anyone,* and *anybody.*

Because such singular pronoun usage may become complicated and awkward, a better solution is to change things a bit so that both pronoun and antecedent are plural, as this version shows:

> *Correct:* When it comes to giving to charity, <u>people</u> must be able to satisfy <u>their</u> own consciences.

When you make both pronoun and antecedent plural, you produce a sentence that is simple, direct, *and* nonsexist.

6. Have you kept all elements parallel? To maintain *parallelism* in your writing, you must make sure that you present all similar, connected elements in the same form. To correct weaknesses in parallelism, first locate any elements you've presented in pairs or groups, especially those connected by *and* and *or,* and then make sure that the elements are set up the same way. Look at this example, with the nonparallel element underlined:

> *Incorrect:* Copies of this document are available in the local library, at city hall, <u>the statehouse</u>, and in the town newspaper's computer file.

As you can see, four elements, *in the local library, at city hall, the statehouse,* and *in the town newspaper's computer file,* are connected by *and;* unlike the other three, however, *the statehouse* isn't a prepositional phrase. Correcting the faulty parallelism here is a simple matter of making this element a prepositional phrase, as this version shows:

> *Correct:*   Copies of this document are available in the local library, at city hall, <u>at</u> the statehouse, and in the town newspaper's computer file.

Since problems with parallelism can also occur when you connect elements with the correlative conjunctions *both/and, either/or, neither/nor, not only/but also,* and *whether/or,* double-check for weaknesses in parallelism whenever you use these words. Also check any passage in which you compare elements by using *than* or *as;* make sure that you have expressed the elements of the comparison with the same form.

Although these six types of errors represent the most common problems writers face, you may find that this list doesn't exactly suit your own needs. If you find that you are not prone to one or more of these weaknesses or that you are tripped up by a weakness not listed among these common problems, adapt this list so that it is tailored to your own particular problems. Setting up a consistent, personalized system of proofreading will help you make sure that your final draft is error free.

The Relationship between Your Purpose and the Rhetorical Modes

In addition to having a thorough understanding of the writing process itself, you also need to understand the connection between your aim — your *purpose* — and the patterns or types of writing you use — the *rhetorical modes: narration, description, example, process, definition, comparison and contrast, cause and effect,* and *division and classification.* As noted earlier, people generally write for one of three reasons: to inform, to entertain, or to persuade. With some essays, you'll concentrate almost exclusively on one of these purposes, but in most cases, you'll probably find that your essays fulfill multiple purposes. Most of the time, you don't think about the purpose of your paper, in large part because the assignment you face suggests the purpose you'll fulfill — but the purpose is there nevertheless.

As the next nine chapters demonstrate, you use the rhetorical modes in a variety of combinations to fulfill the purpose in your essay. You'll soon discover that one mode dominates in most papers, with several other modes providing additional support, depending on the specific needs of that assignment. A paper in which you examine two forms of government, for instance, will no doubt feature comparison and contrast as the primary mode, but it is also likely to feature examples to illustrate the types of government, cause and effect to specify how each type evolved, process to explain how each type functions, and so on. All of this happens naturally, most of the time without your even being aware of it as you work to fulfill the purpose of your essay.

Incidentally, since persuasion is one of the three aims of writing, *argument* is presented as an aim rather than a mode. When you write an argument essay, you take a stand and attempt to convince the reader that the point of view expressed is valid and reasonable. To argue effectively, you use whatever modes best help you fulfill that intent.

Remember as you work through the remainder of the book that the names of the various modes are merely loose titles rather than all-encompassing categories. In fact, you'll discover some degree of overlap in the modes. Narration, for example, involves relating *a series of events* in order, whereas process involves presenting *a series of steps* in order. Description involves using details to make a scene, character, or situation *accessible* to a reader, whereas definition involves using details *to specify the elements or characteristics* of a scene, character, or situation. Don't worry too much about such overlap; concentrate instead on using the modes to fulfill the purpose of the assignment. If you do, the result will be an effective essay.

Exercises

1. As the first part of this chapter indicates, the work you do before you begin to write your ideas in an organized fashion is all-important to your success. Several prewriting techniques are suggested on pages 15–18. In order to decide which technique — or combination of techniques — works best for you, try each of them, choosing from among the following subjects. Keep these practice sessions to ten or fifteen minutes.

your first date	a person's right to privacy
required collegiate courses	objectionable advertisements
steroid use in sports	stress in your life
sexism in society	political term limitations
reincarnation	virtual reality

2. As pages 19–20 indicate, an effective essay is composed of three sections: the introduction, body, and conclusion. Read the following two essays and identify the three sections in each: "Everything Has a Name" by Helen Keller (pp. 65–67) and "Taking Type into Account in Education" by Isabel Briggs Myers (pp. 307–312).

3. The part of an essay that expresses the main point is the thesis (pp. 20–23). Its location is determined on the basis of where it will best serve the reader. Identify the theses in "Cow Tools" by Gary Larson (pp. 167–170) and "The Opposite Sex" by Steven Doloff (pp. 224–226), and in a brief paragraph suggest why you feel the writers have chosen these particular locations.

4. As pages 23–24 indicate, one of the most important aspects of an essay is that it be reader-centered rather than writer-centered, that it must communicate its ideas to someone other than the writer. Certain documents — for instance, your classroom notes — are likely to be more writer-centered than reader-centered. Take a page of your

notes from a class and rewrite this material so that it is now reader-centered.

5. An effective essay is effectively organized. Using the material on pages 26–29 to guide you, identify the method of organization in "Exposed Toes" by Diane Riva (pp. 316–318) and "The Discus Thrower" by Richard Selzer (pp. 89–92).

6. One of the best ways to maintain coherence is to include clear transitions to guide your reader. Choose an excerpt of about three hundred words from one of your textbooks or a magazine in which you identify the transitional elements. Refer to the discussion on transition and the list of transitional elements on pages 29–30.

3

Narration

The Technique

They are part of the framework of all cultures: the story-tellers. Long before there were books or any other documents from which people could learn and be entertained, the story-tellers were the teachers and the entertainers. What all cultures and all stories have in common is *narration,* the mode through which a series of events is presented. No matter what your subject and purpose, you'll frequently rely on narration to explain the sequence of some incident or event. Besides using narration as a supporting technique, you may often find that certain assignments will call for narration as a dominant mode; the essays in this chapter exemplify such writing. To make sure your narrative writing is effective, you must

- present the information in *the proper sequence;*
- recognize the most *effective point of view;* and
- provide *a thorough presentation.*

THE PROPER SEQUENCE

For your writing to be effective, you must present it so that the reader is able to understand it fully. *Chronological order,* the order in which the incidents or events actually occurred, is the logical choice with narration, since it enables the reader to follow the incidents or events of the story as they happened.

You may occasionally find, however, that purposely presenting one of the incidents out of sequence, called a *flashback,* will help you emphasize some point. Imagine you were writing an essay about how you overcame terrible stage fright in a public-speaking course. Including a flashback about the incident that led you to develop such a fear — being left onstage for what seemed like hours by your first-grade teacher, who was angry when you forgot your lines in the spring pageant — would make it far easier for your reader to understand how hard it was to overcome your severe anxiety.

Look how Amy Tan, in her 1989 novel *The Joy Luck Club,* uses chronological order in this brief passage about a talent-show performance:

> And I started to play. It was so beautiful. I was so caught up in how lovely I looked that at first I didn't worry how I would sound. So it was a surprise to me when I hit the first wrong note and I realized that something didn't sound quite right. And then I hit another and another followed that. A chill started at the top of my head and began to trickle down. Yet I couldn't stop playing, as though my hands were bewitched. I kept thinking my fingers would adjust themselves back, like a train switching to the right track. I played this strange jumble through two repeats, the sour notes staying with me all the way to the end.

EFFECTIVE POINT OF VIEW

With much of the narration, you will write from a *first-person point of view,* that is, with you as the participant and teller of the story, using *I, me,* and so on. With essays about your own experience, it clearly makes sense to tell the story from this vantage point, as author Annie Dillard does in this brief excerpt from her essay, "God in the Doorway":

> One cold Christmas Eve I was up unnaturally late because we had all gone out to dinner — my parents, my baby sister, and I. We had come home to a warm living room, and Christmas Eve. Our stockings dropped from the mantel; beside them, a special table bore a bottle of ginger ale and a plate of cookies.
>
> I had taken off my fancy winter coat and was standing on the heat register to bake my shoe soles and warm my bare legs. There was a commotion at the front door; it opened, and cold wind blew around my dress.
>
> Everyone was calling me. "Look who's here! Look who's here!" I looked. It was Santa Claus. Whom I never — ever — wanted to meet. Santa Claus was looming in the doorway and looking around for me. My mother's voice was thrilled: "Look who's here!" I ran upstairs.

With some narration, though, you will be writing about events that you witnessed or learned about. In these cases, you will write from the *third-person point of view,* that is, observing and recording the story, using *he, she, they,* and so on. Look at this example of third-person point of view from Willa Cather's short story, "Paul's Case," in which Paul contemplates suicide:

> He rose and moved about with a painful effort, succumbing now and again to attacks of nausea. It was the old depression exaggerated; all the world had become Cordelia Street. Yet somehow he was not afraid of anything, was absolutely calm; perhaps because he had looked into the dark corner at last and knew. It was bad enough, what he saw there, but somehow not so bad as his long fear of it had been. He saw everything clearly now. He had a feeling that he had made the best of it, that he had lived the type of life he was meant to live, and for half an hour he sat staring at the revolver. But he told himself that was not the way, so he went downstairs and took a cab to the ferry.

A THOROUGH PRESENTATION

With any type of writing, your reader depends on you to provide sufficient information. To make sure you meet these needs, you need to avoid two main problems: providing too little specific information and becoming sidetracked.

Consider again the essay about overcoming the stage fright you developed as a child. Because the overall experience is so vivid for you, such a subject is a natural choice for a paper. Ironically, though, because you had lived with the fear day after day following that first-grade incident, you might tend to undercut your explanation of what your life was like whenever you faced any kind of public presentation. Yet, the fear that became almost routine for you is anything but routine for your reader. Therefore, you must make sure to spell out in thorough detail what happened to you.

The other potential difficulty, the danger of becoming sidetracked, also results from your intimate knowledge of the event. Perhaps you learned some years later that your first-grade teacher had suffered the death of a parent shortly before that spring pageant and that his anger with you was a reaction to his own loss. Unless the focus of your paper is to be your reunion with this teacher during which he apologized for having caused you such pain, however, you shouldn't include this information.

In this brief passage from his masterpiece, *The Adventures of Huckleberry Finn,* Mark Twain is careful to provide plenty of detail and to stay on track. Here, Huck explains how he staged his own murder in order to escape from the cabin in which his father had imprisoned him:

> I took the ax and smashed in the door. I beat it and hacked it considerable doing it. I fetched the pig in, and took him back nearly to the table and hacked into his throat with the ax and laid him down on the ground to bleed; I say ground because it *was* ground — hard-packed, and no boards. Well, next I took an old sack and put a lot of big rocks in it — all I could drag — and I started it from the pig, and dragged it to the door and through the woods down the river and dumped it in, and down it sunk, out of sight. You could easy see that something had been dragged over the ground.

AN ANNOTATED EXAMPLE

Langston Hughes

Salvation

How terrible it must feel to be a child and be the only one left out of a group. Imagine how much worse it must feel when the group consists of souls who have been granted eternal bliss and have thus earned the admiration of all. This is the situation Langston Hughes presents in this autobiographical essay. One of the influential voices in modern American literature, Hughes was also a leader of the Harlem Renaissance, the flowering of African American writing, culture, and art in New York during the 1920s. In this piece, Hughes uses narration to bring the reader back to this crossroad of his own youth: his unsuccessful struggle to risk shame by choosing honesty over hypocrisy.

Is it better to stand by your principles or tell a convenient lie?

First-person point of view

These opening sentences serve as the introduction.

Chronological order is used throughout (note transitional words).

I was saved from sin when I was going on thirteen. But not really saved. It happened like this. There was a big revival at my Auntie Reed's church. Every night for weeks there had been much preaching, singing, praying, and shouting, and some very hardened sinners had been brought to Christ, and the membership of the church had grown by leaps and bounds. <u>Then just</u> before the revival ended, they held a special meeting for children, "to bring the young lambs to the fold." My aunt spoke of it for days ahead. <u>That night I</u> was escorted to the front row and placed on the mourners' bench with all the other young sinners, who had not yet been brought to Jesus.

1

My aunt told me that when you   2
were saved you saw a light, and something happened to you inside! And
Jesus came into your life! And God was
with you from then on! She said you
could see and hear and feel Jesus in
your soul. I believed her. I had heard a
great many old people say the same
thing and it seemed to me they ought
to know. So I sat there calmly in the
hot, crowded church, waiting for Jesus
to come to me.

Good details

The preacher preached a wonder-   3
ful rhythmical sermon, all moans and
shouts and lonely cries and dire pictures of hell, and then he sang a song
about the ninety and nine safe in the
fold, but one little lamb was left out
in the cold. Then he said: "Won't you
come? Won't you come to Jesus?
Young lambs, won't you come?" And
he held out his arms to all us young
sinners there on the mourner's bench.
And the little girls cried. And some of
them jumped up and went to Jesus
right away. But most of us just sat
there.

He provides a
thorough presentation
with plenty of specific
examples and good
description.

A great many old people came and   4
knelt around us and prayed, old women
with jet-black faces and braided hair,
old men with work-gnarled hands. And
the church sang a song about the lower
lights are burning, some poor sinners
to be saved. And the whole building
rocked with prayer and song.

Note the
transitional words.

Still I kept waiting to *see* Jesus.   5

Finally, all the young people had   6
gone to the altar and were saved, but
one boy and me. He was a rounder's
son named Westley. Westley and I were

He avoids becoming sidetracked with the story of Westley.

surrounded by sisters and deacons praying. It was very hot in the church and getting late now. <u>Finally</u> Westley said to me in a whisper: "God damn! I'm tired o' sitting here. Let's get up and be saved." So he got up and was saved.

<u>Then I was left</u> all alone on the 7 mourners' bench. My aunt came and knelt at my knees and cried, while prayers and songs swirled all around me in the little church. The whole congregation prayed for me alone, in a mighty wail of moans and voices. <u>And I kept waiting</u> serenely for Jesus, waiting, waiting — but he didn't come. I wanted to see him, but nothing happened to me. Nothing! I wanted something to happen to me, but nothing happened.

Chronological order is used throughout (note transitional words).

I heard the songs and the minister 8 saying: "Why don't you come? My dear child, why don't you come to Jesus? Jesus is waiting for you. He wants you. Why don't you come? Sister Reed, what is this child's name?"

"Langston," my aunt sobbed. 9

"Langston, why don't you come? 10 Why don't you come and be saved? Oh, Lamb of God! Why don't you come?"

<u>Now it was</u> really getting late. <u>I</u> 11 <u>began</u> to be ashamed of myself, holding everything up so long. I began to wonder what God thought about Westley, who certainly hadn't seen Jesus either, but who was now sitting proudly on the platform, swinging his knickerbockered legs and grinning down at me, surrounded by deacons and old women on their knees praying. God had not struck Westley dead for taking his name in

vain or for lying in the temple. <u>So I de-</u>cided that maybe to save further trouble, I'd better lie, too, and say that Jesus had come, and get up and be saved.

Note all the transitional words.

<u>So I got up.</u>   *12*

<u>Suddenly</u> the whole room broke   *13*
into a sea of shouting, as they saw me rise. Waves of rejoicing swept the place. Women leaped in the air. My aunt threw her arms around me. The minister took me by the hand and led me to the platform.

<u>When things quieted down,</u> in a   *14*
hushed silence, punctuated by a few ecstatic "Amens," all the new young lambs were blessed in the name of God. Then joyous singing filled the room.

<u>That night,</u> for the last time in my   *15*
life but one — for I was a big boy twelve years old — I cried. I cried, in bed alone, and couldn't stop. I buried my head under the quilts, but my aunt heard me. She woke up and told my uncle I was crying because the Holy Ghost had come into my life, and because I had seen Jesus. But I was really

The conclusion spells out the significance — the irony of Langston losing faith rather than gaining faith.

crying because I couldn't bear to tell her that I had lied, that I had deceived everybody in the church, that I hadn't seen Jesus, and that now I didn't believe there was a Jesus any more, since he didn't come to help me.

Your Turn: Responding to the Subject

a. Childhood is full of adventures and experiences that in retrospect seem so clear and simple, sometimes even silly. But that's not the way the experiences felt at the time, when you were delighted or amazed or terrified. For this assignment, focus on one of your childhood recollections — for example, a situation you faced in school, within your family, during a religious service, at a summer camp, during a sporting event, and so on — that you understand differently now as an adult.

b. Adults put children through a number of situations: some, such as religious or social customs, because the adults want the children to follow family tradition; others, such as Little League or dance or music lessons, because these adults think children should be active; and others, such as camp, because adults decide the children want them. For this assignment, focus on one of the stories from your own childhood (or from somebody else's past) in which an individual was subjected to something entirely against his or her personal interest.

Paul F. Fletcher
Nightwatch

For more than four decades, Paul F. Fletcher has been a highly ef-fective educator, teaching literature and writing at both the high school and college levels. During the last twenty-five years, he has served as a professor of English and the assistant dean of humani-ties at Bristol Community College in Massachusetts. In addition to working as an educator, Fletcher has pursued interests in freelance writing and in local history. In this essay, he recounts a terrible in-cident of racism and police brutality committed under the cover of night in a small New England coastal community.

When those wielding power are also infected with prejudice, what consequences await those who dare to speak out?

It is a quiet spring night. In the oak-paneled living room of   1
one of the gussied-up old houses that line Main Street, my
daughter, Rosemary, and her boyfriend, Dan, are watching TV.
A fire burns in the nicely detailed fireplace.

Crash. Tinkle, tinkle, bang!   2

Dan leaps up.   3

"Damn! If that's my car. . . ."   4

He throws open the front door and runs out, with Rose-   5
mary at his heels.

The driver's side of Dan's station wagon is, as they might   6
have said years ago in this old seacoast town, "stove in." Dan
and Rosemary are just in time to see a Mustang take off.

Then, unaccountably, the car comes to a halt; it slowly   7
backs into a driveway and stands there, idling. In the moonlight, one can just make out the head and shoulders of the driver, a young woman.

By now, several neighbors are out on the street, under the   8
bare horse-chestnut trees. Against the old Colonial church, the
shadows of the trees look like the ghosts of slaves. In the half-
light, their bony arms seem to be warding off an overseer's whip.

60

From the back of the historic house on the corner, a young   9
black man emerges. He is followed by another, and another,
and yet another, until there are five young black men standing across the street from the driveway where the young
woman sits in the Mustang.

The great tower of the old church, which has watched over   10
the town since the days of the slave trade, chimes one.

A police car, its blue lights flashing, pulls up, and a young   11
officer approaches the young woman in the car. She appears to
be dazed. She is blonde, well dressed, in the preppie fashion —
apparently a student at the local college.

"I didn't do any damage," she moans, more to herself or   12
her absent parents than to anyone else.

Dan shakes his head as he looks at the large strip of chrome   13
from his station wagon protruding from her front-wheel
sprockets.

Under the great church tower, there in the moonlight,   14
everyone seems to be frozen in time: the young woman; the
police officer, joined now by a backup; the neighbors; the five
young black men — all members, it turns out, of the college's
basketball team. One of them seems to know the woman, and
he steps toward her, to try to calm her.

"Take it easy," he seems to say, though his voice is muffled   15
by those of the bystanders.

It appears that the young woman is intoxicated. One of   16
the police officers tries to conduct a sobriety test, and she
stands there flailing her slender arms as she tries to connect
with the tip of her nose.

"Be cool," encourages the young man.   17

"Get away from her!" barks the officer. His even features   18
turn distorted with rage.

"Get away from her!" he repeats.   19

"I'm only trying to help."   20

Now everything speeds up, and it seems that the police-   21
man has struck the youth.

"That'll teach you," he says.   22

Did he jab the young man in the kidneys? Despite the   23
bright, brittle moonlight, it's too dark to see.

Murmurs of protest emanate from the onlookers. The po-   24
lice officers hustle the young man into one of the patrol cars.

The church clock watches. 25

Gradually, the distorted mien of the angry policeman reverts to normal. He strides over to Dan. 26

"You wouldn't mind signing this report, would you, sir?" he says. "Just to witness that this young man was disorderly — don't want any stuff about police brutality." 27

Dan refuses. "I saw you manhandle that young man. He was only trying to quiet the girl." 28

The patrol car with the young woman and the young man drives off. Rosemary turns to go back into the house with Dan. She looks up at the church tower, which looms over the peaceful skyline of our old town, as it has always done, since the time when black people here were traded and transported. 29

Understanding the Significance

1. After damaging Dan's car, what does the driver of the other vehicle do?
2. Given all the details Paul Fletcher provides, what would you identify as the cause of the accident?
3. What is it that so enrages the investigating officer?
4. In your judgment, why does the officer presume that Dan will sign the report?

Discovering the Writer's Purpose

1. Why does Fletcher emphasize the darkness of the scene?
2. Fletcher makes it a point to highlight the appearance and background of the young men involved. Why does he underscore these details?
3. In paragraph 23, Fletcher presents important information in the form of a question. Why do you think he phrases it in this manner?
4. In paragraph 28, Dan refuses to sign the police report. Why doesn't Fletcher include the officer's response to Dan's refusal?

Examining the Writer's Method

1. Rather than providing a more traditional introductory paragraph that gives an overview of the essay to follow, Fletcher uses the first several paragraphs to ease his reader into the body of the essay. Given this particular story, do you think this technique is a good choice? Explain.
2. Fletcher includes a good deal of dialogue. How would his essay have been affected had he chosen to use paraphrase instead of the dialogue?
3. Fletcher presents this story largely from a third-person point of view. In what ways would the essay be different if he had told it from a first-person point of view? From Dan's point of view? From the young man's point of view?
4. The last paragraph serves as the conclusion. In what way does it capture and reiterate Fletcher's thesis?

Considering Style and Language

1. Why do you think Fletcher chose to personify the trees and the church tower?
2. In paragraph 14, Fletcher notes that the scene is "frozen in time." Then, in paragraph 21, he states that the action "speeds up." What effect does he create by freezing the scene? What effect does he create when he puts events back in motion?
3. In the final paragraph, Fletcher uses the word *transported*. To what meaning of *transported* is he alluding? What point is he making?
4. What do the following words mean in the context of the writing? Gussied, detailed (para. 1); unaccountably, idling (para. 7); warding, overseer (para. 8); sprocket (para. 13); sobriety, flailing (para. 16); distorted, rage (para. 18); brittle (para. 23); murmurs, emanate (para. 24); mien, revert (para. 26); brutality (para. 27); looms (para. 29).

Your Turn: Responding to the Subject

a. As Paul Fletcher's compelling piece shows, writing that recounts a traumatic incident makes for great reading. And
from a writer's standpoint, because of the stunning and
disturbing nature of such situations, memories seem as if
they jump out of your head and onto the paper. For this
assignment, focus on a traumatic incident, one that you
actually experienced or witnessed or one that — like
Fletcher's piece — reconstructs an episode that you somehow learned about.

b. One point that Fletcher's writing underscores is that people sometimes behave quite differently when they believe
they are hidden from view than they would if they were
out in the open. Have you ever been part of or witnessed
an incident in which you or someone else acted in this
fashion? If so, tell that story.

Helen Keller
Everything Has a Name

As an infant, Helen Keller lost her vision and hearing and for nearly five years lived in a world of complete silence and darkness. As the play The Miracle Worker *(and the various movie versions based on the play) show, her world changed with the arrival of her teacher, Anne Mansfield Sullivan, who put Keller in touch once again with the world around her. In this selection, an excerpt from her autobiography,* The Story of My Life, *Keller uses narration to bring the reader to that pivotal moment when she began to understand the significance of language.*

What does it feel like suddenly to understand something that had completely eluded you before?

The most important day I remember in all my life is the one 1
on which my teacher, Anne Mansfield Sullivan, came to me. I
am filled with wonder when I consider the immeasurable contrast between the two lives which it connects. It was the third
of March, 1887, three months before I was seven years old.

On the afternoon of that eventful day, I stood on the 2
porch, dumb, expectant. I guessed vaguely from my mother's
signs and from the hurrying to and fro in the house that something unusual was about to happen, so I went to the door and
waited on the steps. The afternoon sun penetrated the mass of
honeysuckle that covered the porch, and fell on my upturned
face. My fingers lingered almost unconsciously on the familiar leaves and blossoms which had just come forth to greet the
sweet southern spring. I did not know what the future held of
marvel or surprise for me. Anger and bitterness had preyed
upon me continually for weeks and a deep languor had succeeded this passionate struggle.

Have you ever been at sea in a dense fog, when it seemed 3
as if a tangible white darkness shut you in, and the great
ship, tense and anxious, groped her way toward the shore with

plummet and sounding-line, and you waited with beating heart for something to happen? I was like that ship before my education began, only I was without compass or sounding-line, and had no way of knowing how near the harbour was. "Light! give me light!" was the wordless cry of my soul, and the light of love shone on me in that very hour.

I felt approaching footsteps. I stretched out my hand as I 4 supposed to my mother. Some one took it, and I was caught up and held close in the arms of her who had come to reveal all things to me, and, more than all things else, to love me.

The morning after my teacher came she led me into her 5 room and gave me a doll. The little blind children at the Perkins Institution had sent it and Laura Bridgman [the first deaf and blind person to be educated in the United States] had dressed it; but I did not know this until afterward. When I had played with it a little while, Miss Sullivan slowly spelled into my hand the word "d-o-l-l." I was at once interested in this finger play and tried to imitate it. When I finally succeeded in making the letters correctly I was flushed with childish pleasure and pride. Running downstairs to my mother I held up my hand and made the letters for doll. I did not know that I was spelling a word or even that words existed: I was simply making my fingers go in monkey-like imitation. In the days that followed I learned to spell in this uncomprehending way a great many words, among them *pin, hat, cup,* and a few verbs like *sit, stand* and *walk.* But my teacher had been with me several weeks before I understood that everything has a name.

One day, while I was playing with my new doll, Miss Sul- 6 livan put my big rag doll into my lap also, spelled "d-o-l-l" and tried to make me understand that "d-o-l-l" applied to both. Earlier in the day we had had a tussle over the words "m-u-g" and "w-a-t-e-r." Miss Sullivan had tried to impress it upon me that "m-u-g" is *mug* and that "w-a-t-e-r" is *water,* but I persisted in confounding the two. In despair she had dropped the subject for the time, only to renew it at the first opportunity. I became impatient at her repeated attempts and, seizing the new doll, I dashed it upon the floor. I was keenly delighted when I felt the fragments of the broken doll at my feet. Neither sorrow nor regret followed my passionate outburst. I had not loved the doll. In the still, dark world in which I lived there was no strong sentiment or tenderness. I felt my teacher sweep the fragments to one side of the hearth, and I had a sense of satisfaction that the cause of my discomfort was removed. She brought me my hat, and I knew I was going out into the warm sunshine. This thought, if a wordless sensation may be called a thought, made me hop and skip with pleasure.

We walked down the path to the well-house, attracted by   7
the fragrance of the honeysuckle with which it was covered. Some one was drawing water and my teacher placed my hand under the spout. As the cool stream gushed over one hand she spelled into the other the word *water*, first slowly, then rapidly. I stood still, my whole attention fixed upon the motions of her fingers. Suddenly I felt a misty consciousness as of something forgotten — a thrill of returning thought; and somehow the mystery of language was revealed to me. I knew then that "w-a-t-e-r" meant the wonderful cool something that was flowing over my hand. That living word awakened my soul, gave it light, hope, joy, set it free! There were barriers still, it is true, but barriers that could in time be swept away.

I left the well-house eager to learn. Everything had a   8
name, and each name gave birth to a new thought. As we returned to the house every object which I touched seemed to quiver with life. That was because I saw everything with the strange, new sight that had come to me. On entering the door I remembered the doll I had broken. I felt my way to the hearth and picked up the pieces. I tried vainly to put them together. Then my eyes filled with tears; for I realized what I had done, and for the first time I felt repentance and sorrow.

I learned a great many new words that day. I do not re-   9
member what they all were; but I do know that *mother, father, sister, teacher* were among them — words that were to make the world blossom for me, "like Aaron's rod, with flowers." It would have been difficult to find a happier child than I was as I lay in my crib at the close of that eventful day and lived over the joys it had brought me, and for the first time longed for a new day to come.

Understanding the Significance

1. In the opening paragraph, Helen Keller refers to the "immeasurable contrast" between her life before and after the arrival of Anne Mansfield Sullivan. What does she mean?
2. In paragraph 5, Keller relates how she quickly learned the signs that her teacher taught her. What then prevented her from fully understanding and communicating?
3. How did Sullivan finally get through to Keller?
4. If you had to describe the feelings that Keller had for Sullivan, how would you characterize them?

Discovering the Writer's Purpose

1. What point do you feel Keller is trying to make by telling the story of the doll that she breaks with "neither sorrow nor regret" and then repents over? In paragraph 8, Keller explains that once she returned to the house with her new understanding of language, she went first to the spot where she had broken the doll and, unable to repair it, felt sorrow and remorse. What point is Keller trying to make about language and responsibility?
2. In paragraph 3, Keller describes her deprivation so beautifully as a "tangible white darkness." Imagine yourself in her place; briefly describe what you think it would be like to be blind.
3. Explain what kind of person Helen Keller was before her transformation.
4. In the opening paragraph, Keller refers to the "immeasurable contrast" between her life before Sullivan's arrival and her life after this "most important day." Summarize this contrast.

Examining the Writer's Method

1. The first sentence of this excerpt is also the thesis: "The most important day I remember in all my life is the one

on which my teacher, Anne Mansfield Sullivan, came to me." What advantage does she gain by beginning in this fashion?

2. Helen Keller has chosen to tell the story in strict chronological order. If she had begun with the episode of realization related in paragraph 7 and then told the rest of the story in flashback, how would the story have been affected?

3. Which of the numerous details that Keller relates gives you the greatest sense of what her life of isolation was like?

4. Keller's explanation of how the concept of language was awakened within her seems limited. If she had explained it in any greater detail, would it seem less like the mystery she describes it as? Explain.

Considering Style and Language

1. How does Keller use details to emphasize her blindness?

2. In paragraph 3, Keller uses an analogy — an extended comparison — to explain what her life was like before the arrival of her teacher. What point is she trying to make?

3. In paragraph 6, Keller spells out the words *doll, mug,* and *water* letter by letter. What is the effect of presenting these words this way?

4. What do the following words mean in the context of the writing? Languor, passionate (para. 2); tangible, groped, plummet, sounding-line (para. 3); flushed (para. 5); tussle, confounding, keenly (para. 6); fragrance (para. 7); quiver, vainly, repentance, (para. 8).

Your Turn: Responding to the Subject

a. Sometimes, as Keller's story illustrates, people learn the answer to some vexing question of life in a sudden burst of awareness. In other cases, however, people expend great amounts of energy — and, occasionally, agony — to gain that understanding. Discuss one of those moments when you understood for the first time the significance of some action or individual in your life — for instance, when you realized what caused you to grow apart from a close friend or family member, decided on your path in life, figured out what may have motivated an apparently successful person to commit suicide, and so on.

b. Keller's essay is about someone who made a difference in her life. Think of a person who has inspired you or influenced your life — a teacher, close friend, historical or political figure, and so on. Relate the episode that, in your view, truly showed this person's abilities.

Ken Weber

He Understands.
He Always Did.

Coming to terms with the ebb and flow of life is among life's most difficult lessons, especially when the issue is aging, the subject of this selection by Ken Weber. For several years Weber, copy editor with the Providence Journal-Bulletin, *has written a popular weekly feature on nature in the* Journal. *This piece, however, which appeared on the paper's editorial pages, departs from his usual subject. Weber instead writes about a journey to his Midwestern home, which forces him to come to terms with the effects that inexorable time has had on his father.*

Given a second chance, how should one say a final farewell to a loved one?

I drive on and on, straight west. A light rain is falling but I   1
hardly notice. Nor do I really see the string of tiny villages this
highway — U.S. 224 — passes through in its push across Ohio.
My mind is on the man I'm hurrying to see. My thoughts are
of my father.

It's my first trip back in winter in many years. I usually   2
visit only in summer, when farmland is lush and lively. I've
forgotten how empty the fields are now. There is a stark barrenness in winter. Severed corn stalks poke through the thin
snow cover, row after row of them, acre after acre. The stubble
of last year's other crops stand sere and lifeless. Fields already
plowed for spring resemble lumpy deserts of white. When I
lived here, I never realized how desolate, depressing, the fields
are in winter.

But maybe the desolation is only in my mind, in my mood.   3
I'm here to visit a man of the soil, a man who took great pleasure in plowing and planting this land. My father developed
his love for farming as a boy before World War I, behind a team
of horses. He took pride in the straight furrow, the field free of

71

weeds, the granary filled after harvest. He worked many jobs in his time but farming was his favorite, the anchor, the basis to which he returned whenever he could.

Dad won't plow these fields again. He is 87 now, and con-   4
fined to a nursing home. A stroke last summer left his right arm useless, his right leg nearly so. He is often disoriented, confused, forgetful. Heretofore soft-spoken and unemotional, he is now subject to fits of uncontrolled crying, and some-times belligerence. His speech is hard to understand, and that, combined with the loss of most of his hearing 50 years ago, makes communication most difficult.

He doesn't know I'm coming. I asked other family mem-   5
bers not to tell him, in case weather problems force me to can-cel or delay my plans. Time weighs heavily on him now; his days are empty between visits by my mother and brothers and sisters. Having him expect me, and then not being able to come, might have been more cruel than staying away.

Lately they've told me, he has been asking for me. I   6
haven't been back since shortly after he was stricken. It didn't appear that he could last more than a few weeks. He was still in the hospital when I last saw him, and I recall saying good-bye. As I walked from his room, feeling, *knowing,* that I would never see this kind, gentle man alive again, my knees buckled and I sagged against a wall, tears streaming down my face. The sense of loss was great, but the helplessness and frustration were overwhelming.

For months, the whole family has been saying it shouldn't   7
be this way. A man like Dad, a man so active and so healthy for so long, should not have to live his final days and weeks and months like this, unable to care for himself. He should have been allowed to die quickly and painlessly, with dignity. Even Dad, whose faith has withstood countless setbacks over the years, including the loss of his hearing, without com-plaint, began to question his God. Why had this happened? What had he done to deserve this punishment?

As we near Ottoville, my hometown, I tell my wife of my   8
apprehension. I've been anxious to come here, but a part of me has been dreading it. I don't really want to see him as a helpless invalid; I'd rather remember him as he was. Would I be able to talk with him? Would he even know me?

I'm feeling guilty for not coming sooner. All through the   *9*
fall and winter I made calls back here to check on his condition. One week he would seem a little stronger, the next he
would be weakening. Up and down. Back and forth. And all
the time, I kept expecting the final call, the one that would
mean it was all over.

Finally, though, when Christmas passed and I learned he was   *10*
asking for me, I knew I had to come. I should have visited him
more. We're a large family, and somebody is with him nearly
every day. Perhaps I told myself that it didn't matter if I came, as
long as my mother and brothers and sisters were around. But it
did matter to him, and now I realize it matters to me.

We stop first at the farm, where my mother is now living   *11*
alone for the first time in her life. She seems tired and frail, but
as warm and intellectually lively as ever. She tells of Dad's
"good days" and "bad days" and that she never knows what
to expect when she visits. He can be calm and resigned, or lash
out angrily at her, something totally out of character for him.
In their 58 years of marriage, I doubt that he had even raised
his voice to her until now.

Within an hour, a brother and a sister call, both trying to   *12*
prepare me for the visit, warning me to expect a great deal of
emotion and many tears from Dad, whom I never saw cry in
the first 40 years of my life. My apprehension grows.

I steel myself for the worst as we enter the nursing home.   *13*
It's lunch time. Most of the patients are in the dining room,
but others, in wheelchairs, are positioned in a long corridor,
outside their rooms.

Just as we start walking, I catch sight of Dad, in his chair,   *14*
trying to feed himself with his left hand. At nearly the same instant, he glances up, and even though we're many yards away
and I had never before worn a beard, he immediately recognizes me and calls out my name. And he bursts into tears.

The visit goes far better than I expected. We're unable to   *15*
make out much of what he's trying to tell us, but enough
comes through so that we can communicate. I feel like the
Prodigal Son returned as he gives us a tour of the home and
attempts to introduce us to his nurses and some of the other
patients. There is no hint of resentment over my long absence.
As usual, he's more interested in our lives and children than

in talking about himself. His crying fits are sudden and fre-
quent, but brief. He at first says he doesn't know why he cries.
Later he says the tears come because he's so happy.

> We stay about two hours, until he tires, and return the   16
next day. His voice is weaker this time, possibly from all the
talking the previous day, but his mood is as upbeat and appreciative. We've caught him on two "good days" and for that
I'm thankful. Mom says our visits will do him good, but I
know I'm getting as much or more from this trip than he is.

> Too quickly, it is time to return to Rhode Island. On our   17
last visit, I leave by saying something I've felt all my life but
had never put in words before. Looking directly into his face,
to make sure he understands, I say "Dad, I love you." A simple sentence that I should have said a thousand times but
somehow could not. His fingers tighten on my hand, and tears
fill his eyes. He doesn't say anything. He simply nods his head,
and gives me the slightest of smiles. He understands. He always did.

Understanding the Significance

1. How do the details in the first two paragraphs set the tone
   for Ken Weber's essay?
2. In paragraphs 3 and 4, Weber provides contrasting pictures of his father. As Weber explains it, how has his father
   changed?
3. Does Weber's first meeting with his father in the nursing
   home live up to his expectations? Explain.
4. At the end of paragraph 16, Weber states, "Mom says our
   visits will do him good, but I know I'm getting as much or
   more from this trip than he is." What does he mean?

Discovering the Writer's Purpose

1. In many ways, Ken Weber's story is less about going to see
   his father than it is about leaving his father for the last

time. Why do you feel Weber focuses the bulk of his essay on the journey and lead-up to the visit rather than on their final moments as father and son?

2. Two scenes from this essay are especially touching: in paragraph 14, when Weber's father recognizes his son, and in the final paragraph when Weber tells his father, "I love you." In both cases, Weber presents the episodes without including his own reaction. Why do you feel Weber excludes his own feelings from these scenes? Would the episodes have been better had he included them?

3. In paragraph 7, Weber relates that his entire family felt that Weber's father "should have been allowed to die quickly and painlessly, with dignity" rather than become a mere shade of his former self. But how do you think Weber truly felt? Remember — had his father died quickly and painlessly, Weber would never have been able to have his memorable moment with him.

4. Dealing with a highly personal, highly emotional subject is among the most difficult tasks any writer faces. Weber's essay contains several powerful moments. If you had been seated at Weber's desk, which of these moments would you have found hardest to express in words? Why?

Examining the Writer's Method

1. In paragraph 3, Weber paints a powerful, positive image of his father. In your view, what words and details enable Weber to create that image?

2. A key element in this story is paragraph 6, which details Weber's previous visit to his father, a meeting that he had presumed would be the last time he would see his father alive. Why do you feel Weber has placed this episode roughly in the middle of the essay rather than right at the beginning?

3. In paragraph 6, Weber powerfully underscores his grief over his father's declining health when he states that during his earlier visit, he left his ailing father "feeling, *knowing,* that I

would never see this kind, gentle man alive again"; yet, as the rest of the essay indicates, Weber has another — and better — chance to see his father. What point does Weber make by emphasizing what he had felt on his previous visit?

4. Overall, Weber's essay is moving because he has included plenty of details and examples. In which paragraph or paragraphs do you feel Weber's presentation is most complete and effective? Why?

Considering Style and Language

1. Rather than using the opening paragraph to express his main idea, Weber spreads out his main idea over the first six paragraphs. Why do you think he chose this strategy over a more conventional introduction? Do you agree with his choice? Explain.

2. In paragraph 7, Weber relates how his formerly patient father had begun to question the fairness of his fate. What does this episode tell the reader about Weber's father?

3. In paragraph 15, Weber states that he feels like "the Prodigal Son returned," a reference to a famous parable from the New Testament. The parable relates the story of a son who returns home to his father after squandering the money that represented his inheritance, and to his surprise, he is greeted joyfully by his father. In what way are the situations comparable?

4. What do the following words mean in the context of the writing? Lush, stark, barrenness, sere, desolate (para. 2); disoriented, heretofore, belligerence (para. 4); resigned (para. 11); apprehension (para. 12); steel (para. 13); appreciative (para. 16).

Your Turn: Responding to the Subject

a. To a great degree, Weber's essay is moving because it deals so effectively with familiar, personal life situations: the struggles to deal with the mortality of others and to communicate the most basic of messages, "I love you." For this assignment, write as Weber has done about one of your own tender moments — for example, of a time when you expressed your love; told someone good-bye; welcomed someone home; held a niece, nephew, godchild, or even your own child for the first time; and so on.

b. What is the most emotional moment you've ever observed? Tell that story. Was it when a child received a special toy? When a parent made a plea for assistance in finding her lost child? A movie scene in which someone finally understood his importance? A scene from a book? Tell your reader that story.

Other Possibilities for Using Narration

Here are some additional topics for papers that feature narration. Of course, these subjects are merely starting points. As you work your way through the writing process, adapt or develop the topic you choose so that you fulfill your purpose.

- a time you witnessed a crime
- a trip to the "big city"
- an encounter with the police
- a traumatic experience
- a meeting with an unusual, famous, or otherwise memorable person
- a special day in your life
- the worst phone call you ever received
- an embarrassing episode
- an accident you witnessed
- a trip to the principal's office
- a "first time" experience
- an experience from driving school
- a family (or school, team, or club) reunion
- an unusual date
- a time that you were caught in a lie

Practical Application: Narration

Congratulations! In yesterday's mail, you received a letter notifying you that, on the basis of your grades, you have been nominated by your academic adviser for induction into a prestigious national honor society for students. As the letter explains, the nomination is only the first step. Not all nominees are accepted. Final selection is based on a *three hundred to five hundred word* (*two typewritten pages* maximum) personal statement, written by the nominee on a subject determined by the national organization. This year's nominees have been asked to tell about the best lesson they've been taught, either in school or on the streets.

You immediately go to see your adviser to thank her for recommending you and to seek her advice on writing the personal statement. She graciously offers you a copy of Nicole C. Kelly's winning statement from the previous year, dealing with Kelly's personal philosophy of education. Use Kelly's "My Philosophy of Education" as a model for *approach* and *format* as you create your personal statement on the best lesson you have ever been taught.

My Philosophy of Education

When very young children are first learning to paint, their pictures generally incorporate some version of a landscape — sun shining in a narrow strip of sky at the top of the page, a stripe of green grass at the bottom, with the space between sporting an irregular house or car and perhaps some (proportionally) six-foot tall flowers. Within only a few short years, however, a remarkable change begins to take place. Notwithstanding varying levels of individual ability and interest, the painted landscapes of a fourth-grade class differ from those of a kindergarten class in terms of one consistent detail. The sky, once an isolated slash at the very edge of the paper, suddenly surrounds the whole scene; the blue stretches all the way down to the grass.

It seems to me that any really effective method of education must always involve itself with leading students through a similar process of realization. As a would-be teacher of English, I find that many students are intimidated by the subject — by the idea of writing a complex story or paper, by the intricacy (and often, idiocy) of grammar, or by the very sound of the word "literature." This apprehension lends itself to a mindset which is restrictive in that it is also, in most cases, untrue. "I hate to read/write," I have been told by friends, relatives, and other students. Yet, all too frequently the message behind the message is something more moderate, but also more destructive: "I know that 'real' reading/writing is beyond the reach of someone like me."

In such instances, I believe the key to good teaching often lies in helping discouraged students change the way they view their own capacity for understanding. In other words, the secret is to reassure them that all writing is "real," and all expression valuable, and that literature belongs to and can (should, MUST) be accessible to everybody. English is a wonderful subject in large part because language can be explored on such a variety of levels, none of which is mutually exclusive and all of which are equally important and essential. As a teacher, I would hope to convey the subject's unique mixture of dynamism and security by reminding students of something they suddenly discovered while learning to draw. I firmly believe that, in literature, as in most things, the sky we reach for ultimately stretches down to the grass we stand on. And, from there, there is nowhere to go but everywhere — and up.

4

Description

The Technique

Since effective writing of any kind depends on the inclusion of specific details, description is a mode that you will frequently depend on. More often than not, you'll use description as a supporting technique rather than as the primary mode in an essay. For example, in an essay proposing that existing nuclear power plants should be closed until greater safety measures are developed, you might include a passage that illustrates the actual damage that occurred in the Chernobyl nuclear disaster in the former Soviet Union several years ago. But sometimes you will find that a particular assignment calls for a more thorough use of description. An essay about riding out a storm at sea in a small sailboat is a good example of an essay that would be dominated by description, as would an essay about a fiery confrontation with an unfair supervisor.

Whether you are using description as support or as the dominant mode in an essay, you need to

- draw upon *sensory details;*
- rely on both *objective and subjective description;* and
- consider using *spatial order.*

SENSORY DETAILS

Vivid experiences create vivid memories. Think for a moment of the aroma the last time you walked into a bakery or the sensation you felt the last time you plunged into a swimming pool on a hot summer day. *Sensory details,* what you perceive through sight, hearing, tasting, smelling, and touching, enable you to communicate these experiences to your reader.

An essay about a vacation at a tropical resort, for example, would no doubt benefit from the use of sensory details. The first part of such an essay might focus on your impressions as you arrived at your hotel. In order to make it easier for your reader to walk in your shoes, you might focus on the fragrance of the various flowers, the notes from a distant guitar, the sensation of intense humidity, and so on.

Here's a passage from F. Scott Fitzgerald's masterful novel *The Great Gatsby,* in which narrator Nick Carraway describes the sound of his cousin (and Gatsby's love interest) Daisy Buchanan's voice:

> I looked back at my cousin, who began to ask me questions in her low, thrilling voice. It was the kind of voice that the ear follows up and down, as if each speech is an arrangement of notes that will never be played again. Her face was sad and lovely with bright things in it, bright eyes and a bright passionate mouth, but there was an excitement in her voice that men who had cared for her found difficult to forget: a singing compulsion, a whispered "Listen," a promise that she had done gay, exciting things just a while since and that there were gay, exciting things hovering in the next hour.

OBJECTIVE AND SUBJECTIVE DESCRIPTION

When you focus on objects, situations, or people as they appear, without dealing with the impressions they generate, you are using *objective description*. When you focus on the way such things make you feel, you are using *subjective description*. Of course, you use both types of description when you write, generally without giving much thought to which type you are employing. In a passage concerning a carpentry shop you visited as a child, you might provide objective description to note that the shop was filled with racks of lumber, three large power saws, and a workbench covered with various carpentry tools and coffee cans full of nails and screws. In the same piece, you might use subjective description to explain how nervous you felt around the enormous machinery, especially the overhead saw with its exposed blade, and how sweet the sawdust smelled.

In this brief passage from *Night,* Elie Weisel's powerful memoir of his experiences in Nazi death camps, look at how Weisel mixes objective and subjective description as he recounts one evening when he and his father and other prisoners traveled from one camp to the next:

> I lay down and tried to force myself to sleep, to doze a little, but in vain. God knows what I would not have given for a few moments of sleep. But, deep down, I felt that to sleep would mean to die. And something within me revolted against this death. All round me death was moving in, silently, without violence. It would seize upon some sleeping being, enter into him, and consume him bit by bit. Next to me there was someone trying to wake up his neighbor, his brother, perhaps, or a friend. In vain. Discouraged in the attempt, the man lay down in his turn, next to the corpse, and slept too. Who was there to wake him up?

SPATIAL ORDER

An effective essay depends on effective arrangement, and with description you will probably frequently use *spatial order.* As pages 27–28 explain, this method of arrangement locates the elements in relation to each other, enabling a reader to visualize a scene.

In writing about the tropical resort, for instance, you might use spatial order to explain where your room was in relation to the pool and the ocean. As a result, your reader gains a greater understanding of why your experience in paradise was so wonderful — or horrible. In the essay about the carpentry shop, you might use spatial order to indicate that the huge overhead saw was hanging from the ceiling in the middle of the shop, in front of the large table saw but behind the well-worn workbench. Such an arrangement would make it clear for your reader why that one piece of machinery dominated your recollection of the shop.

Look at this passage from *The Sea around Us* by nature writer Rachel Carson, in which she uses spatial order to explain the location of the Sargasso Sea:

> The central oceanic regions, bounded by the currents that sweep around the ocean basins, are in general the deserts of the sea. There are few birds and few surface feeding fishes, and indeed there is little surface plankton to attract them. The life of these regions is largely confined to deep water. The Sargasso Sea is an exception, not matched in the anticyclonic centers of other ocean basins. It is so different from any other place on earth that it may well be considered a definite geographic region. A line drawn from the mouth of Chesapeake Bay to Gibraltar would skirt its northern border; another from Haiti to Dakar would mark its southern boundary. It lies all about Bermuda and extends more than halfway across the Atlantic, its entire area being roughly as large as the United States.

AN ANNOTATED EXAMPLE

Sullivan Ballou
My Dearest Sarah

Anyone who thinks that history is boring and lifeless has never been exposed to documents like the letter that Union Army Major Sullivan Ballou wrote to his wife during the Civil War. Some 129 years after it was written, Sullivan Ballou's private letter became public when Ken Burns included it in the first segment of his critically acclaimed PBS documentary, The Civil War. *As a result, Ballou was transformed from an obscure casualty in a terrible episode in American history to the celebrated author of an extraordinary love letter, written a week before the battle from which he would not return. In this letter, Ballou used description to express his struggle to balance duty with the love he felt for his wife and family.*

What must it feel like when, to perform the duty you feel you owe to your country, you must face the prospect of death far from the family you love?

"Head-Quarters," Camp Clark
Washington, D.C., July 14, 1861
My Very Dear Wife:

His first paragraph serves as the introduction, outlining his situation and concerns.

Indications are very strong that we 1 shall move in a few days, perhaps tomorrow. Lest I should not be able to write you again, I feel impelled to write a few lines, that may fall under your eye when I shall be no more.

He gives objective details of time, place, and so on.

Our movement may be one of a few 2 days duration and full of pleasure — and it may be one of severe conflict and death to me. Not my will, but thine, O God, be done. If it is necessary that I should fall on the battle-field for my country, I am ready. I have no misgivings about, or lack of confidence in, the cause in which I am engaged, and my courage does not halt or falter. I know how strongly American civilization now leans upon the triumph of government, and how great a debt we owe to those who went before us through the blood and suffering of the Revolution, and I am willing, perfectly willing to lay down all my joys in this life to help maintain this government, and to pay that debt.

But, my dear wife, when I know, 3 that with my own joys, I lay down nearly all of yours, and replace them in

He expresses his love for country conflicting with his love of family.

this life with care and sorrows, — when, after having eaten for long years the bitter fruit of orphanage myself, I must offer it, as their only sustenance, to my dear little children, is it weak or dishonorable, while the banner of my purpose floats calmly and proudly in the breeze, that my unbounded love for you, my darling wife and children, should struggle in fierce, though useless, contest with my love of country.

He expresses his emotions at his possible death.

I cannot describe to you my feelings on this calm summer night, when two thousand men are sleeping around me, many of them enjoying the last, perhaps, before that of death, — and I, suspicious that Death is creeping behind me with his fatal dart, am communing with God, my country and thee. **4**

I have sought most closely and diligently, and often in my breast, for a wrong motive in this hazarding the happiness of those I loved, and I could not find one. A pure love of my country, and of the principles I have often advocated before the people, and "the name of honor, that I love more than I fear death," have called upon me, and I have obeyed. **5**

He uses subjective description to emphasize his love for his family.

Sarah, my love for you is deathless. It seems to bind me with mighty cables, that nothing but Omnipotence can break; and yet, my love of country comes over me like a strong wind, and bears me irresistibly on with all those chains, to the battlefield. The memories of all the blissful moments I have spent with you, come crowding over me, and I feel most deeply grateful to God and you, that I have enjoyed them so long. And how hard it is for me to **6** give them up, and burn to ashes the hopes of future years, when, God willing, we might still have lived and loved together, and seen our boys grow up to honorable manhood around us.

I know I have but few claims upon   7
Divine Providence, but something whispers to me, perhaps it is the wafted prayer of my little Edgar, that I shall return to my loved ones unharmed. If I do not, my dear Sarah, never forget how much I love you, nor that, when my last breath escapes me on the battle-field, it will whisper your name.

He uses powerful subjective details.

Forgive my many faults, and the   8
many pains I have caused you. How thoughtless, how foolish I have oftentimes been! How gladly would I wash out with my tears, every little spot upon your happiness, and struggle with all the misfortune of this world, to shield you and my children from harm. But I cannot. I must watch you from the spirit land and hover near you, while you buffet the storms with your precious little freight, and wait with sad patience till we meet to part no more.

Note his beautiful phrasing about his love.

But, O Sarah, if the dead can come   9
back to this earth, and flit unseen around those they loved, I shall always be near you — in the garish day, and the darkest night — amidst your happiest scenes and gloomiest hours — always, always; and, if the soft breeze fans your cheek, it shall be my breath; or the cool air cools your throbbing temples, it shall be my spirit passing by.

Sarah, do not mourn me dear; think   10
I am gone, and wait for me, for we shall meet again.

He uses his conclusion to reemphasize his love for his family.

As for my little boys, they will grow   *11*
as I have done, and never know a father's love and care. Little Willie is too
young to remember me long, and my
blue-eyed Edgar will keep my frolics
with him among the dimmest memories of his childhood. Sarah, I have unlimited confidence in your maternal
care, and your development of their
characters. Tell my two mothers, I call
God's blessing upon them. O Sarah, I
wait for you there! Come to me, and
lead thither my children.

"Sullivan."

Your Turn: Responding to the Subject

a. The impetus for Sullivan Ballou's letter was the separation
   from his wife and family, a separation from which he
   feared he would not return. If you've ever been separated
   from a special person or persons in your life because of an
   extended camp or school experience, a separation or divorce, work or military obligations, and so forth, write
   about that experience, detailing the way you felt as a result of that separation.

b. What do you imagine it would be like to face the prospect
   of your own death? What would you be glad you had
   done? What would you regret not having done? Would
   you be bitter? Fearful? Prepared? Imagine that you are now
   set to embark on a journey or adventure from which, like
   Sullivan Ballou, you might not return. Write a letter to the
   individual who would be most affected, expressing your
   feelings.

Richard Selzer

The Discus Thrower

When a surgeon operates, it is to correct some problem a patient is suffering from. But that patient is much more than just the part or system needing repair; alleviating the problem — or being unable to alleviate it — affects the whole person. Richard Selzer, a working surgeon, is certainly aware of this, as his essay shows. In addition to his medical career, Selzer has enjoyed a successful writing career with both fiction and essays, including Confessions of a Knife *(1979), from which the following selection is taken, and* Letters to a Young Doctor *(1982), as well as articles in such periodicals as* Harper's, Esquire, *and* Redbook. *His work often draws upon the world of medicine and his vantage point as a physician. In this essay, his description brings to life a patient he calls the "discus thrower," enabling the reader to understand that this patient's behavior each morning was a result of the patient's frustration and isolation brought about by his condition.*

How should a person facing grief and pain respond to these feelings?

I spy on my patients. Ought not a doctor to observe his patients   1
by any means and from any stance, that he might the more fully assemble evidence? So I stand in the doorways of hospital rooms and gaze. Oh, it is not all that furtive an act. Those in bed need only look up to discover me. But they never do.

From the doorway of Room 542 the man in the bed seems   2
deeply tanned. Blue eyes and close-cropped white hair give him the appearance of vigor and good health. But I know that his skin is not brown from the sun. It is rusted, rather, in the last stage of containing the vile repose within. And the blue eyes are frosted, looking inward like the windows of a snowbound cottage. This man is blind. This man is also legless — the right leg missing from midthigh down, the left from just below the knee. It gives him the look of a bonsai, roots and branches pruned into the dwarfed facsimile of a great tree.

Propped on pillows, he cups his right thigh in both hands.   *3*
Now and then he shakes his head as though acknowledging
the intensity of his suffering. In all of this he makes no sound.
Is he mute as well as blind?

The room in which he dwells is empty of all possessions   *4*
— no get-well cards, small, private caches of food, day-old
flowers, slippers, all the usual kick-shaws of the sickroom.
There is only the bed, a chair, a nightstand, and a tray on
wheels that can be swung across his lap for meals.

"What time is it?" he asks.   *5*

"Three o'clock."   *6*

"Morning or afternoon?"   *7*

"Afternoon."   *8*

He is silent. There is nothing else he wants to know.   *9*

"How are you?" I say.   *10*

"Who is it?" he asks.   *11*

"It's the doctor. How do you feel?"   *12*

He does not answer right away.   *13*

"Feel?" he says.   *14*

"I hope you feel better," I say.   *15*

I press the button at the side of the bed.   *16*

"Down you go," I say.   *17*

"Yes, down," he says.   *18*

He falls back upon the bed awkwardly. His stumps, un-   *19*
weighted by legs and feet, rise in the air, presenting themselves. I unwrap the bandages from the stumps, and begin to
cut away the black scabs and the dead, glazed fat with scissors
and forceps. A shard of white bone comes loose. I pick it away.
I wash the wounds with disinfectant and redress the stumps.
All this while, he does not speak. What is he thinking behind
those lids that do not blink? Is he remembering a time when
he was whole? Does he dream of feet? Of when his body was
not a rotting log?

He lies solid and inert. In spite of everything, he remains   *20*
impressive, as though he were a sailor standing athwart a
slanting deck.

"Anything more I can do for you?" I ask.   *21*

For a long moment he is silent.   *22*

"Yes," he says at last and without the least irony. "You can   *23*
bring me a pair of shoes."

In the corridor, the head nurse is waiting for me.   *24*

"We have to do something about him," she says. "Every   *25*
morning he orders scrambled eggs for breakfast, and, instead
of eating them, he picks up the plate and throws it against the
wall."

"Throws his plate?"   *26*

"Nasty. That's what he is. No wonder his family doesn't   *27*
come to visit. They probably can't stand him any more than
we can."

She is waiting for me to do something.   *28*

"Well?"   *29*

"We'll see," I say.   *30*

The next morning I am waiting in the corridor when the   *31*
kitchen delivers his breakfast. I watch the aide place the tray
on the stand and swing it across his lap. She presses the button to raise the head of the bed. Then she leaves.

In time the man reaches to find the rim of the tray, then   *32*
on to find the dome of the covered dish. He lifts off the cover
and places it on the stand. He fingers across the plate until he
probes the eggs. He lifts the plate in both hands, sets it on the
palm of his right hand, centers it, balances it. He hefts it up
and down slightly, getting the feel of it. Abruptly, he draws
back his right arm as far as he can.

There is the crack of the plate breaking against the wall at   *33*
the foot of his bed and the small wet sound of the scrambled
eggs dropping to the floor.

And then he laughs. It is a sound you have never heard. It   *34*
is something new under the sun. It could cure cancer.

Out in the corridor, the eyes of the head nurse narrow.   *35*

"Laughed, did he?"   *36*

She writes something down on her clipboard.   *37*

A second aide arrives, brings a second breakfast tray, puts   *38*
it on the nightstand, out of his reach. She looks over at me
shaking her head and making her mouth go. I see that we are
to be accomplices.

"I've got to feed you," she says to the man.   *39*

"Oh, no you don't," the man says.   *40*

"Oh, yes I do," the aide says, "after the way you just did.   *41*
Nurse says so."

"Get me my shoes," the man says.   *42*

"Here's oatmeal," the aide says. "Open." And she touches   *43*
the spoon to his lower lip.
    "I ordered scrambled eggs," says the man.   *44*
    "That's right," the aide says.   *45*
    I step forward.   *46*
    "Is there anything I can do?" I say.   *47*
    "Who are you?" the man asks.   *48*
    In the evening I go once more to that ward to make my   *49*
rounds. The head nurse reports to me that Room 542 is deceased. She has discovered this quite by accident, she says. No,
there had been no sound. Nothing. It's a blessing, she says.
    I go into his room, a spy looking for secrets. He is still there   *50*
in his bed. His face is relaxed, grave, dignified. After a while, I
turn to leave. My gaze sweeps the wall at the foot of the bed,
and I see the place where it has been repeatedly washed, where
the wall looks very clean and very white.

Understanding the Significance

1. What is it that Richard Selzer finds so fascinating about
   this patient?
2. In telling this story, what is Selzer trying to say about the
   practice of medicine?
3. Why does Selzer include his dialogue with the discus
   thrower?
4. How does Selzer emphasize this man's isolation?

Discovering the Writer's Purpose

1. With little exception, Selzer keeps himself — and his
   emotions — out of the piece. How do you think this writing would have been different had he broken down that
   barrier and allowed more of his feelings to come through
   in his dealings with the discus thrower?
2. It is clear that Selzer and the nurses who care for the discus thrower hold different opinions about this patient.
   Specify the differences in their points of view.

3. The nurse who reports the discus thrower's death says his passing is "a blessing," an expression that people sometimes use when someone who has suffered before death finally dies. Considering all that Selzer relates about this patient, including the frustration of dealing with him day after day, what do you feel the nurse might mean by this expression?
4. After reading this essay, how do you feel about the discus thrower? Which emotions does he trigger in you — pity, sadness, frustration, anger, or some combination? Why?

Examining the Writer's Method

1. Throughout the essay, Selzer provides a number of vivid sensory details. What point do you feel Selzer makes by using these sensory details?
2. Selzer's use of subjective description accounts for much of the power in this essay. Of the subjective description that Selzer provides, which image affected you most? Why?
3. Selzer ends his essay with a striking piece of description: he enters the room where his now-dead patient lies and then notes that the wall the patient had used as a target "looks very clean and very white." What message do you think Selzer is trying to impart with this description?
4. Selzer never explains why the patient erupts in laughter after throwing his plate. Why do you think the discus thrower laughs when his plate of scrambled eggs hits the wall?

Considering Style and Language

1. From what you can infer, how does Selzer feel about patients like the discus thrower? Explain.
2. Throughout the essay, Selzer describes the discus thrower from the viewpoint of an objective observer. Does he break away from this stance at any point? Explain.
3. In paragraph 34, Selzer provides this description of how the man laughs when he realizes that his breakfast plate

has hit its target: "It is a sound you have never heard. It is
something new under the sun. It could cure cancer." What
does he mean? Why did he choose this type of description
rather than saying he "laughs hilariously" or "howls" or
"guffaws"?

4. What do the following words mean in the context of the
writing? Furtive (para. 1); vigor, vile, bonsai (para. 2); shard
(para. 19); hefts (para. 32); accomplices (para. 38); dignified (para. 50).

Your Turn: Responding to the Subject

a. As Selzer explains in the second sentence, he observes
while he works. His essay stems from his efforts to "spy"
and "gaze" on the people he serves, an excellent method
for developing a paper. For this assignment, follow Selzer's
lead and spend some time observing people involved in or
served by your current job, or think back to the people you
were in contact with in some previous job. Then, focus on
a specific figure whose actions or words remain with you
today.

b. Choose a place where you regularly spend time — one of
your classes, the school cafeteria, the library, a health club,
and so on — and discuss the various ways that people behave there.

Joan Didion

In Bed

Joan Didion has been a successful working writer for more than forty years. During that time, she has served as a magazine writer and editor, novelist, playwright, and essayist. Her essays have been collected in two volumes: Slouching toward Bethlehem *(1968) and* The White Room *(1979), from which this selection is taken. Among her more recent work is her 1996 book* The Last Thing He Wanted *and her 1996 screenplay* Up Close and Personal. *Anyone who has suffered the intense pain associated with migraine headaches will appreciate the way Didion uses description in this writing to commit her agony to paper; because of Didion's skillful use of description, the lucky ones who have never been through such an ordeal will experience it vicariously through this essay.*

What is it like to live with the potential of experiencing a headache so severe that you simply cannot function?

Three, four, sometimes five times a month, I spend the day in 1
bed with a migraine headache, insensible to the world around
me. Almost every day of every month, between these attacks, I
feel the sudden irrational irritation and the flush of blood into
the cerebral arteries which tell me that migraine is on its way,
and I take certain drugs to avert its arrival. If I did not take the
drugs, I would be able to function perhaps one day in four. The
physiological error called migraine is, in brief, central to the
given of my life. When I was 15, 16, even 25, I used to think
that I could rid myself of this error by simply denying it, character over chemistry. "Do you have headaches *sometimes? frequently? never?*" the application forms would demand. "Check
one." Wary of the trap, wanting whatever it was that the successful circumnavigation of that particular form could bring (a
job, a scholarship, the respect of mankind and the grace of
God), I would check one. *"Sometimes,"* I would lie. That in fact
I spent one or two days a week almost unconscious with pain

seemed a shameful secret, evidence not merely of some chemical inferiority but of all my bad attitudes, unpleasant tempers, wrongthink.

For I had no brain tumor, no eyestrain, no high blood   *2*
pressure, nothing wrong with me at all: I simply had migraine headaches, and migraine headaches were, as everyone who did not have them knew, imaginary. I fought migraine then, ignored the warnings it sent, went to school and later to work in spite of it, sat through lectures in Middle English and presentations to advisers with involuntary tears running down the right side of my face, threw up in washrooms, stumbled home by instinct, emptied ice trays onto my bed and tried to freeze the pain in my right temple, wished only for a neurosurgeon who would do a lobotomy on house call, and cursed my imagination.

It was a long time before I began thinking mechanistically   *3*
enough to accept migraine for what it was: something with which I would be living, the way some people live with diabetes. Migraine is something more than the fancy of a neurotic imagination. It is an essentially hereditary complex of symptoms, the most frequently noted but by no means the most unpleasant of which is a vascular headache of blinding severity, suffered by a surprising number of women, a fair number of men (Thomas Jefferson had migraine, and so did Ulysses S. Grant, the day he accepted Lee's surrender), and by some unfortunate children as young as two years old. (I had my first when I was eight. It came on during a fire drill at the Columbia School in Colorado Springs, Colorado. I was taken first home and then to the infirmary at Peterson Field, where my father was stationed. The Air Corps doctor prescribed an enema.) Almost anything can trigger a specific attack of migraine: stress, allergy, fatigue, an abrupt change in barometric pressure, a contretemps over a parking ticket. A flashing light. A fire drill. One inherits, of course, only the predisposition. In other words I spent yesterday in bed with a headache not merely because of my bad attitudes, unpleasant tempers, and wrongthink, but because both my grandmothers had migraine, my father has migraine and my mother has migraine.

No one knows precisely what it is that is inherited. The   *4*
chemistry of migraine, however, seems to have some connection with the nerve hormone named serotonin, which is nat-

urally present in the brain. The amount of serotonin in the blood falls sharply at the onset of migraine, and one migraine drug, methysergide, or Sansert, seems to have some effect on serotonin. Methysergide is a derivative of lysergic acid (in fact Sandoz Pharmaceuticals first synthesized LSD-25 while looking for a migraine cure), and its use is hemmed about with so many contraindications and side effects that most doctors prescribe it only in the most incapacitating cases. Methysergide, when it is prescribed, is taken daily, as a preventive; another preventive which works for some people is old-fashioned ergotamine tartrate, which helps to constrict the swelling blood vessels during the "aura," the period which in most cases precedes the actual headache.

Once an attack is under way, however, no drug touches it. 5 Migraine gives some people mild hallucinations, temporarily blinds others, shows up not only as a headache but as a gastrointestinal disturbance, a painful sensitivity to all sensory stimuli, and abrupt overpowering fatigue, a strokelike aphasia, and a crippling inability to make even the most routine connections. When I am in a migraine aura (for some people the aura lasts fifteen minutes, for others several hours), I will drive through red lights, lose the house keys, spill whatever I am holding, lose the ability to focus my eyes or frame coherent sentences, and generally give the appearance of being on drugs, or drunk. The actual headache, when it comes, brings with it chills, sweating, nausea, a debility that seems to stretch the very limits of endurance. That no one dies of migraine seems, to someone deep into an attack, an ambiguous blessing.

My husband also has migraine, which is unfortunate for 6 him but fortunate for me; perhaps nothing so tends to prolong an attack as the accusing eye of someone who has never had a headache. "Why not take a couple of aspirin," the unafflicted will say from the doorway, or "I'd have a headache, too, spending a beautiful day like this inside with all the shades drawn." All of us who have migraine suffer not only from the attacks themselves but from this common conviction that we are perversely refusing to cure ourselves by taking a couple of aspirin, that we are making ourselves sick, that we "bring it on ourselves." And in the most immediate sense, the sense of why we have a headache this Tuesday and not last Thursday, of course we often do. There certainly is what doctors call a "migraine personality," and that personality tends to be ambitious, inward, intolerant of error, rather rigidly organized, perfectionist. "You don't look like a migraine personality," a doctor once said to me. "Your hair's messy. But I suppose you're a compulsive housekeeper." Actually my house is kept even more negligently than my hair, but the doctor was right nonetheless: perfectionism can also take the form of spending most of a week writing and rewriting and not writing a single paragraph.

But not all perfectionists have migraine, and not all migrainous people have migraine personalities. We do not escape heredity. I have tried in most of the available ways to escape my own migrainous heredity (at one point I learned to give myself two daily injections of histamine with a hypodermic needle, even though the needle so frightened me that I had to close my eyes when I did it), but I still have migraine. And I have learned now to live with it, learned when to expect it, how to outwit it, even how to regard it, when it does come, as more friend than lodger. We have reached a certain understanding, my migraine and I. It never comes when I am in real trouble. Tell me that my house is burned down, my husband has left me, that there is gunfighting in the streets and panic in the banks, and I will not respond by getting a headache. It comes instead when I am fighting not an open but a guerrilla war with my own life, during weeks of small household confusions, lost laundry, unhappy help, canceled appointments, on days when the telephone rings too much and I get no work done and the wind is coming up. On days like that my friend comes uninvited.

And once it comes, now that I am wise in its ways, I no longer fight it. I lie down and let it happen. At first every small apprehension is magnified, every anxiety a pounding terror. Then the pain comes, and I concentrate only on that. Right there is the usefulness of migraine, there in the imposed yoga, the concentration on the pain. For when the pain recedes, ten or twelve hours later, everything goes with it, all the hidden resentments, all the vain anxieties. The migraine has acted as a circuit breaker, and the fuses have emerged intact. There is a pleasant convalescent euphoria. I open the windows and feel the air, eat gratefully, sleep well. I notice the particular nature of a flower in a glass on the stair landing. I count my blessings.

Understanding the Significance

1. What is Joan Didion trying to convince her reader to see about migraine headaches? Is she successful? Explain.
2. Would Didion's essay have been as effective if she were not a migraine sufferer herself? Why or why not?
3. Why does Didion include the details about the physical cause of migraine?
4. In the final paragraph, Didion explains that the headache acts as a "circuit breaker." Explain what she means.

Discovering the Writer's Purpose

1. Didion's essay concerns two types of pain: the actual physical pain from the headaches and the psychological pain of being misunderstood. Which pain does she suggest is worse? Explain her reasons.
2. How do you think Didion's essay would have been different had she written about someone else having to deal with migraine headaches — her husband, for instance, who is also a migraine sufferer?
3. In paragraph 3, Didion recounts her first headache, its aftermath, and her subsequent treatment. What point is she trying to make with this description?
4. One of the most intriguing lines in Didion's essay occurs at the end of paragraph 5, following a list of symptoms related to migraine headaches: "That no one dies of migraine seems, to someone deep into an attack, an ambiguous blessing." What do you think Didion is trying to say?

Examining the Writer's Method

1. Didion's essay is effective because of the brilliant description that she provides throughout. In your judgment, which part of her essay contains the most powerful description? Why do you think so?

2. Didion's essay contains an outstanding mixture of objective and subjective description. What do you think the result would have been had she focused on objective or subjective description only?
3. The sensory details in Didion's piece are among the most powerful elements in this essay. Which one of these sensory details do you feel is most effective? Why?
4. In spelling out the ordeal she has suffered as a result of migraine headaches, Didion provides more objective description than subjective description. Why do you think this particular balance of details works so well?

Considering Style and Language

1. What is Didion's dominant attitude about her affliction? Explain.
2. In paragraph 3, Didion briefly sums up her own first experience with migraine. Why do you think she included this incident in parentheses? Was it a good choice? Explain.
3. Why do you think Didion includes the detail about her husband suffering from migraine?
4. What do the following words mean in the context of the writing? Avert, circumnavigation (para. 1); involuntary, instinct, lobotomy (para. 2); mechanistically, neurotic, hereditary, vascular, severity, contretemps, predisposition (para. 3); derivative, contraindications, aura (para. 4); aphasia, debility, ambiguous (para. 5); perversely, compulsive (para. 6); guerrilla (para. 7); recedes, euphoria (para. 8).

Your Turn: Responding to the Subject

a. Didion's essay deals in large part with pain, a sensation that is difficult to describe. A paper cut and a serious laceration are both painful, for example, but to different degrees; the same is true for the pain from the disappointment over a failed exam compared with the breakup of a love affair or friendship. For this assignment, write about the pain that you've had to deal with — or that you've witnessed some- one else suffer.

b. What's it like to deal with something that others don't un- derstand? Take a subject about which you have some spe- cial insight, for example, a physical disability, depression, lack of self-esteem, a fear or phobia, physical or sexual abuse, and so forth, and as Didion has done, explain your experiences with this subject.

John Steinbeck
From *The Grapes of Wrath*

*The winner of the 1962 Nobel Prize for literature, John Steinbeck
enjoyed a distinguished career as a writer, beginning in 1935 with
the publication of the novel* Tortilla Flat. *His many published works
include such popular successes as* In Dubious Battle, Of Mice and
Men, Cannery Row, *and* East of Eden. *The impact of his powerful epic novel* The Grapes of Wrath *(1939) far eclipsed his other
work, however. In* The Grapes of Wrath, *Steinbeck relates the terrible struggle of the Joad family as they are forced to abandon their
lives in Oklahoma and travel west in a vain search for work, security, and dignity. In this passage, Chapter 25 of the novel, Steinbeck
uses description to bring forth the cruel irony of people being allowed to starve in the midst of plenty.*

*Is it possible for land to be too fertile and for agricultural tech-
nology to be too advanced?*

The spring is beautiful in California. Valleys in which the fruit   *1*
blossoms are fragrant pink and white waters in a shallow sea.
Then the first tendrils of the grapes, swelling from the old
gnarled vines, cascade down to cover the trunks. The full green
hills are round and soft as breasts. And on the level vegetable
lands are the mile-long rows of pale green lettuce and the spindly
little cauliflowers, the gray-green unearthly artichoke plants.

And then the leaves break out on the trees, and the petals   *2*
drop from the fruit trees and carpet the earth with pink and
white. The centers of the blossoms swell and grow and color:
cherries and apples, peaches and pears, figs which close the
flower in the fruit. All California quickens with produce, and
the fruit grows heavy, and the limbs bend gradually under the
fruit so that little crutches must be placed under them to support the weight.

Behind the fruitfulness are men of understanding and   *3*
knowledge and skill, men who experiment with seed, end-

lessly developing the techniques for greater crops of plants whose roots will resist the million enemies of the earth: the molds, the insects, the rusts, the blights. These men work carefully and endlessly to perfect the seed, the roots. And there are the men of chemistry who spray the trees against pests, who sulphur the grapes, who cut out disease and rots, mildews and sicknesses. Doctors of preventive medicine, men at the borders who look for fruit flies, for Japanese beetle, men who quarantine the sick trees and root them out and burn them, men of knowledge. The men who graft the young trees, the little vines, are the cleverest of all, for theirs is a surgeon's job, as tender and delicate; and these men must have surgeons' hands and surgeons' hearts to slit the bark, to place the grafts, to bind the wounds and cover them from the air. These are great men.

Along the rows, the cultivators move, tearing the spring 4 grass and turning it under to make a fertile earth, breaking the ground to hold the water up near the surface, ridging the ground in little pools for the irrigation, destroying the weed roots that may drink the water from the trees.

And all the time the fruit swells and the flowers break out 5 in long clusters on the vines. And in the growing year the warmth grows and the leaves turn dark green. The prunes lengthen like little green bird's eggs, and the limbs sag down against the crutches under the weight. And the hard little pears take shape, and the beginning of the fuzz comes out on the peaches. Grape blossoms shed their tiny petals and the hard little beads become green buttons, and the buttons grow heavy. The men who work in the fields, the owners of the little orchards, watch and calculate. The year is heavy with produce. And men are proud, for of their knowledge they can make the year heavy. They have transformed the world with their knowledge. The short, lean wheat has been made big and productive. Little sour apples have grown large and sweet, and that old grape that grew among the trees and fed the birds its tiny fruit has mothered a thousand varieties, red and black, green and pale pink, purple and yellow; and each variety with its own flavor. The men who work in the experimental farms have made new fruits: nectarines and forty kinds of plums, walnuts with paper shells. And always they work, selecting, grafting, changing, driving themselves, driving the earth to produce.

And first the cherries ripen. Cent and a half a pound. Hell,   *6*
we can't pick 'em for that. Black cherries and red cherries, full and sweet, and the birds eat half of each cherry and the yellowjackets buzz into the holes the birds made. And on the ground the seeds drop and dry with black shreds hanging from them.

The purple prunes soften and sweeten. My God, we can't   *7*
pick them and dry and sulphur them. We can't pay wages, no matter what wages. And the purple prunes carpet the ground. And first the skins wrinkle a little and swarms of flies come to feast, and the valley is filled with the odor of sweet decay. The meat turns dark and the crop shrivels on the ground.

And the pears grow yellow and soft. Five dollars a ton. Five   *8*
dollars for forty fifty-pound boxes; trees pruned and sprayed, orchards cultivated — pick the fruit, put it in boxes, load the trucks, deliver the fruit to the cannery — forty boxes for five dollars. We can't do it. And the yellow fruit falls heavily to the ground and splashes on the ground. The yellowjackets dig into the soft meat, and there is a smell of ferment and rot.

Then the grapes — we can't make good wine. People can't   *9*
buy good wine. Rip the grapes from the vines, good grapes, rotten grapes, wasp-stung grapes. Press stems, press dirt and rot.

But there's mildew and formic acid in the vats.   *10*

Add sulphur and tannic acid.   *11*

The smell from the ferment is not the rich odor of wine,   *12*
but the smell of decay, and chemicals.

Oh, well. It has alcohol in it, anyway. They can get drunk.   *13*

The little farmers watched debt creep up on them like the   *14*
tide. They sprayed the trees and sold no crop, they pruned and grafted and could not pick the crop. And the men of knowledge have worked, have considered, and the fruit is rotting on the ground, and the decaying mash in the wine vats is poisoning the air. And taste the wine — no grape flavor at all, just sulphur and tannic acid and alcohol.

This little orchard will be a part of a great holding next   *15*
year, for the debt will have choked the owner.

This vineyard will belong to the bank. Only the great own-   *16*
ers can survive, for they own the canneries too. And four pears peeled and cut in half, cooked and canned, still cost fifteen cents. And the canned pears do not spoil. They will last for years.

The decay spreads over the State, and the sweet smell is a   *17*
great sorrow on the land. Men who can graft the trees and make
the seed fertile and big can find no way to let the hungry people eat their produce. Men who have created new fruits in the
world cannot create a system whereby their fruits may be eaten.
And the failure hangs over the State like a great sorrow.

The works of the roots of the vines, of the trees, must be   *18*
destroyed to keep up the price, and this is the saddest, bitter-
est thing of all. Carloads of oranges dumped on the ground.
The people came for miles to take the fruit, but this could not
be. How would they buy oranges at twenty cents a dozen if
they could drive out and pick them up? And men with hoses
squirt kerosene on the oranges, and they are angry at the
crime, angry at the people who have come to take the fruit. A
million people hungry, needing the fruit and kerosene sprayed
over the golden mountains.

And the smell of rot fills the country.   *19*

Burn coffee for fuel in the ships. Burn corn to keep warm,   *20*
it makes a hot fire. Dump potatoes in the rivers and place
guards along the banks to keep the hungry people from fish-
ing them out. Slaughter the pigs and bury them, and let the
putrescence drip down into the earth.

There is a crime here that goes beyond denunciation.   *21*
There is a sorrow here that weeping cannot symbolize. There
is a failure here that topples all our success. The fertile earth,
the straight tree rows, the sturdy trunks, and the ripe fruit.
And children dying of pellagra must die because a profit cannot be taken from an orange. And coroners must fill in the
certificates — died of malnutrition — because the food must
rot, must be forced to rot.

The people come with nets to fish for potatoes in the river,   *22*
and the guards hold them back; they come in rattling cars to
get the dumped oranges, but the kerosene is sprayed. And they
stand still and watch the potatoes float by, listen to the
screaming pigs being killed in a ditch and covered with quick-
lime, watch the mountains of oranges slop down to a putre-
fying ooze; and in the eyes of the people there is the failure;
and in the eyes of the hungry there is a growing wrath. In the
souls of the people the grapes of wrath are filling and growing
heavy, growing heavy for the vintage.

Understanding the Significance

1. What is John Steinbeck's attitude about the scientists who have made increases in yield possible?
2. In paragraph 15, Steinbeck says that these small farms will become part of a large farm the next year. Will this cycle continue — even with the change, will the waste continue?
3. Does not being able to make a profit justify destroying food that might have fed starving people?
4. What has gone wrong in this situation? Is it the single-mindedness and determination of the scientists, the greed of the farmers, or some other factor? Explain.

Discovering the Writer's Purpose

1. As this excerpt shows, irony is a powerful tool that enables a writer to hammer home some point. What message do you think Steinbeck is trying to make with his use of irony?
2. Steinbeck takes his reader through the full agricultural cycle: from cultivation, to the harvest, and to the aftermath of the harvest. In which section do you feel he most effectively uses description? Why?
3. It's impossible to miss the tragedy inherent in the situation Steinbeck describes. Without a doubt, the migrant workers lose and suffer terribly, but the farmers lose and suffer as well. So who wins? What do you think Steinbeck's point is?
4. In the final sentence of this excerpt, Steinbeck echoes "The Battle Hymn of the Republic," the song from which he draws the title of the book: "In the souls of the people the grapes of wrath are filling and growing heavy, growing heavy for the vintage." On the basis of what you've read, explain what Steinbeck might mean by the "grapes of wrath."

Examining the Writer's Method

1. This excerpt from John Steinbeck's masterpiece is moving, thanks to the powerful description he includes. Which of

the details affected you more, the objective images or the subjective ones? Why?

2. In contrast to the rest of the excerpt, Steinbeck uses dialogue in paragraphs 6–9. What advantage does he gain in doing so?

3. Steinbeck's use of subjective description enables him to capture the absolute horror involved in this scene. Is there any spot in the piece where you would like to see additional subjective detail?

4. One of the elements that makes this piece so remarkable is Steinbeck's use of sensory details. Which sensory detail — or details — did you find most effective? Why?

Considering Style and Language

1. Why do you think Steinbeck begins with the beauty of spring? Wouldn't the piece have been just as effective if he began with paragraph 6, once the fruit had begun to ripen?

2. Would the description of the various fruits rotting on the vine have been less effective if Steinbeck had not already included the description of those plants when they are ripe? Explain.

3. The beauty of the California valley masked a terrible horror. What message is Steinbeck sending about true success and our relationship with nature?

4. What do the following words mean in the context of the writing? Tendrils, gnarled, cascade, spindly (para. 1); blights, quarantine, grafts (para. 3); ridging (para. 4); decay, shrivels (para. 7); ferment (para. 8); putrescence (para. 20); denunciation, pellagra (para. 21); wrath (para. 22).

Your Turn: Responding to the Subject

a. Few experiences sear a person's memories more than being exposed to the type of human tragedy that Steinbeck captures in this passage. Fortunately, not many people come face-to-face with such horror; through the medium of television, however, most people have been exposed to gripping scenes of some disaster or calamity, either as the events are still occurring or as they have been hypothesized about or reconstructed in a documentary. For this assignment, choose a human tragedy that you have been exposed to — for example, news film from one of the world's apparently perennial hot spots such as Northern Ireland or the Middle East; documentaries on the Civil Rights Movement or the Vietnam War; and so on — and focus on one event, detailing what you saw.

b. As this selection from Steinbeck shows, things are not always as they seem to be. What appears to be an ideal family situation to an outsider may in fact not be. Or an apparently run-down neighborhood may actually be the setting for a very close-knit group of people. For this assignment, use your writing to show your reader the reality behind the appearance.

Other Possibilities for Using Description

Here are some additional topics for a paper that features description. As you work through the writing process, adapt and develop the subject you choose in whatever way necessary to help you turn the general idea into an effective essay.

- a normally busy place, now deserted
- a memorable sunrise or sunset you've witnessed
- the thrill of success you felt when you made the big basket, won a part in a play, received an award, graduated from school, and so on
- backstage during a play or performance
- an unusual person you've met
- what you see in a painting or photograph
- a special possession
- an unusual room you've visited
- the scene at a concert or athletic event
- a physical injury or bout with illness
- a distinctive, renowned, or unique restaurant, deli, bakery, or bar
- an accident scene
- a special place — an amusement park, a zoo, a swimming area — that you remember from your childhood
- what you envision as you listen to a piece of music
- the feeling of being alone

Practical Application: Description

A month ago you became an intern at Fine, Howard, and Fine, a small advertising and marketing firm. Your first two weeks on the job were a blur as you tried to learn as much as you could about the advertising business. It's a good thing that you have paid close attention, because your supervisor has just pulled you aside to give you your first real assignment: to help develop the copy for the advertising campaign of Diego Valdez House, the region's fastest growing chain of gourmet coffee bars.

Mr. Maxwell Folger, CEO of Diego Valdez House, Inc., was impressed with the successful advertising campaign that Timothy Matos of Fine, Howard, and Fine had developed for Azores Resorts, and he has provided a copy of the successful print advertisement than ran in several travel magazines and newspapers last year. Your supervisor has asked you to develop a statement of *approximately three hundred words* that captures the aroma and atmosphere of a Diego Valdez House coffee bar, much as Matos had captured the sense of the Azorean Island resort. Use Matos's copy as a model in terms of *approach* and *format*.

Your Azorean Getaway

The Ponta Delgada Island Resort is a quaint white-washed Iberian style hotel located on the lush island of São Miguel. The brisk mornings are pleasantly spent enjoying a cup of freshly ground coffee on your warm sunbathed beach-side verandah. As you bask in the salty-sweet smell of an Atlantic breeze, the haunting melodies of the Fado, the traditional Portuguese folk music, pull your attention from the hypnotic murmur of the sea to a distant vision of the countryside. In the songs, the tormented wails of an unseen voice sound out loud the quiet desperation of the people, the Açorianos.

Our tour guides will show you the lamented places described in these songs, the sights of love gone astray. The boiling crystal-clear waters of Furnas, the blue and green lagoons of Sete Cidades, and the daunting heights of Pico de Vara exist, it seems, simply to provide the perfect setting for drama and romance of the highest order.

Yet this is only half of what the island has to offer, for hidden in the vast canopy of greenery are tiny villages, each with its own unique flavor. There you can sample rich cheeses, bold homemade wines, and the famous cozido (meat and vegetables boiled on the volcanic earth). The savory smell of the boiling meats is so strong that it even overwhelms the primeval incense of volcanic sulfur.

Finally, as the mild evening sun sets into the ocean, the cobblestone streets of the charming little city lead you back to the coastline. Your long day ends in a walk along black sand beaches which seem almost to vanish in the total darkness. Sometimes, it feels as if you will too.

5

Example

The Technique

As might be expected, example is frequently used as a supporting technique in writing. In an essay against capital punishment, for instance, including cases of innocent individuals who were wrongfully executed would clearly reinforce the point that with capital punishment, mistakes cannot be rectified. In some cases, though, an assignment — a paper concerning the difficulties involved in hunting for a job — will call for example to be the dominant mode.

Whether example is a supporting mode or the dominant technique, you need to

- ensure that you use *specific and relevant examples;*
- include *multiple examples* to make your point; and
- provide *an effective arrangement.*

SPECIFIC AND RELEVANT EXAMPLES

Whenever you write, your reader depends on you to support or illustrate your essay's points, and it is through example that you accomplish this. In order for an essay to be successful, however, the examples must be *specific* (detailed and particular) and *relevant* (directly related to the point being made).

Making an example specific is a matter of providing enough information so that your reader can understand its meaning and significance. To make sure that the examples are specific in an essay about the federal government's efforts to reduce water pollution, you would spell out as fully as possible the changes Congress now demands of its cities and towns. Specific examples would include required upgrading of current wastewater treatment plants to remove more pollutants, mandatory reconstruction of sewer systems to eliminate any untreated flow into waterways, permanent bans on individual septic systems within one hundred yards of any body of water, and so on.

To ensure that your examples are relevant, you must keep your focus narrow. For instance, one of the problems with the government's steps to reduce water pollution is that municipalities are being saddled with astronomical costs, leaving some older, midsize cities with potential expenses of $150 million or more in order to comply with the regulations. Because it is directly related to the changes demanded, a discussion of the expense of such measures in your essay would definitely be relevant.

In this brief passage from his 1985 book, *Illiterate America*, notice how Jonathan Kozol keeps his examples of the consequences of adult illiteracy both specific and relevant:

> Illiterates cannot read the letters that their children bring home from their teachers. They cannot study school department circulars that tell them of the courses that their children must be taking if they hope to pass the SAT exams. They cannot help with homework. They cannot write a letter to the teacher. They are afraid to visit in the classroom. They do not want to humiliate their children or themselves.

MULTIPLE EXAMPLES

As page 24 shows, an essay that paints a full picture for a reader is one that is fully developed or *amplified*. Sometimes a paper with a single extended example can make a point effectively. In many cases, though, with a paper that features example as the dominant mode, the means to achieving this goal is to provide multiple examples.

In an essay about sexism in society, examples about sexist language and stereotypes in the entertainment world would be good, but by themselves they wouldn't be enough to make the point fully. Other examples would bring the point across more clearly: recent research showing that boys receive far more attention from teachers than girls do, statistics showing that women still receive on average fifty-eight cents for every dollar earned by men, the disparity between the number of male and female elected officials (exemplified by the predominantly male U.S. Senate), and so on.

The following paragraph on agoraphobia, the abnormal fear of open places, provides several examples of what those affected by this disorder experience:

> When you have agoraphobia, the everyday things that people take for granted become major problems. For example, taking a ride in a car, even to the corner store, becomes a heart-pounding nightmare. You get in the car, and your heart begins to race. You're covered with a cold sweat, and you feel faint. As you move farther from home, the feelings intensify. Your heart pounds so hard you can hear it in your ears, you can't breathe, and you feel certain that you are going to die. The feeling starts to lessen only when you return to your home, a refuge which might as well be your prison.

AN EFFECTIVE ARRANGEMENT

How the material in an essay is presented is also important. Sometimes you will write an essay focusing on a single episode or experience as an example, with chronological order as the method of arrangement. Occasionally your essay will be composed of multiple examples, each having about the same degree of impact, so the order of arrangement is less of a concern. In other cases, however, some of the examples are more striking or powerful than others. As pages 28–29 illustrate, *emphatic order,* in which you build up to your strongest example, is the most effective way to arrange such a paper.

Consider an essay discussing situations in which dishonesty is justified. In such a paper, emphatic order would ensure that the main point is most effectively supported. For instance, showing enthusiasm for a gift you don't actually like would be a strong example, and pretending not to hear someone's off-color language would be a stronger one. Stealing to save someone from starvation would clearly be the strongest example of all, however, since it deals with life and death. Saving it for last allows the paper to build in intensity and thus maintain the reader's interest.

Here is a brief excerpt from a psychology text written by Carol Tarvis and Carole Wade, in which they use emphatic order to present different interpretations of common hand gestures:

> Even the simplest gesture is subject to misunderstanding and offense. The sign of the University of Texas football team, the Longhorns, is to extend the index finger and the pinkie. In Italy and other parts of Europe this gesture means a man's wife has been unfaithful to him — a serious insult! Anita Rowe, a consultant who advises businesses on cross-cultural customs, tells of a newly hired Asian engineer in a California company. As the man left his office to lead the first meeting of his project team, his secretary crossed her fingers to wish him luck. Instead of reassuring him, her gesture thoroughly confused him: In his home country, crossing one's fingers is a sexual proposition.

AN ANNOTATED EXAMPLE

Betty Friedan
The Problem that Has No Name

One of the names most often associated with the women's movement in the United States is Betty Friedan. Over the last thirty years, her writings about the roles of women in society and women's rights have appeared in numerous publications, including Mademoiselle, Ladies' Home Journal, McCall's, *and the* New York Times Magazine. *More recently, Friedan has turned her attention to aging and society's reaction to it with her 1993 book* The Fountain of Age. The Feminine Mystique, *her landmark book from which this excerpt is taken, initially appeared in 1963 and was reissued on the tenth and twentieth anniversaries of its publication, irrefutable testimony to its continuing impact and influence.*

How does Friedan's use of example help her express the shared sense of emptiness and despair that countless post-World War II American women experienced?

Gradually I came to realize that the problem that has no name was shared by countless women in America. As a magazine writer I often interviewed women about problems with their children, or their marriages, or their houses, or their communities. But after a while I began to recognize the telltale signs of this other problem. I saw the same signs in suburban ranch houses and split-levels on Long Island and in New Jersey and Westchester County; in colonial houses in a small Massachusetts town; on patios in Memphis; in suburban and city apartments; in living rooms in the Midwest. Sometimes I sensed the problem, not as a reporter, but as a suburban housewife, for during this time I was also bringing up my own three children in Rockland County, New York. I heard echoes of the problem in college dormitories and semi-private maternity wards, at PTA meetings and luncheons of the League of Women Voters, at suburban cocktail parties, in station wagons waiting for trains, and in snatches of conversations overheard at Schrafft's. The groping words I heard from other women, on quiet afternoons when children were at school or on quiet

She includes several examples of the problem as her introduction.

She uses an episode from her own experience as an example.

1

evenings when husbands worked late, I think I understood first as a woman long before I understood their larger social and psychological implications.

She gives examples of possible causes of the problem.

Just what was this problem that has 2 no name? What were the words women used when they tried to express it? Sometimes a woman would say, "I feel empty somehow . . . incomplete." Or she would say, "I feel as if I don't exist." Sometimes she blotted out the feeling with a tranquilizer. Sometimes she thought the problem was with her husband, or her children, or that what she really needed was to redecorate her house, or move to a better neighborhood, or have an affair, or another baby. Sometimes, she went to a doctor with symptoms she could hardly describe: "A tired feeling . . . I get so angry with the children it scares me . . . I feel like crying without any reason." (A Cleveland doctor called it "the housewife's syndrome.")

Note the powerful example.

A number of women told me about great bleeding blisters that break out on their hands and arms. "I call it the housewife's blight," said a family doctor in Pennsylvania. "I see it so often lately in these young women with four, five and six children who bury themselves in their dishpans. But it isn't caused by detergent and it isn't cured by cortisone."

Sometimes a woman would tell me 3 that the feeling gets so strong she runs out of the house and walks through the streets. Or she stays inside her house and cries. Or her children tell her a joke, and she doesn't laugh because she doesn't hear it. I talked to women who had spent years on the analyst's couch,

She uses the women's own words to support her examples.

working out their "adjustment to the feminine role," their blocks to "fulfill-ment as a wife and mother." But the desperate tone in these women's voices, and the look in their eyes, was the same as the tone and the look of other women, who were sure they had no problem, even though they did have a strange feeling of desperation.

A mother of four who left college　4
at nineteen to get married told me:

She uses emphatic order — moves from strong example to stronger to strongest.

I've tried everything women are supposed to do — hobbies, garden-ing, pickling, canning, being very social with my neighbors, joining committees, running PTA teas. I can do it all, and I like it, but it doesn't leave you anything to think about — any feeling of who you are. I never had any career ambitions. All I wanted was to get married and have four children. I love the kids and Bob and my home. There's no problem you can even put a name to. But I'm desperate. I begin to feel I have no personality. I'm a server of food and a putter-on of pants and a bedmaker, somebody who can be called on when you want some-thing. But who am I?

She continues to use women's own words to support her examples.

A twenty-three-year-old mother in　5
blue jeans said:

I ask myself why I'm so dissatisfied. I've got my health, fine children, a lovely new home, enough money. My husband has a real future as an electronics engineer. He doesn't have any of these feelings. He says

She continues to use women's own words to support her examples.

maybe I need a vacation, let's go to New York for a weekend. But that isn't it. I always had this idea we should do everything together. I can't sit down and read a book alone. If the children are napping and I have one hour to myself I just walk through the house waiting for them to wake up. I don't make a move until I know where the rest of the crowd is going. It's as if ever since you were a little girl, there's always been somebody or something that will take care of your life: your parents, or college, or falling in love, or having a child, or moving to a new house. Then you wake up one morning and there's nothing to look forward to.

A young wife in a Long Island de- 6
velopment said:

She saves her strongest example for last; the final sentence is truly powerful.

I seem to sleep so much. I don't know why I should be so tired. This house isn't nearly so hard to clean as the cold-water flat we had when I was working. The children are at school all day. It's not the work. I just don't feel alive.

Your Turn: Responding to the Subject

a. At least part of the problem that has no name is the burden that women have had to bear in the so-called traditional marriage. In such an arrangement, the husband's role is to provide financial support for the family, and the wife's role is to take care of all domestic matters, including child rearing. As Betty Friedan's excerpt illustrates, however, an enormous number of women find their duties and responsibilities in these marriages overwhelmingly mindless and stifling. For this assignment, suggest a more equitable arrangement for marriage, providing plenty of examples of ways you would adjust responsibilities.

b. No doubt at least part of the problem that has no name is miscommunication or worse, lack of communication. For this assignment, focus on examples of what happens when people in situations other than marriage don't listen to or understand each other.

Steven A. Holmes
It's Terrible News! And It's Not True. . . .

Some days, if all the news reports are to be believed, it seems as if the world is just falling apart — that our environment is completely ru-ined, that society is without morals, that we're on the brink of anni-hilation, and so on. The problem, as Steven A. Homes explains in this article from the New York Times, *is that such reports aren't always accurate. According to Holmes, sometimes the media offers only a superficial — and therefore, misleading — look at controversial sub-jects. Furthermore, reporters sometimes fail to do the kinds of research or checking and double-checking of facts that they should. As a re-sult, some of the news stories we read or hear simply aren't credible.*

What happens when legitimate news organizations publish or broadcast inaccurate or misleading news stories?

The reports were shocking, even enraging. They were the types 1
of reports that can make one wonder where American society is headed.

In 1995, several research organizations reported that a hefty 2
percentage — in one study, 65 percent — of teenage mothers had babies by adult men. The image of lecherous men seduc-ing troubled young girls prompted several states to step up en-forcement of statutory rape laws.

There was one problem, though. The concept was largely 3
wrong.

What many news reports on the studies neglected to men- 4
tion was that 62 percent of the teenage mothers were 18 or 19 years old and, therefore, like the fathers of their babies, adults. Also ignored was the fact that the researchers did not differ-entiate between married and single teenagers.

Subsequent studies found that, of those age 15 to 17 who 5
gave birth, only 8 percent were unmarried and made pregnant by men five or more years older.

122

The tale of the predatory males is just one example of 6 what has become a disquieting trend. Call it the "whoops factor," a phenomenon that starts with shoddy research or the misinterpretation of solid research, moves on quickly to public outcry, segues swiftly into the enactment of new laws or regulations and often ends with news organizations and some public-policy mavens sounding like the late Gilda Radner's character, Emily Litella, as they sheepishly chirp, "Never mind!"

The public has been buffeted by reports suggesting a 7 campaign to torch black churches, a surge in juvenile crime, rampant day-care-center child abuse, a rape crisis on college campuses and the continued poisoning of the country by cancer-causing chemicals such as alar, saccharin or cyclamates, or by electromagnetic forces emanating from high-voltage power wires.

Recently, a panel of scientists from the National Cancer Institute and some leading hospitals reported — after an exhaustive study — that there is no evidence that living near power lines causes elevated rates of childhood leukemia. The link had been suggested by a poorly designed 1979 University of Colorado study. After that study was reported, parents of children with cancer sued power companies, and property values near power lines plummeted. 8

While there tends to be enough truth in many of these 9 claims to warrant serious investigation and remedial action, some of the initial reports are so overblown as to produce panic and then cynicism.

"It's what I call the Weather Channel phenomenon," said 10 Robert Thompson, a Syracuse University professor of radio and television. "Five minutes into watching it, you're convinced that you have to be really concerned about that front moving in. The next thing you know you've turned off the TV in a state of panic . . ."

When the brewing problem is exposed as a kind of Comet 11 Kohoutek of social pathology, there is a sense of betrayal, complacency and, finally, attention is drawn away from the true extent of the problem to the methodology that was used to unearth it.

"A brilliant sleight-of-hand gets achieved," Thompson 12 said. "These are problems that are difficult to solve. And if we divert attention to a debate on how they are covered or how they are measured, then we don't have to make the tough choices on how to actually address them."

Underneath the embarrassing retreats from what in hind-   *13* sight seems shabby research, superficial journalism or a triumph of politically motivated public relations lies a much deeper problem: Americans' willingness, almost eagerness, to accept a Hobbesian view of man as a brutish thug who, if left unchecked, would sow chaos and destruction. In this atmosphere, even reports like the one claiming that one-quarter of all female college students are raped each year are readily believed.

Moreover, "people are always looking for one single-bullet   *14* answer," said Kristin Moore, president of Child Trends Inc., a Washington-based research organization specializing in adolescent sexual issues. "But things are more complicated than people want them to be."

And they are more complicated than many reporters and   *15* editors want them to be. Cramped by space and time, and usually not having much knowledge of statistics, journalists often are bamboozled by "experts" bearing impressive numbers or they fail to put the numbers in historical or demographic perspective.

"The media do not have the time, inclination or skill to   *16* really dig deeply into reports of research or claims made by political leaders," said Alfred Blumstein, a professor of criminology at Carnegie Mellon University in Pittsburgh. "It merely transmits them, and transmits them in a way to make headlines or sound bites on TV."

Thus, when the Department of Health and Human Ser-   *17* vices estimated in 1983 that 1.5 million children are reported missing each year, few people questioned the information. With the imprimatur of the federal government, a national campaign sprang up that included pictures of missing children on milk cartons and campaigns instructing children how to avoid being kidnapped.

Later, more rigorous studies would find that 3,200 to   *18* 4,600 children a year are abducted by strangers. To be sure, that is a large number. But it is dwarfed by the more than 350,000 children who, the Justice Department estimated later, are snatched by a parent in custody disputes, and it is nowhere near 1.5 million.

The definition of a particular group as victims — often   *19*
with solid historical and contemporary evidence — also helps
color the public's receptivity to studies or claims about them.

For example, last year, a spate of fires at African-American   *20*
churches conjured images of white night-riders running amok
or a reprise of the 1963 Birmingham, Ala., church bombing.
President Clinton appointed a task force to look into the problem. This past month, the task force reported that there was
no national conspiracy of hate groups; the fires stemmed in
part from racism but also from financial profit, burglary and
personal revenge. Indeed, about one-third of the 76 people ar-
rested in the church cases between Jan. 1, 1995, and May 27,
1997, were black.

Often, the unwillingness of reporters to ask hard questions   *21*
or of policy-makers to provide a context for data can lead reg-
ulators and lawmakers into broad-brush policies that waste resources and political capital.

In May, the U.S. House of Representatives, in response to   *22*
reports of surging juvenile crime and an increase in the number of young killers, voted to offer states $1.5 billion in finan-
cial incentives to require that juveniles accused of violent
crimes be tried as adults. Even as the House acted, the Bureau
of Criminal Justice Statistics reported that while juvenile homicides had risen, they were highly concentrated.

The bureau determined that in 1995, one-third took place   *23*
in just 10 of the counties in the nation. It added that 84 percent of the nation's counties had no juvenile homicides at all.

Understanding the Significance

1. What was incorrect about the story of teenage girls having
   babies fathered by adult men?
2. As Steven Holmes explains it, what is the "whoops factor"?
3. When the kind of claims on which Holmes focuses prove
   to be false, what are the two primary outcomes?
4. What did the task force investigating claims of a national
   conspiracy of hate groups intent on burning down black
   churches ultimately determine?

Discovering the Writer's Purpose

1. Throughout this writing, is Holmes more interested in the errors in these stories or in the effects that such misstatements have on society? Explain.
2. In paragraph 7, Holmes lists crises recently reported in the news. What point is he trying to make by listing these disasters or problems in this way?
3. While explaining the reasons people believe news stories that reflect the worst about themselves and the world, Holmes quotes Kristin Moore, a researcher, who states that people are "looking for one single-bullet answer" (paragraph 14) when faced with disturbing news reports. What do you think Moore means?
4. What is Holmes saying about the role of the media in perpetuating these stories?

Examining the Writer's Method

1. Holmes opens his essay with a story about teenage girls having babies fathered by older men, a story that he reveals in the third and fourth paragraphs is not at all what it appears. Is beginning his writing in this way a good technique, given his subject? Explain.
2. Of the examples Holmes supplies, which one in your judgment does the best job of supporting his thesis? Why?
3. Would Holmes's paper be more — or less — effective if he provided less explanation or analysis of the stories and more examples of inaccurate or untrue stories? Explain.
4. Do you agree with the way Holmes has arranged his examples or would you suggest changing the order? Why?

Considering Style and Language

1. How does Holmes avoid making the same mistake that the writers of the stories featured in his article had made?

2. Holmes's approach in presenting and discussing the examples of inaccurate or untrue news stories is calm and straightforward. How would his article have been different if he had instead emphasized his outrage with the media's failure to do its job thoroughly?

3. In his essay, Holmes includes such expressions as the "whoops" factor (para. 6), "the Weather Channel phenomenon" (para. 10), and "a kind of Comet Kohoutek of social pathology (para. 11). How does his use of such expressions affect the tone of his writing?

4. What do the following words mean in the context of the writing? Lecherous, seducing, statutory (para. 2); subsequent (para. 5); predatory, disquieting, shoddy, segues, maven (para. 6); buffeted, rampant, emanating (para. 7); plummeted (para. 8); cynicism (para. 9); pathology, complacency (para. 11); sleight-of-hand (para. 12); Hobbesian, chaos (para. 13); bamboozled, demographic (para. 15); imprimatur (para. 17); rigorous (para. 18); spate, reprise (para. 20).

Your Turn: Responding to the Subject

a. Holmes states that journalists often don't fully understand the findings they report or are misled by experts who twist information to fit specific agendas. All in all, Holmes presents a picture of the media as more interested in the shock value of the story than its accuracy. What has been your experience? Can you think of other examples of stories reported by the media — newspaper, magazine, television, radio, Internet — that have proven to be erroneous? For this assignment, write about those examples.

b. A few years ago a story circulated around the country about a man who awoke in a bathtub full of ice cubes after a night on the town, with a sign taped to his side informing him to call a doctor immediately because his kidneys had been removed, presumably to be sold on the black market to an organ broker. Although this story was repeated and believed by many, of course it was not true; it

was an "urban myth." Urban myths are stories of out-
landish government conspiracies, incurable deadly dis-
eases, unspeakable violence, and so forth, that travel from
one person to the next, often growing as the storytellers
unconsciously — or intentionally — embellish them. With
the wide availability of the Internet, the number, variety,
and complexity of urban myths seem to have grown enor-
mously. For this assignment, relate and explain several
urban myths that you've heard.

Perri Klass

She's Your Basic L.O.L. in N.A.D.

Whether the subject is professional athletics, show business, mortuary science, law, and so on, an insider's insights are always intriguing. Perri Klass, who published this essay in 1984 while a student at Harvard Medical School, is clearly an insider when it comes to the world of medicine. Now a pediatrician and an instructor at the Boston University School of Medicine, she is also an accomplished writer, with short stories and articles in such periodicals as the Antioch Review, Mademoiselle, Discover, *and the* New York Times *to her credit. In addition, she has published two novels, a collection of short stories, and two collections of her essays, including* A Not Entirely Benign Procedure: Four Years as a Medical Student, *from which this essay is taken.*

How does Perri Klass use example in this essay to translate the sometimes funny, sometimes serious, and sometimes ironic abbreviations and acronyms that physicians use as they deal with their patients?

"Mrs. Tolstoy is your basic L.O.L. in N.A.D., admitted for a soft   1
rule-out M.I.," the intern announces. I scribble that on my patient list. In other words Mrs. Tolstoy is a Little Old Lady in No Apparent Distress who is in the hospital to make sure she hasn't had a heart attack (rule out a myocardial infarction). And we think it's unlikely that she has had a heart attack (a *soft* rule-out).

If I learned nothing else during my first three months of   2
working in the hospital, as a medical student, I learned endless jargon and abbreviations. I started out in a state of primeval innocence, in which I didn't even know that "s̄ C.P., S.O.B., N/V" meant "without chest pain, shortness of breath, or nausea and vomiting." By the end I took the abbreviations so for granted that I would complain to my mother the English

129

Professor, "And can you believe I had to put down *three* NG tubes last night?"

"You'll have to tell me what an NG tube is if you want me   *3*
to sympathize properly," my mother said. NG, nasogastric — isn't it obvious?

I picked up not only the specific expressions but also the   *4*
patterns of speech and the grammatical conventions; for example, you never say that a patient's blood pressure fell or that his cardiac enzymes rose. Instead, the patient is always the subject of the verb: "He dropped his pressure." "He bumped his enzymes." This sort of construction probably reflects the profound irritation of the intern when the nurses come in the middle of the night to say that Mr. Dickinson has disturbingly low blood pressure. "Oh, he's gonna hurt me bad tonight," the intern may say, inevitably angry at Mr. Dickinson for dropping his pressure and creating a problem.

When chemotherapy fails to cure Mrs. Bacon's cancer,   *5*
what we say is, "Mrs. Bacon failed chemotherapy."

"Well, we've already had one hit today, and we're up next,   *6*
but at least we've got mostly stable players on our team." This means that our team (group of doctors and medical students) has already gotten one new admission today, and it is our turn again, so we'll get whoever is next admitted in emergency, but at least most of the patients we already have are fairly stable, that is, unlikely to drop their pressures or in any other way get suddenly sicker and hurt us bad. Baseball metaphor is pervasive: A no-hitter is a night without any new admissions. A player is always a patient — a nitrate player is a patient on nitrates, a unit player is a patient in the intensive-care unit and so on, until you reach the terminal player.

It is interesting to consider what it means to be winning,   *7*
or doing well, in this perennial baseball game. When the intern hangs up the phone and announces, "I got a hit," that is not cause for congratulations. The team is not scoring points; rather, it is getting hit, being bombarded with new patients. The object of the game from the point of view of the doctors, considering the players for whom they are already responsible, is to get as few new hits as possible.

These special languages contribute to a sense of closeness   *8*
and professional spirit among people who are under a great deal of stress. As a medical student, it was exciting for me to discover

that I'd finally cracked the code, that I could understand what doctors said and wrote and could use the same formulations myself. Some people seem to become enamored of the jargon for its own sake, perhaps because they are so deeply thrilled with the idea of medicine, with the idea of themselves as doctors.

I knew a medical student who was referred to by the interns   9
on the team as Mr. Eponym because he was so infatuated with eponymous terminology, the more obscure the better. He never said "capillary pulsations" if he could say "Quincke's pulses." He would lovingly tell over the multinamed syndromes — Wolff-Parkinson-White, Lown-Ganong-Levine, Henoch-Schonlein — until the temptation to suggest Schleswig-Holstein or Stevenson-Kefauver or Baskin-Robbins became irresistible to his less reverent colleagues.

And there is the jargon that you don't ever want to hear   10
yourself using. You know that your training is changing you, but there are certain changes you think would be going a little too far.

The resident was describing a man with devastating termi-   11
nal pancreatic cancer. "Basically he's C.T.D.," the resident concluded. I reminded myself that I had resolved not to be shy about asking when I didn't understand things. "C.T.D.?" I asked timidly.

The resident smirked at me. "Circling The Drain."   12

The images are vivid and terrible. "What happened to   13
Mrs. Melville?"

"Oh, she boxed last night." To box is to die, of course.   14

Then there are the more pompous locutions that can make   15
the beginning medical student nervous about the effects of medical training. A friend of mine was told by his resident, "A pregnant woman with sickle-cell represents a failure of genetic counseling."

Mr. Eponym, who tried hard to talk like the doctors, once   16
explained to me, "An infant is basically a brainstem preparation." A brainstem preparation, as used in neurological research, is an animal whose higher brain functions have been destroyed so that only the most primitive reflexes remain, like the sucking reflex, the startle reflex and the rooting reflex.

The more extreme forms aside, one most important function   17
of medical jargon is to help doctors maintain some distance

from their patients. By reformulating a patient's pain and problems into a language that the patient doesn't even speak, I suppose we are in some sense taking those pains and problems under our jurisdiction and also reducing their emotional impact. This linguistic separation between doctors and patients allow conversations to go on at the bedside that are unintelligible to the patient. "Naturally, we're worried about adeno-C.A.," the intern can say to the medical student, and lung cancer need never be mentioned.

I learned a new language this past summer. At times it thrills me to hear myself using it. It enables me to understand my colleagues, to communicate effectively in the hospital. Yet I am uncomfortably aware that I will never again notice the peculiarities and even atrocities of medical language as keenly as I did this summer. There may be specific expressions I manage to avoid, but even as I remark them, promising myself I will never use them, I find that this language is becoming my professional speech. It no longer sounds strange in my ears — or coming from my mouth. And I am afraid that as with any new language, to use it properly you must absorb not only the vocabulary but also the structure, the logic, the attitudes. At first you may notice these new alien assumptions every time you put together a sentence, but with time and increased fluency you stop being aware of them at all. And as you lose that awareness, for better or for worse, you move closer and closer to being a doctor instead of just talking like one. *18*

Understanding the Significance

1. Perhaps more than any other professionals, physicians are granted tremendous status by American society. Why do you believe this is so? Do physicians deserve this high ranking? Explain.

2. In paragraph 8, Perri Klass maintains that the special language shared by physicians contributes "to a sense of closeness and professional spirit among people who are under a great deal of stress." In your view, how does a special language hold any group of individuals together?

3. Several of Klass's examples, especially those in paragraphs 11–14, are instances of black humor, that is, humor focusing on the morbid or absurd aspects of life. Do you find these examples funny? Why do you feel people resort to this kind of humor?

4. In paragraph 17, Klass suggests that one function of medical jargon is to reduce the "emotional impact" a patient faces because it allows "conversations to go on at the bedside that are unintelligible to the patient." Is she correct? If you were a patient, would you be comforted or concerned by a discussion of your condition that you couldn't understand? Explain.

Discovering the Writer's Purpose

1. Some people might feel that the examples Klass supplies in paragraphs 11–14 are shocking and perhaps offensive. Why do you think Klass included them? Do you think she made the right decision? Explain.

2. Who Mrs. Tolstoy is, or whether she is one person or an amalgam of several patients encountered by Klass, is not especially important. Her story serves only to illustrate the way physicians converse while on the job. Why, then, do you think Klass bothered to give her a name? Would the anecdote have been less effective if Mrs. Tolstoy were referred to as merely "a female patient"?

3. In paragraph 17, Klass suggests that one of the most important functions of this jargon is "to help doctors maintain some distance from their patients." Does this statement surprise you or change the way you feel about your physician? Why?

4. In her concluding paragraph, Klass says, "I am afraid that as with any new language, to use it properly, you must absorb not only the vocabulary but also the structure, the logic, the attitudes." What do you feel she is trying to say about her profession?

Examining the Writer's Method

1. Klass has certainly included a large number of examples in her essay. In your judgment which is the most effective? Why?
2. Klass saves the most serious examples for the end of her essay. How might the overall effect of her paper have been changed if she had begun with the serious examples and kept the lighter ones for the end?
3. Klass's point in this essay is that physicians rely on this jargon to help them deal with the difficulties of their profession. Explain how paragraphs 4 and 5, which deal with "the patterns of speech and the grammatical conventions" of some of the jargon, support this point.
4. In paragraphs 9 and 16, Klass discusses a classmate nicknamed Mr. Eponym, and the picture she paints of him isn't particularly flattering. Why do you feel Klass has included two paragraphs that focus on him?

Considering Style and Language

1. Klass opens her essay with an anecdote. How does the story of Mrs. Tolstoy help to set the tone for the rest of the essay?
2. Part of Klass's purpose is to emphasize the human side of a profession that requires almost superhuman reactions. How do the examples in her essay provide that insight?
3. In her final sentence, Klass states that as physicians-in-training become accustomed to the specialized language, they move "closer and closer to being a doctor instead of just talking like one." What point does she make by closing her paper in this way?
4. What do the following words mean in the context of the writing? Intern (para. 1); jargon, primeval (para. 2); conventions (para. 4); metaphor, pervasive, terminal (para. 6); perennial (para. 7); formulations, enamored (para. 8); epo-

nym, infatuated, obscure, reverent (para. 9); devastating, timidly (para. 11); pompous, locutions (para. 15); jurisdiction, linguistic, unintelligible (para. 17); peculiarities, atrocities, fluency (para. 18).

Your Turn: Responding to the Subject

a. What Klass offers with this essay is a glimpse at a profession from the vantage point of an insider. And as her essay shows, the view from the inside is clearly different from the view from the outside. Consider some subject that you have studied, some field you have mastered, some event you have gone through, and so on, and write an essay that takes your reader behind the curtain separating the experienced from the inexperienced. For example, you are now a college insider. If you were preparing a handbook for incoming students to help them over the confusion of the first few weeks, what examples would you include?

b. Physicians, Klass explains, sometimes use language to help them maintain a distance between themselves and the less pleasant aspects of their jobs. Have you observed or faced other people who have worked to maintain some degree of impersonality or distance? For this assignment, focus on these examples, perhaps exploring why such restraint is necessary.

Michael Demarest
The Fine Art of Putting Things Off

For some people, procrastination is a way of life, but even the most diligent and orderly among us occasionally delay in completing tasks. In this essay, Michael Demarest uses an extensive series of examples to reassure us that putting things off is a long-standing tradition shared by the famous and not-so-famous throughout history. Demarest, who has written extensively for newspapers and magazines and who has been associated with Time *as a foreign correspondent, award-winning senior writer, and editor, combines a gently ironic tone with an extensive use of example to create a delightful study of why people don't do what they are supposed to do when they are supposed to do it.*

Is Demarest suggesting that procrastination is something we should be concerned with, or something we should not worry about until tomorrow, or the day after, or . . . ?

"Never put off till tomorrow," exhorted Lord Chesterfield in 1749, "what you can do today." That the elegant earl never got around to marrying his son's mother and had a bad habit of keeping worthies like Dr. Johnson cooling their heels for hours in an anteroom attests to the fact that even the most well-intentioned men have been postponers ever. Quintus Fabius Maximus, one of the great Roman generals, was dubbed *"Cunctator"* (Delayer) for putting off battle until the last possible *vinum* break. Moses pleaded a speech defect to rationalize his reluctance to deliver Jehovah's edict to Pharaoh. Hamlet, of course, raised procrastination to an art form.   1

The world is probably about evenly divided between delayers and do-it-nowers. There are those who prepare their income taxes in February, prepay mortgages and serve precisely   2 planned dinners at an ungodly 6:30 P.M. The other half dine happily on leftovers at 9 or 10, misplace bills and file for an extension of the income tax deadline. They seldom pay credit-card bills until the apocalyptic voice of Diners threatens doom from Denver. They postpone, as Faustian encounters, visits to barbershop, dentist or doctor.

Yet for all the trouble procrastination may incur, delay can   3 often inspire and revive a creative soul. Jean Kerr, author of many successful novels and plays, says that she reads every soup-can and jam-jar label in her kitchen before settling down to her typewriter. Many a writer focuses on almost anything but his task — for example, on the Coast and Geodetic Survey of Maine's Frenchman Bay and Bar Harbor, stimulating his imagination with names like Googins Ledge, Blunts Pond, Hio Hill and Burnt Porcupine, Long Porcupine, Sheep Porcupine and Bald Porcupine islands.

From *Cunctator's* day until this century, the art of post-   4 ponement had been virtually a monopoly of the military ("Hurry up and wait"), diplomacy and the law. In former times, a British proconsul faced with a native uprising could comfortably ruminate about the situation with Singapore Sling in hand. Blessedly, he had no nattering Telex to order in machine guns and fresh troops. A U.S. general as late as World War II could agree with his enemy counterpart to take a sporting day off, loot the villagers' chickens and wine and go back to battle a day later. Lawyers are among the world's most addicted post-poners. According to Frank Nathan, a nonpostponing Beverly Hills insurance salesman, "The number of attorneys who die without a will is amazing."

Even where there is no will, there is a way. There is a dif-   5 ference, of course, between chronic procrastination and purposeful postponement, particularly in the higher echelons of business. Corporate dynamics encourage the caution that breeds delay, says Richard Manderbach, Bank of America group vice president. He notes that speedy action can be embarrassing or extremely costly. The data explosion fortifies those seeking excuses for inaction — another report to be read, another authority to be consulted. "There is always," says Manderbach, "a delicate edge between having enough information and too much."

His point is well taken. Bureaucratization, which flourished   6
amid the growing burdens of government and the greater complexity of society, was designed to smother policy-makers in
blankets of legalism, compromise and reappraisal — and thereby prevent hasty decisions from being made. The centralization of government that led to Watergate has spread to
economic institutions and beyond, making procrastination a
worldwide way of life. Many languages are studded with phrases
that refer to putting things off — from the Spanish *mañana* to
the Arabic *bukra fil mishmish* (literally "tomorrow in apricots,"
more loosely "leave it for the soft spring weather when the apricots are blooming").

Academe also takes high honors in procrastination.   7
Bernard Sklar, a University of Southern California sociologist
who churns out three to five pages of writing a day, admits
that "many of my friends go through agonies when they face
a blank page. There are all sorts of rationalizations: the pressure of teaching, responsibilities at home, checking out the
latest book, looking up another footnote."

Psychologists maintain that the most assiduous procrasti-   8
nators are women, though many psychologists are (at $50-
plus an hour) pretty good delayers themselves. Dr. Ralph
Greenson, a U.C.L.A. professor of clinical psychiatry (and Marilyn Monroe's onetime shrink), takes a fairly gentle view of
procrastination. "To many people," he says, "doing something, confronting, is the moment of truth. All frightened
people will then avoid the moment of truth entirely, or evade
or postpone it until the last possible moment." To Georgia
State Psychologist Joen Fagan, however, procrastination may
be a kind of subliminal way of sorting the important from the
trivial. "When I drag my feet, there's usually some reason,"
says Fagan. "I feel it, but I don't yet know the real reason."

In fact, there is a long and honorable history of procrasti-   9
nation to suggest that many ideas and decisions may well improve if postponed. It is something of a truism that to put off
making a decision is itself a decision. The parliamentary process is essentially a system of delay and deliberation. So, for
that matter, is the creation of a great painting, or an entrée, or
a book, or a building like Blenheim Palace, which took the
Duke of Marlborough's architects and laborers 15 years to construct. In the process, the design can mellow and marinate.

Indeed, hurry can be the assassin of elegance. As T. H. White, author of *Sword in the Stone,* once wrote, time "is not meant to be devoured in an hour or a day, but to be consumed delicately and gradually and without haste." In other words, *pace* Lord Chesterfield, what you don't necessarily have to do today, by all means put off until tomorrow.

Understanding the Significance

1. Michael Demarest arranges his examples in groups of historical figures, everyday people, writers, and so on. Of these groups, which do you feel receives the most attention? Why do you feel he focuses on this group?
2. It seems likely that the unnamed writer in paragraph 3 is Demarest himself. In what way would the essay have been different had he specifically identified himself as the student of obscure maps?
3. In paragraph 5, Demarest makes a distinction "between chronic procrastination and purposeful postponement." Explain the difference as you understand it.
4. In his final paragraph, Demarest states that "there is a long and honorable history of procrastination to suggest that many ideas and decisions may well improve if postponed." On the basis of the examples he has provided throughout the essay, do you feel Demarest is making a serious point — that putting off something can actually be beneficial — or is he winking at the reader once again and excusing his own tendency to procrastinate?

Discovering the Writer's Purpose

1. Demarest divides the world into "delayers" and "do-it-nowers." Do you agree with him, or do you feel that even the most ardent do-it-nower avoids a task once in a while? Give an example to support your answer.

2. At several points in his essay, Demarest defends procrastination as a potentially beneficial or justifiable activity. Have
   you ever discovered any benefit from putting off something? Explain.
3. In paragraph 8, Demarest refers to a psychiatrist who the-
   orizes that the main reason people procrastinate is fear. Do
   you agree? Why or why not?
4. In your judgment, what is Demarest's overall point about
   procrastination?

Examining the Writer's Method

1. In his introduction, Demarest features several examples.
   Why do you think he followed this strategy rather than
   focus on one example?
2. Demarest provides a large number of excellent examples
   in his essay. Which one do you feel is strongest? Why?
3. In paragraph 8, Demarest offers psychologists' explanations of why people procrastinate. Do you feel that this
   material would have changed the overall effect of the
   paper if it had been presented elsewhere in the essay? Why
   or why not?
4. Demarest begins and ends his paper with a reference to the
   same historical figure, Lord Chesterfield. In what way does
   this repetition affect his essay?

Considering Style and Language

1. Part of the appeal of Demarest's essay is his use of tongue-
   in-cheek humor, that is, humor that is ironic or facetious
   for effect. How does this technique help Demarest make
   his point?
2. At the end of paragraph 4 and again at the end of paragraph 8, Demarest presents a quotation expressing someone's view of procrastination, but in neither case does he

comment on the assessment. Why do you think he followed this strategy?

3. How does Demarest's use of emphatic order to present his examples affect the overall impact of the essay?

4. What do the following words mean in the context of the writing? Exhorted, anteroom, dubbed, rationalize, edict (para. 1); apocalyptic, Faustian (para. 2); geodetic (para. 3); virtually, monopoly, diplomacy, ruminate, nattering (para. 4); purposeful, echelons, dynamics, fortifies (para. 5); centralization, studded (para. 6); academe, churns (para. 7); assiduous, subliminal, trivial (para. 8); truism, mellow, marinate (para. 9).

Your Turn: Responding to the Subject

a. In this essay Demarest provides a series of examples in order to support his position that procrastination doesn't necessarily deserve its bad reputation. Of course, another writer might have taken exactly the opposite opinion — that procrastination is indeed every bit as bad as some people claim — and provided a series of examples to illustrate this point of view. For this assignment, take this second position.

b. Examine another questionable activity that people engage in — teasing, exaggerating, nagging, playing practical jokes, fibbing, and so on — and write a paper in which you, as Demarest did, reconsider the reputation of the activity. If after you consider the subject you decide it serves little useful purpose, you might write a paper in which you provide examples showing that this activity deserves its reputation.

Other Possibilities for Using Example

Here are some additional topics from which you might develop a paper that features example. Keep in mind that these are only general starting points. Make whatever changes necessary to develop the idea into a full essay.

- negative political advertisements
- college challenges
- highway dangers
- shortcomings in today's high schools
- dating complications
- fads
- duties as a pet owner
- true heroism
- pet peeves
- outstanding leaders — historical or current — in a field (literature, entertainment, sports, medicine, scientific research, etc.)
- boring hobbies
- diets
- corruption in society, government, religion, and so on
- superstitions
- proper manners

Practical Application: Example

Last year, your uncle began a small mail-order business from his home. His speciality is a gift item perfect for birthdays and anniversaries: old newspapers — not facsimiles but actual old newspapers — each in a clear plastic case. The concept has been such a hit that your uncle has taken a partner, moved the business out of his house and into a small office, and hired you to work there part time. Your job is take orders over the phone, contact the suppliers at the warehouses where the old papers are kept and cataloged, and record the transactions.

Right from your first day on the job, you have been amazed at how old-fashioned and inefficient your uncle's method of operation is. Everything, from ordering to keeping inventory to writing the copy for advertisements, is done by hand — paper and pencil. It is obvious to you that if this business is going to grow, it needs to be streamlined, and the perfect way to do so is to computerize.

When you suggest this innovation to your uncle, he is hesitant. He doesn't know much about computers, he explains, and he isn't convinced that spending money on a computer system at this point makes sense. But he is willing to consider discussing the prospect with his partner if you will prepare a *three hundred to five hundred word* report on ways that computerizing will help a small business such as his. To give you an idea of what he is looking for, your uncle gives you the following report prepared by business consultant Jessica A. Fletcher on ways that small businesses can cut expenses without compromising quality. Now get to work, using Fletcher's report to guide you in terms of *approach* and *format*.

Reduce Costs — Increase Quality

Any type of business can increase profits by increasing sales or reducing costs. Methods for increasing sales need to be considered on an individual basis for each because every business is dif-

ferent. However, there are several ways every business can reduce costs without reducing efficiency.

Saving money by cutting your company's cost expense must
be based on the concept of an organized, planned program. First
of all, adequate financial records must be maintained through a
proper accounting system in order to ascertain and analyze costs.
Rather than hiring an accountant, purchasing a software package
such as Peachtree Accounting or Quicken that can be specifically
tailored to your company's needs is more cost-effective and equally
time-effective. In addition, your taxes can be done by using a similar program, like Kiplinger's Tax Cut series.

In short, the owner-manager must understand the nature of
expenses and how expenses interrelate with sales, inventories,
cost of goods sold, gross profits, and net profits in order to effectively be able to reduce expenditures.

When thinking of ways to reduce costs, consider the following:

- **Computerize your business**
  Aside from the accounting aspect, a computer can be used
  to create and produce your own letterheads, invoices, and
  memos — the list is endless. You can even use the computer now as a marketing aspect by utilizing the Internet.
  The savings with time and money will by far outweigh the
  initial cost of becoming computerized. If you aren't proficient
  with a PC there are generally inexpensive courses offered at
  your local community college.
- **Cut out the middle man**
  A perfect example is to stop paying a payroll service — use
  direct deposit. Electronic banking for most businesses is free
  or offered for a minimal fee from most major banks. The
  money you will save from using a paper check system is
  quite substantial.
- **Advertise your business**
  There are several places to advertise that are relatively inexpensive and yet can generate a great response. Consider all
  of your options besides the obvious phone book, TV, and
  billboards. Don't forget local places such as mailers or other

companies' methods of advertising such as the back of menus or health newsletters, etc. And don't forget the Internet. It's a great way to spread the name of your business around.

- **Work smarter not harder**
  Make sure you are working to your full potential. Is your work space adequate? Are supplies accessible and useful in saving time? Remember — time is money.

There is really no end to the ways a small business can lower costs. And by doing so, quality does not have to suffer. In fact, by becoming cost-efficient, your business may actually discover new avenues of service to offer to your clients, thereby benefiting all parties concerned. In the end, your business can't afford not to.

6

Process

The Technique

As with the rest of the modes, process often serves as a supporting technique in an essay. A paper concerning the first night working at a pizza parlor, for example, might include the initially confusing list of steps involved in preparing the pizza, and an essay about the dangers of the use of anabolic steroids might include a section that details the physical and emotional changes a user experiences following a cycle of use.

Process will also sometimes be the primary focus of an essay, and it can be classified in one of three ways. One type is a *set of instructions* (often called *how-to writing*), which explains how to do something; the second type, *process analysis*, outlines how a condition or activity occurred; and the third type, *process narrative*, spells out how you or somebody else completed some task or action. Regardless of the focus you choose when you use process, you must make sure to

- keep the writing *clear and direct;*
- divide the process into *simple, logical steps;* and
- rely on *linear order.*

CLARITY AND DIRECTNESS

Your reader depends on you to make an essay clear and direct, but in no case is that need greater than with a paper that focuses primarily on process. No matter how familiar a process may seem to you as a writer, you must take into account that the reader may have a very limited understanding of it. And the more complex or technical the subject, the greater the chance that the reader won't have much of an understanding of it. Therefore, you must fully explain all specialized terms and steps. A paper about how nitrites in prepared foods can trigger serious allergic reactions wouldn't be effective without the explanation that nitrites are preservatives, added to such items as hot dogs, bologna, and some Chinese food.

With a set of instructions, an additional way to ensure that the writing communicates the various steps effectively is to address the reader directly through use of the *imperative mood,* commonly referred to as *command.* In the imperative mood, the subject of the sentence is not stated but is understood to be the person reading the piece.

Note the use of the imperative mood in this brief excerpt from the *Claris Works 5.0 User's Guide* that explains how to integrate different types of information in a single document by using a *frame,* a special object that serves as a conduit or window into another type of document:

> To create a frame, click to select a frame tool in the tool panel, position the pointer over the page, and then hold down the mouse button and drag the pointer until the frame is the size you want. You can now work in the frame, and you see the appropriate menu commands for that frame (for example, you see spreadsheet commands when you work in a spreadsheet frame).

SIMPLE, LOGICAL STEPS

With a paper featuring process as a dominant mode, the gap between what you and your reader know is often greater than it is with other types of writing. After all, a reader generally seeks out a process writing piece in order to gain a greater understanding of some task, condition, or phenomenon. When you write a process paper, you are essentially an expert presenting information to someone less knowledgeable, so you must make sure to break the process into easily understandable steps and then explain each step fully.

For example, you could describe how people see by explaining the process by which an image is viewed by the eye and translated by the brain, but such an explanation would be vastly inadequate. A far better method would be to break the process of vision into these four steps:

1. Light enters the lens of the eye and strikes specialized photoreceptor cells — called rods and cones — in the retina, the tissue at the back of the eye.
2. The light stimulates the photoreceptor cells to record the image within the range of the lens.
3. The photoreceptor cells send the visual message captured on the retina along the optic nerves to the visual cortex, the vision center of the brain.
4. The visual cortex translates the signals into a mental image.

With the process divided into smaller units like these, all that would remain would be to provide supporting examples or explanations so that the purpose and function of the various elements that allow us to see are clear for the reader.

Note how physician Herbert Benson takes one stage of the process of relaxation and breaks it into easy-to-follow steps in this brief passage from his book *Beyond the Relaxation Response*:

> Starting with your feet and progressing up to your calves, thighs, and abdomen, relax the various muscle groups in your body.
>
> Loosen up your head, neck, and shoulders by gently rolling your head around and shrugging your shoulders slightly. As for your arms and hands, stretch and then relax them, and then let them drape naturally into your lap. Avoid grasping your knees or legs or holding your hands tightly together.

LINEAR ORDER

One of the attributes that distinguish process writing from other types of writing is that it often features *linear order,* meaning that the steps are presented in the order in which they occur or must be completed. A paper dealing with how a hurricane develops or an essay on how the corruption in the Nixon administration was discovered are examples of subjects that would be arranged in linear order.

Not all papers with process as a dominant mode feature linear order, of course. An essay explaining how to lose weight and tone up would contain such elements as taking the stairs rather than using elevators or escalators; walking; jogging; swimming; eliminating snacks between meals; cutting back on fatty foods; and so on. But successfully completing the process doesn't require that these steps be done in a particular order.

Taking a photograph properly with a 35-millimeter camera, however, is a process that requires adherence to linear order. First you adjust the focus, then you change the setting to allow the proper amount of light through the lens, and then you push the shutter button to take the picture. Linear order is called for here because if these steps were rearranged in any other way, the resulting photograph would not likely be particularly pleasing.

In this brief excerpt from *The Education of Koko,* their fascinating book dealing with a study of the language abilities of apes, psychologist Francine Patterson and writer Eugene Linden use linear order to describe part of the daily routine that Koko, the female lowland gorilla who is the primary subject of the study, follows:

> I wake Koko up at 8:00 or 8:30 A.M. if she has not already been roused by Michael's [another gorilla involved in the study] antics. Following a breakfast of cereal or rice bread (rice and cereals plus raisins baked into a cake), milk, and fruit, Koko helps with the daily cleaning of her room. She enjoys going over both her room and Michael's with a sponge. Often these cleaning sessions end when Koko, seized by some urge, rips the sponge to shreds.

Then, some mornings, she sits on a chair before an electric teletype keyboard in the kitchen for a thirty-minute lesson in the production of English. Gorillas cannot generate the sounds necessary to speak, but through this Auditory Language Keyboard, which is linked to a voice synthesizer, we have given Koko a device that enables her to talk as well as generate signs. Other mornings we videotape or audiotape our work with flash cards.

AN ANNOTATED EXAMPLE

Diane Ackerman

Why Leaves Turn Color in the Fall

Diane Ackerman has enjoyed a prolific and varied writing career. A graduate of Pennsylvania State University and Cornell University, Ackerman is a highly acclaimed poet as well as the author of a number of successful nonfiction texts that explore the world of science and natural history, including The Moon by Whale Light, and Other Adventures among Bats, Penguins, Crocodilians, and Whales *(1991) and* The Rarest of the Rare: Vanishing Animals, Timeless Worlds *(1995). She is also the author of* A Natural History of Love *(1994), a collection of essays examining the phenomenon of romantic love. In addition, she has directed the writing program at Washington State University, been a writer in residence or visiting writer at several colleges such as the College of William and Mary and Columbia University, served as a staff writer for the* New Yorker, *and hosted the PBS* Mystery of the Senses. *This selection, taken from her 1992 text* A Natural History of the Senses, *details how the color change associated with fall occurs.*

How is the brilliant green that signifies spring and summer transformed into the rainbow of colors that characterizes fall?

Goldfinch, yellow,
and red-winged *are*
key words, signaling
the color change to be
discussed in the body
of the paper.

The opening
paragraph serves as
an overview of the
entire process — from
green leaves to bare
limbs.

This piece is process
analysis, *so it is*
presented in the third-
person point of view.

Note the use of a
rhetorical question to
signal the focus of the
essay.

How the tree prepares
for winter is
presented.

The stealth of autumn catches one un- 1
aware. Was that a goldfinch perching in
the early September woods, or just the
first turning leaf? A red-winged black-
bird or a sugar maple closing up shop
for the winter? Keen-eyed as leopards,
we stand still and squint hard, looking
for signs of movement. Early-morning
frost sits heavily on the grass, and turns
barbed wire into a string of stars. On a
distant hill, a small square of yellow appears to be a lighted stage. At last the
truth dawns on us: Fall is staggering in,
right on schedule, with its baggage of
chilly nights, macabre holidays, and
spectacular, heart-stoppingly beautiful
leaves. Soon the leaves will start cring-
ing on the trees, and roll up in clenched
fists before they actually fall off. Dry
seedpods will rattle like tiny gourds. But
first there will be weeks of gushing color
so bright, so pastel, so confettilike, that
people will travel up and down the East
Coast just to stare at it — a whole season of leaves.

Where do the colors come from? 2
Sunlight rules most living things with
its golden edicts. When the days begin
to shorten, soon after the summer sol-
stice on June 21, a tree reconsiders its
leaves. All summer it feeds them so they
can process sunlight, but in the dog
days of summer the tree begins pulling
nutrients back into its trunk and roots,
pares down, and gradually chokes off its
leaves. A corky layer of cells forms at the
leaves' slender petioles, then scars over.
Undernourished, the leaves stop pro-
ducing the pigment chlorophyll, and
photosynthesis ceases. Animals can mi-

grate, hibernate, or store food to prepare for winter. But where can a tree go? It survives by dropping its leaves, and by the end of autumn only a few fragile threads of fluid-carrying xylem hold leaves to their stems.

The process of green fading away, revealing actual color, is described.

A turning leaf stays partly green at 3 first, then reveals splotches of yellow and red as the chlorophyll gradually breaks down. Dark green seems to stay longest in the veins, outlining and defining them. During the summer, chlorophyll dissolves in the heat and light, but it is also being steadily replaced. In the fall, on the other hand, no new pigment is produced, and so we notice the other colors that were always there, right in the leaf, although chlorophyll's shocking green hid them from view. With their camouflage gone, we see these colors for the first time all year, and marvel, but they were always there, hidden like a vived secret beneath the hot glowing greens of summer.

How color changes occur differently in different geographical regions is explained.

The most spectacular range of fall 4 foliage occurs in the northeastern United States and in eastern China, where the leaves are robustly colored, thanks in part to a rich climate. European maples don't achieve the same flaming reds as their American relatives, which thrive on cold nights and sunny days. In Europe, the warm, humid weather turns the leaves brown or mildly yellow. Anthocyanin, the pigment that gives apples their red and turns leaves red or red-violet, is produced by sugars that remain in the leaf after the supply of nutrients dwindles. Unlike the carotenoids, which color

The chemical process of color change is presented.

carrots, squash, and corn, and turn leaves orange and yellow, anthocyanin varies from year to year, depending on the temperature and amount of sunlight. The fiercest colors occur in years when the fall sunlight is strongest and the nights are cool and dry (a state of grace scientists find vexing to forecast). This is also why leaves appear dizzyingly bright and clear on a sunny fall day: The anthocyanin flashes like a marquee.

The process as it affects different species is noted.

Not all leaves turn the same colors. 5 Elms, weeping willows, and the ancient ginkgo all grow radiant yellow, along with hickories, aspens, bottlebrush buckeyes, cottonweeds, and tall, keening poplars. Basswood turns bronze, birches bright gold. Water-loving maples put on a symphonic display of scarlets. Sumacs turn red, too, as do flowering dogwoods, black gums, and sweet gums. Though some oaks yellow, most turn a pinkish brown. The farmlands also change color, as tepees of cornstalks and bales of shredded-wheat-textured hay stand drying in the fields. In some spots, one slope of a hill may be green and the other already in bright color, because the hillside facing south gets more sun and heat than the northern one.

An odd feature of the colors is that 6 they don't seem to have any special purpose. We are predisposed to respond to their beauty, of course. They shimmer with the colors of sunset, spring flowers, the tawny buff of a colt's pretty rump, the shuddering pink of a blush. Animals and flowers color for a reason — adaptation to their environment — but there is no adaptive reason for leaves to color so beautifully in the fall any more than there is for the sky or ocean to be blue. It's just one of the haphazard marvels the planet bestows every year. We find the sizzling colors thrilling, and in a sense they dupe us. Colored like living things, they signal death and disintegration. In time, they will become fragile and, like the body, return to dust. They are as we hope our own fate will be when we die: Not to vanish, just to sublime from one beautiful state into another. Though leaves lose their green life, they bloom with urgent colors, as the woods grow mummified day by day, and Nature becomes more carnal, mute, and radiant.

How the name of the season evolved is explained.

We call the season "fall," from the Old English *feallan,* to fall, which leads back through time into the Indo-European *phol,* which also means to fall. So the word and the idea are both extremely ancient, and haven't really changed since the first of our kind needed a name for fall's leafy abundance. As we say the word, we're reminded of that other Fall, in the garden of Eden, when fig leaves never withered and scales fell from our eyes. Fall is the time when leaves fall from the trees, just as spring is when flowers spring up, summer is when we simmer, and winter is when we whine from the cold.   7

Children love to play in piles of leaves, hurling them into the air like confetti, leaping into soft unruly mattresses of them. For children, leaf fall is just one of the odder figments of Nature, like hailstones or snowflakes. Walk   8 down a lane overhung with trees in the never never land of autumn, and you will forget about time and death, lost in the sheer delicious spill of color. Adam and Eve concealed their nakedness with leaves, remember? Leaves have always hidden our awkward secrets.

Another rhetorical question is used to begin the discussion of the next aspect of the process.

But how do the colored leaves fall? 9 As a leaf ages, the growth hormone, auxin, fades, and cells at the base of the petiole divide. Two or three rows of small cells, lying at right angles to the axis of the petiole, react with water, then come apart, leaving the petioles hanging on by only a few threads of xylem. A light breeze, and the leaves are airborne.

The steps involved in the separation of leaf from branch are presented.

They glide and swoop, rocking in invisible cradles. They are all wing and may flutter from yard to yard on small whirlwinds or updrafts, swiveling as they go. Firmly tethered to earth, we love to see things rise up and fly — soap bubbles, balloons, birds, fall leaves. They remind us that the end of a season is capricious, as is the end of life. We especially like the way leaves rock, careen, and swoop as they fall. Everyone knows the motion. Pilots sometimes do a maneuver called a "falling leaf," in which the plane loses altitude quickly and on purpose, by slipping first to the right, then to the left. The machine weighs a ton or more, but in one pilot's mind it is a weightless thing, a falling leaf.

A comparable process is included.

She has seen the motion before, in the Vermont woods where she played as a child. Below her the trees radiate gold, copper, and red. Leaves are falling, although she can't see them fall, as she falls, swooping down for a closer view.

The concluding paragraph emphasizes the eternal nature of the seasons.

At last the leaves leave. But first 10 they turn color and thrill us for weeks on end. Then they crunch and crackle underfoot. They *shush*, as children drag their small feet through leaves heaping along the curb. Dark, slimy mats of leaves cling to one's heels after a rain. A damp, stuccolike mortar of semidecayed leaves protects the tender shoots with a roof until spring, and makes a rich humus. An occasional bulge or ripple in the leafy mounds signals a shrew or a field mouse tunneling out of sight. Sometimes one finds in fossil stones the imprint of a leaf, long since disintegrated, whose outlines remind us how detailed, vibrant, and alive are the things of this earth that perish.

Your Turn: Responding to the Subject

a. In this piece, Diane Ackerman explains a process in nature that we observe and appreciate but often don't fully understand. For this assignment, choose another aspect or element of nature that we experience or witness without, for the most part, considering how that aspect or element came to be. For instance, how does rain or snow form? How does beach erosion or beach transformation occur? How do various animals in cold climates prepare for winter? How does the Gulf Stream or an atmospheric condition such as El Niño change weather patterns? How does the lunar cycle occur? Because of your own academic background or interests, you may already understand the process you choose. If you lack the specialized information that would help you explain this process, however, plan to do a little research in the library or on the Internet so that you will be prepared to explain the various steps to your reader.

b. In the sixth paragraph of this excerpt, Ackerman suggests that the change in the color of leaves gives us hope that we too will become more vibrant as we move through our cycle of life. The idea that we pass through stages of life is one that has always captivated philosophers and writers. Here, for instance, is how Shakespeare characterized the cycle of life in his wonderful pastoral comedy, *As You Like It*:

All the world's a stage,
And all the men and women merely players.
They have their exits and entrances,
And one man in his time plays many parts,
His acts being seven ages. At first, the infant,
Mewling and puking in the nurse's arms.
Then the whining schoolboy, with his satchel
And shining morning face, creeping like a snail
Unwillingly to school. And then the lover,
Sighing like furnace, with a woeful ballad
Made to his mistress' eyebrow. Then a soldier,
Full of strange oaths and bearded like the pard,
Jealous in honour, sudden and quick in quarrel,
Seeking the bubble reputation
Even in the cannon's mouth. And then the justice,
In fair round belly with good capon lin'd
With eyes severe and beard of formal cut,
Full of wise saws and modern instances;
And so he plays his part. The sixth age shifts
Into the lean and slipper'd pantaloon,
With spectacles on nose and pouch on side;
His youthful hose, well sav'd, a world too wide
For his shrunk shank, and his big manly voice,
Turning again toward childish treble, pipes
And whistles in his sound. Last scene of all,
That ends this strange eventful history,
Is second childishness and mere oblivion,
Sans teeth, sans eyes, sans taste, sans everything.
(Act II, Scene 7, lines 138–165)

For this assignment, consider the stages of life we go through, either as Shakespeare spells them out or as you envision them. Then explain how you think people progress from one phase to the next.

Betty Edwards
Drawing Realistically through Pure Contour Drawing

To date, Betty Edwards's remarkable book, Drawing on the Right Side of the Brain, *has sold more than a million copies and has been translated into ten foreign languages, overwhelming testimony to its impact. In the text, she applies the results of brain research, principally on the differences between the two halves of the brain, to the teaching of drawing. Her approach is to introduce a number of techniques and exercises to help the right hemisphere of the brain, the seat of creativity, overcome the stifling control of the dominant left hemisphere, the center of verbal and analytical abilities. In this excerpt, she explains how to execute* pure contour drawing, *a method that enables a person to create a realistic drawing by focusing on the edges of the objects in the scene.*

How can drawing without looking at the paper and the hand doing the drawing enable one to become a better artist?

The technique is called "pure contour drawing," and your left 1
hemisphere is probably not going to like it. Introduced by a respected art teacher, Kimon Nicolaides, in his 1941 book, *The
Natural Way to Draw,* the method has been widely used by art
teachers. I believe that our new knowledge about how the brain
divides its work load provides a conceptual basis for understanding *why* pure contour drawing is effective as a teaching
method. At the time of writing his book, Nicolaides apparently
felt that the reason the pure contour method improved students' drawing was that it caused students to use both senses of
sight *and* touch: Nicolaides recommended that students imagine that they were *touching* the form as they drew. It seems more
likely now that the method works because the left brain rejects
the slow, meticulous, complex perceptions of spatial, relational

information, thus allowing access to R-mode processing. In short, pure contour drawing doesn't suit the left brain's style; it suits the style of the right brain — again, just what we want.

Before describing the method, I'll define some terms.   *2*

In drawing, a *contour* is defined as an *edge as you perceive it.*   *3* As a method, pure contour drawing (which is sometimes termed "blind contour drawing") entails close, intense observation as you draw the edges of a form *without looking at the drawing* while it is in progress.

An *edge,* as the term is used in drawing, is the *place where*   *4* *two things meet.* In drawing your hand, for example, the places where the *air* (which in drawing is thought of as *background* or *negative space*) meets the surface of your hand, the place where a fingernail meets the surrounding skin, the place where two folds of skin meet to form a wrinkle, and so on, are *shared edges.* The shared edge (called a *contour*) can be described — that is, *drawn* — as a single line, which is called a *contour line.*

This concept of edges is a fundamental concept in art, hav-   *5* ing to do with *unity,* perhaps the most important principle in art. Unity is achieved when everything in a composition fits together as a coherent whole, each part contributing to the wholeness of the total image.

To firmly set in your mind the concept of unified shapes   *6* and spaces that share edges, do the following exercise in imaging and seeing edges:

1. See in your mind's eye a disassembled child's jigsaw puzzle   *7* of six or eight painted pieces. The pieces will go together to form a picture of a sailboat on a lake. Imagine that the jigsaw pieces are shaped like the forms: a single white piece is the sail; a red piece, the boat, etc. Imagine the rest of the pieces in your own way — land, dock, clouds, whatever.
2. Now assemble the pieces in your imagination. See that the   *8* two edges come together to form a *single line* (imagine this as a precision-cut puzzle). These shared edges form *contour lines.* All of the pieces — spaces (sky and water) and shapes (boat, sail, land, etc.) — fit together to form the whole puzzle.

3. Next regard your own hand, one eye closed to flatten the   *9*
   image (closing one eye removes binocular depth perception). Think of your hand and the air around it as a jigsaw
   puzzle, the spaces (negative spaces) between the fingers
   sharing edges with the fingers; the shape of the flesh
   around each fingernail sharing an edge with the fingernail;
   two areas of skin sharing an edge to form a wrinkle. The
   whole image, made up of shapes and spaces, fits together
   like a jigsaw puzzle.
4. Now direct your eyes at one specific edge anywhere on   *10*
   your hand. Imagine in your mind's eye that you are drawing that edge as a single, slow, exact line on a piece of
   paper. As your eyes move slowly along the edge, imagine
   that you can *simultaneously* see the line being drawn, as
   though by some magical recording device.

In my classes, I demonstrate pure contour drawing, de-   *11*
scribing how to use the method as I draw — *if* I can manage
to keep talking (an L-mode function) while I'm trying to use
my right brain for drawing. Usually, I start out all right but
begin trailing off in mid-sentence after five minutes or so. By
that time, however, my students will have the idea.

Following the demonstration, I show examples of previous   *12*
students' pure contour drawings.

Before you begin: To best achieve an approximation of the   *13*
classroom procedure, be sure to read all of the instructions . . .
before beginning your drawing.

1. Find a place where you can be alone and uninterrupted for   *14*
   at least twenty minutes.
2. Set an alarm clock or timer, if you wish, for twenty min-   *15*
   utes just before you start your drawing. (This is to remove
   the necessity of keeping track of time — an L-mode function.) Or, if you have plenty of time and don't care about
   how long you might be drawing, omit the timer.
3. Place a piece of paper on a table and tape it down in any   *16*
   position that seems comfortable. Taping is necessary so
   that the paper won't shift about while you are drawing.

4. You are going to draw a picture of your own hand — your *17* left hand if you are right-handed, your right hand if you are left-handed. Arrange yourself so that your drawing hand, holding the pencil, is ready to draw on the taped-down paper.

5. Face *all the way around* to the opposite direction, gazing at *18* the hand you will draw. Be sure to rest the hand on some support, because you will be holding the same position for quite a long time. You are going to draw your hand *without being able to see what you are drawing*. . . . Facing away from your drawing is necessary to achieve the purpose of the method: first, to *focus your entire attention* on the visual information *out there* in front; and second, to *remove all attention* from the drawing, which might trigger off your old symbolic patterns memorized from childhood as the "way to draw hands." You want to draw only what you see (in spatial R-mode) and not what you know (in symbolic L-mode). Turning all the way around is necessary also because the impulse to look at the drawing is almost overwhelming at first. If you draw in the normal position and say to yourself, "I just won't look," you will very likely find yourself stealing peeks out of the corner of your eye. This will reactivate the L-mode and defeat the purpose of the exercise.

6. In the turned-around position, focus your eyes on some *19* part of your hand and perceive an *edge*. At the same time, place the point of your pencil on the paper (at any place well within the outside borders of the paper).

7. Very slowly, creeping a millimeter at a time, move your eyes *20* along the edge of your hand, *observing every minute variation and undulation of the edge*. As your eyes move, also move your pencil point *at the same slow pace* on the paper, recording each slight change or variation in the edge that you observe with your eyes. Become convinced in your mind that the information originating in the observed object (your hand) is minutely and precisely perceived by your eyes and is simultaneously recorded by the pencil, which *registers everything you are seeing at the moment of seeing*.

8. Do not turn around to look at the paper. Observing your *21* hand, draw the edges you see one bit at a time. Your eyes

will see and your pencil will record bit by bit the changing configuration of the contour. At the same time you will be aware of the relationship of that contour to the whole configuration of complex contours that is the whole hand. You may draw outside or inside contours or move from one to the other and back again. Don't be concerned about whether the drawing will look like your hand. It probably won't, since you can't monitor proportions, etc. By confining your perceptions to small bits at a time, you can learn to see things *exactly as they are,* in the artist's mode of seeing.

9. Match the movement of the pencil exactly with your eye   22
movement. One or the other may attempt to speed up, but don't let that happen. You must record everything at the very instant that you see each point on the contour. Do not pause in the drawing, but continue at a slow, even pace. At first you may feel uneasy or uncomfortable: some students report sudden headaches or a sense of panic. I believe this happens when the left brain senses that pure contour drawing is presenting a serious challenge to its dominance. It realizes, I think, that if you record the intricate, complex tangle of edges in your hand at the slow pace you are drawing, the right brain will have control for a long, long time. Therefore, the left brain says, in effect, "Stop this stupid stuff right now! We don't need to look at things that closely. I've already *named* everything for you, even some small things like wrinkles. Now be reasonable and let's get on with something that's not so boring — if you don't, I'll give you a headache."

Ignore this complaining. Simply persist. As you continue to   23
draw, the protests from the left will fade out and your mind will become quiet. You will find yourself becoming fascinated with the wondrous complexity of the thing you are seeing, and you will feel that you could go deeper and deeper into the complexity. Allow this to happen. You have nothing to fear or be uneasy about. Your drawing will be a beautiful record of your deep perception. We are not concerned about whether the drawing looks like a hand. We want the record of your perceptions.

Understanding the Significance

1. In the first few paragraphs of this selection, Betty Edwards defines several terms. How do these definitions help her make the process clear and understandable for the reader?
2. The subject Edwards writes about is perhaps as abstract as one can get: the way our brains process information and react to it. What parts of her presentation help her make this abstract concept concrete for her reader?
3. In most cases, Edwards explains not only how to complete a particular step but also why. How does this additional information help the reader?
4. How does Edwards's concluding paragraph help to reinforce the overall message of her piece?

Discovering the Writer's Purpose

1. Do you think that it would be more effective to read all the way through the selection before you perform the steps Edwards outlines or to do them as you read them? Why?
2. How might you suggest that Edwards adjust these steps so that an elementary-school audience might take advantage of the process?
3. In the opening paragraph, Edwards explains Kimon Nicolaides's theory, indicating that this method improved students' drawing because it caused them to use both sight and touch. Briefly explain what you think she means by *seeing* and *touching* an object.
4. Try the technique and then explain what step or steps you found hardest and why.

Examining the Writer's Method

1. In this writing Edwards actually includes a process within a process: the exercise in edges (paragraphs 7–10) and the process of contour drawing itself. Which of these process pieces do you feel is more effective? Why?

2. Are there any portions of her presentation that you would like to see spelled out in more detail? Explain your reasoning.

3. Where in the writing do you feel she does the best job of explaining *why* a step should be performed in a particular way?

4. How would the paper have been different had Edwards not relied on the imperative mood?

Considering Style and Language

1. Edwards establishes the tone for her piece with the first sentence. What is that tone, and what words reveal her attitude?

2. In several spots, Edwards emphasizes words and phrases by using italics. What does she accomplish by expressing these words in this way?

3. In paragraph 22, Edwards includes a "conversation" with the left side of the brain. Why do you think she has chosen to express this point in such a whimsical way?

4. What do the following words mean in the context of the essay? Contour, hemisphere, conceptual, meticulous, spatial, relational (para. 1); entails (para. 3); fundamental, composition, coherent (para. 5); binocular (para. 9); simultaneously (para. 10); approximation (para. 13); symbolic (para. 18); variation, undulation, registers (para. 20); configuration, monitor, proportions (para. 21); dominance, intricate, tangle (para. 22).

Your Turn: Responding to the Subject

a. In this excerpt, Edwards guides her readers through a process to help them begin drawing more realistically. For this assignment, take a hobby or craft that you are familiar with — for example, making a holiday decoration, building a homemade kite, creating a floral display — and write a paper explaining the process. Or if you prefer, focus on something else you know well — how to perform a dance step, play a specific card or board game, create a particular hairstyle, work through a video game, and so on — and explain this process.

b. Follow the steps Edwards outlines and then write a process narrative outlining your experience and the result.

Gary Larson
Cow Tools

Before cartoonist Gary Larson retired, his cartoon feature The Far
Side *was syndicated in hundreds of newspapers across the United
States and earned a loyal following because of Larson's droll,
quirky, and sometimes outright bizarre sense of humor. In* The Pre-
History of the Far Side, *his ten-year retrospective analysis of his
cartoon feature, Larson states that his book "is, among other things,
an examination of what went wrong, what went right, and how
rarely any two people seem to agree on which is which." In this excerpt from his book, Larson illustrates this very point as he explains
the process he followed in developing a cartoon titled "Cow Tools,"
which was widely misinterpreted.*

*What assumptions did Larson make about his readers that led
to such confusion?*

The "Cow Tools" episode is one that will probably haunt me   *1*
for the rest of my life. A week after it was published back in
1982, I wanted to crawl into a hole somewhere and die.

Cows, as some Far Side readers know, are a favorite subject   *2*
of mine. I've always found them to be the quintessentially absurd animal for situations even more absurd. Even the name
"cow," to me, is intrinsically funny.

And so one day I started thinking back on an anthropol-   *3*
ogy course I had in college and how we learned that man used
to be defined as "the only animal that made and shaped
tools." Unfortunately, researchers discovered that certain pri-
mates and even some bird species did the same thing — so the
definition had to be extended somewhat to avoid awkward situations such as someone hiring a crew of chimpanzees to re-
model their kitchen.

Inevitably, I began thinking about cows, and what if they,   *4*
too, were discovered as toolmakers. What would they make?
Primitive tools are always, well, primitive-looking — appearing

THE FAR SIDE   By GARY LARSON

Cow tools

rather nondescript to the lay person. So, it seemed to me, whatever a *cow* would make would have to be even a couple notches
further down the "skill-o-meter."

I imagined, and subsequently drew, a cow standing next   5
to her workbench, proudly displaying her handiwork (hoofiwork?). The "cow tools" were supposed to be just meaningless
artifacts — only the cow or a cowthropologist is supposed to
know what they're used for.

The first mistake I made was in thinking this was funny. The   6
second was making one of the tools resemble a crude handsaw

— which made already confused people decide that their only hope in understanding the cartoon meant deciphering what the *other* tools were as well. Of course, they didn't have a chance in hell.

But, for the first time, "Cow Tools" awakened me to the 7 fact that my profession was not just an isolated exercise in the corner of my apartment. The day after its release, my phone began to ring with inquiries from reporters and radio stations from regions in the country where The Far Side was published. Everyone, it seemed, wanted to know what in the world this cartoon *meant!* My syndicate was equally bombarded, and I was ultimately asked to write a press release explaining "Cow Tools." Someone sent me the front page of one newspaper which, down in one corner, ran the tease, "Cow Tools: What does it mean? (See pg. B14.)." I was mortified.

In the first year or two of drawing The Far Side, I always 8 believed my career perpetually hung by a thread. And this time I was convinced it had been finally severed. Ironically, when the dust had finally settled and as a result of all the "noise" it made, "Cow Tools" became more of a boost to The Far Side than anything else.

So, in summary, I drew a really weird, obtuse cartoon that 9 no one understood and wasn't funny and therefore I went on to even greater success and recognition.

Yeah — I like this country. 10

"The Far Side, a single-panel cartoon by Gary Larson, ob- 11 viously went too far to the side some time ago and threw great chunks of the populace into paralytic confusion."

— *Newspaper Columnist, Chicago*

"I asked 37 people to explain the 'Cow Tools' (cartoon) of 12 last week but with no luck. Could you help?"

— *Reader, California*

"Enclosed is a copy of the 'Cow Tools' cartoon. I have 13 passed it around. I have posted it on the wall. Conservatively, some 40-odd professionals with doctoral degrees in disparate disciplines have examined it. No one understands it. Even my 6-year-old cannot figure it out. . . . We are going bonkers. Please help. What is the meaning of 'Cow Tools'? What is the meaning of life?" — *Reader, Texas*

"We give up. Being intelligent, hard-working men, we   *14*
don't often say this, but your cartoon has proven to be beyond any of our intellectual capabilities. . . . Is there some significance to this cartoon that eludes us, or have we been completely foolish in our attempts to unravel the mystery behind 'Cow Tools'?"   — *Readers, California*

"I represent a small band of Fellows from every walk of   *15*
American Life, who have been drawn together by a need to know, a need to understand and a certain perplexity about what to do with this decade. We are a special interest group under the umbrella organization of The Fellowship of the Unexplained. . . . The Cow Tools Fellows have been brought together by the absolute certainty that your cartoon captioned 'Cow Tools' means something. But, as this letter signifies, just what it might mean has escaped us."
                                    — *Reader, California*

"Allow us to introduce ourselves: two humble and dedi-   *16*
cated civil servants who begin every working day with a one-hour review of the funnies. Mister Larson, please write us and let us know the message that this comic drawing is intended to portray. As an artist, you have a professional responsibility to your constituents, especially those whose mental health hinges upon the comic relief provided by your work."   — *Reader, Alabama*

Understanding the Significance

1. What combination of factors originally inspired Gary Larson to create this particular cartoon?
2. What does Larson feel caused his readers' confusion?
3. What did Larson learn from this experience about his comic feature's impact?
4. From the sampling of letters provided, what is the public's attitude about Larson's work?

Discovering the Writer's Purpose

1. In your judgment, how effective would Larson's writing be without his humor?
2. Larson is a highly successful cartoonist. Does his admission in paragraph 8 that early on "I always believed my career perpetually hung by a thread" make you reconsider the way you think about successful people?
3. In paragraph 6, Larson says, "The first mistake I made was in thinking this was funny." In your judgment, was he originally correct — is the cartoon funny or not? Explain.
4. In paragraph 7, Larson says that the reaction to this cartoon "awakened me to the fact that my profession was not just an isolated exercise in the corner of my apartment." Explain what he means.

Examining the Writer's Method

1. Larson presents the experience as it happened. If he had presented it in another order, for instance, using a flashback, how would the overall effect of the essay been changed? Explain.
2. In what way do you feel Larson's introduction fulfills the reader's expectations?
3. Would it have been more effective for Larson to list the readers' responses where he refers to them (paragraph 7)? Why?
4. Why do you think Larson doesn't provide a more traditional conclusion?

Considering Style and Language

1. Larson creates several new words in this piece, including *skill-o-meter, hoofiwork, cowthropologist*. How does the use of these words affect the tone of his writing?
2. Providing transition is one way that a writer can ensure that the reader is able to follow the point being raised. In what part of the piece is Larson's use of transition most effective? Explain.

3. Trying to explain what makes something funny often removes any of the humor from the situation. How does Larson manage to explain the joke and still make his presentation amusing?
4. What do the following words mean in the context of the writing? Quintessentially, absurd, intrinsically (para. 2); inevitably, nondescript (para. 4); artifacts (para. 5); deciphering (para. 6); mortified (para. 7); perpetually (para. 8); obtuse (para. 9); populace, paralytic (para. 11); disparate (para. 13); perplexity (para. 15).

Your Turn: Responding to the Subject

a. Larson's writing is a process narrative in which he explains how he came to develop a widely misinterpreted cartoon. For this essay, use process narrative to trace the steps of something you did. Your subject could be similar to Larson's in that you could discuss how you fouled something up, for example, a project at school or work.
b. Write a paper in which you explain how you did some task: assembled a piece of furniture or a toy, prepared for a party, lost a good deal of weight, and so on.

Carolyn Beard Whitlow
A Poem Is Sculpture

In this essay, poet and professor Carolyn Beard Whitlow offers an enormous picture window through which to view the mysterious process of turning emotions, impressions, and memories into poetry. Beard Whitlow, whose first collection of poems, Wild Meat, *was published in 1986, discovered while working on her dissertation on adult education at Cornell University that her real passion was poetry. She subsequently left that project to pursue an M.A. in creative writing at Brown University, where she received the Rose Low Rome Memorial Poetry Prize. Her work, which explores a variety of subjects including her own African American and Carribean heritage, has also appeared in* Northeast Journal, *the* Indiana Review, Obsidian, *the* Kenyon Review, 13th Moon, *and the* Massachusetts Review.*

What steps does a successful poet follow to turn ordinary words into a striking, engaging poem?

Writers vary as much as pebbles in the sea, each stone its own   *1*
interpretation of wind, wave, and tide. Each writer has the right
and the will to be different, for writing is a creative process. That
which might take my creative juices from simmer to boil might
drown or repel another. Thus, I have to take my own chances
and accept my own responsibility. I guess I choose the writing
process presented here like I choose my underwear.

For me, the creative process to make a poem moves in stages   *2*
from agony to ecstasy to apprehension to euphoria or recycling
to downtime. Then the machinations begin again. (The poetry
making process here described, however, is very different from
generating prose. For, in truth, I hate to write prose. Even generating this paper is most problematical for me.) The end result,
when my artistic endeavors reach fruition, is a poem solid,
sound, and unique as a cherished sculpture. For my job is to
take the "claystuff," the stone, mass, metal, and wood from
which poems are made and to cut, carve, chisel, cast, mold,
weld, and model the mass into form, into art, into poem.

I. THE AGONY

How does a poem begin? Tentatively. Trepidaciously. Hes- 3
itantly. Seldom on purpose. Never on demand. The poetry
process for me is one of daily observations about the every-
dayness of life. I watch people interact constantly, I ponder
scenes, I wonder, always, why. I actively listen, eavesdrop, if
you will. And those overheard snatches of conversation or
mental snapshots or memories or revelations are quickly
recorded in the blank book which I carry everywhere, which
rests at night beside my bed, which waits towel-wrapped on
the floor outside my shower. Some days pass and nothing is
recorded in my book, for nothing transpires of significance.
Other days I record one word. Yet others I capture an image or
a bit of dialogue. Sometimes I write out questions or issues,
sometimes frustrations. But these, most often, are quick jottings. A paragraph is a rarity, and filling a page might take a
month. Then one day, usually on vacation from work because
I need a large block of time, I decide to see whether the MUSE
will emerge. (Always there's music, a jazz CD or Boston Sym-
phony radio.) My muse must be conjured, coaxed, gently encouraged. Most often that happens when I immerse myself in
the written word; simultaneously I juggle books of poetry,
novels, sociology, and history, reading until I'm saturated by
one, sponging off the next. I read, read, read, six, eight hours
from one book to another; relax, rest, sleep. Again, the next
day, read, read, read, and perhaps the next until there's a
catch. Like flint and stone stroked and scratched kindle smoke
and fire, the spark of a poem ignites.

Some idea inflames, some word or phrase pushes me over 4
the brink from "rational" mode to creative mode. That's when
I begin to pace, slowly at first, back and forth, then with agitation, upstairs and down, like the rumblings before a volcanic
eruption. My daughters long ago learned that is the signal I
should not be disturbed, sometimes for days, for days.

II. THE ECSTASY

I'm in ecstasy when I pick up my chisel (pen) and begin to 5
sculpt. Always first with pen and pad, I begin to mold a poem.

Most often, I write down the most immediate thought which triggered the MUSE, that spark of ignition. Then I drag out my "Providence Journals," the chronology of blank books that I've filled over the years, eavesdropping and observing. I cull each book now, lifting notations relevant to my current poetic idea which may have been jotted years before, and transfer them randomly to my pad. I make lists of sounds, words, images, phrases, compile, as it were, all the parts of the poem that were in gestation. Looking back through my journals always allows me to see that the poem I'm currently starting has been in process for a long time, often for years.

From this process to first line comes —   6

"A slip of ice on the river"

I move then to the typewriter, and there's no turning back.   7
In the roost of my third floor bedroom, perched on two   8
pillows atop my wicker seated chair, I place my hands on the keys of my trusty, rusty IBM. My typewriter table holds on its left leaf a pile of recycled paper; stacked on the right leaf two dictionaries (there are more in the living room and the library), a thesaurus, a book of poetic forms, a rhyming dictionary, and a synonym/antonym dictionary. My fingertips dance on the keys, the melody in my head, the typing rhythm like hammer taps. A line forms, then another, the words chisel into place —

"Wearing pelts of rain, I sally
From my saucer, pour
Over lines, meter thoughts,
Cadence chiseled syllables into place . . . "
                    ("For my Red Haired English Teacher,
                    Now Dead," *Wild Meat*)

Hours I sit at the keys, ecstatically. The poem forms, re-   9
forms, rises, and falls. I consult my dictionaries, searching for the just word; I rip off my notes. I chip away, chip away until I find the poem's essence, its core. Every time I add a comma, change or shift the place of a word, I retype the entire poem, no matter its length. A 12 hour exhaustive day at the typewriter

is the norm. The question never asked is how many consecutive days will I sit at these keys, how long will the labor be before birth?

Nights between days are usually sleepless. The lines of the poem appear on a screen in my dreams. Asleep, I realize where I need to edit, awaken and resit my typewriter. Sometimes I type through the night. Meals are taken at the typewriter table, crumbs on the keys, until my famished need to write is satisfied. Then I'm happy, ecstatic.

Always there is a conflict for me between the need to communicate and the need for isolation. Although mine is by nature a personality of silence — conversation must be required or coerced at this stage — I have great need to share verbally my writing experience. Most often I want to yell out the window, "listen to this," bring traffic to a halt. Realistically, though, I must pick up the phone and dial long distance for a listener, especially someone who can evaluate the technical aspects of my work as well as its artistic merit. The numbers to dial are few, the feedback precious.

III. APPREHENSION

After the initial telephone feedback I begin to ponder: Is the poem "ready," "good," "publishable?" Is it better than the last, indicative of intellectual and creative growth? Will anyone else like it? Then I stop waffling and admit that the one who must be satisfied with its quality ultimately is me. For without that strength and resolve, the next part of the process could be undeniably painful. I next must mail the poem off with 2 or 3 others, attempting to publish.

I consult the *International Directory of Little Magazines and Small Presses,* deciding where to mail the sheaf of poems among the journals where I'd like to appear, the journals where I've already appeared, and the journals which publish the types of poetry that I like. I'm most happy when I'm submitting to a journal that has solicited my work. I suffer through the frustration of the unwritten rule that a poem should not be sent to more than one journal simultaneously and the equal frustration that the response time as quoted in the Directory is always an underestimate. A writer is lucky to get an immediate rejection; then at least the poem is not held up for months. It is not unusual for a new poem to be out of circulation for a year, with only one or two rejections. And, ironically, the unspoken expectation is that the longer a poem is held, the more likely it is to be published. Sometimes the wait is unbearable; always I'm apprehensive about the outcome.

IV. EUPHORIA OR DEJECTION

When even one of the sheaf of poems is accepted for publication I'm euphoric; if not one is accepted, I'm dejected. All or nothing, no in-between. But I've learned over the years to mourn, re-read and re-evaluate the poem quickly: A 24-hour turnaround is the ideal. I give myself a pep talk, rewrite the cover letter and submit the poem again possibly with different companion pieces, possibly not-fast. For I know the importance of journal publication of the individual poems before submitting a book manuscript or applying for a grant. And I know journal publication opportunities are "iffy." Sometimes the rejection occurs because the work is marginal; more often, though, reasons may range from the readers not having read closely to an overwhelming number of submissions to a backlog of accepted work to the poem not fitting the thematic interest of that editor or that edition. The standard printed rejection slip really giving no clue.   14

However, occasionally a printed rejection slip includes an ink-scribbled note from the editor. A one-liner which might say "I'd like to see some other work" or "we're overrun with work now, resubmit in 3 months" or somesuch. That message is really recognition and encouragement and those few words are precious feedback.   15

Occasionally, too, one gets a letter of response from the editor, as happened between Marilyn Hacker and me. She wrote to me when I was a graduate student at Brown, suggesting changes in a poem I'd submitted to *13th Moon*. I wrote back refusing to change. She wrote back. I wrote back. Not so ironically, although my poem was ultimately accepted, it never appeared. Marilyn Hacker continues to this day, though, to mentor and encourage me. Most recently, she nominated me for the Barnard New Women Poets Prize. The bottom line in the Euphoria/Dejection stage is that the poet must WAIT, WAIT, WAIT. This process is both exhilarating and debilitating.   16

V. DOWNTIME

Once the poem has been completed and mailed, down-   *17*
time sets in a period of recuperation. The intense effort, the
unbelievably long hours, 12 plus over a period of days, the
concentration and output of emotional energy leave me
drained. The demands of home, friends, family, and work,
which were all sacrificed during the creative period, all coa-
lesce to say there's "no rest for the weary." Thus, the best re-
viver, though the least available, is travel to distant ports
where I can begin afresh the process of observation, eavesdropping, and notetaking, and ignore the calls and demands
of everyday living. I well understand why writers who can escape to Writer's Colonies such as Yaddo and MacDowell.

Downtime from writing is generally when I juggle teach-   *18*
ing six courses per semester, enough to earn a loaf of bread and
a jug of wine. Since I teach literature courses in the main, however, teaching is supportive of my writing. The in-class literature discussions tend to parallel my need to read voraciously
before writing a poem. I need to be surrounded constantly by
the written word to touch, feel, taste, hold the tools of my
trade daily.

Even now, I wish only that my hand held a chisel . . .   *19*

Understanding the Significance

1. Throughout the essay, Carolyn Beard Whitlow compares
   writing a poem to creating a sculpture. In what ways are
   these two processes similar?

2. From what does Beard Whitlow draw her inspiration for
   her poems?

3. Although Beard Whitlow never specifically mentions the
   word *talent* in relation to creating a poem, she does suggest
   that it takes more to write a poem than simply to follow a
   series of steps. How does she communicate this concept?

4. How do her activities during downtime help Beard Whitlow with her poetry writing?

Discovering the Writer's Purpose

1. Does reading Beard Whitlow's explanation of the actual process of writing a poem — the nuts-and-bolts struggle and drudgery — change your attitude about poetry in any way?
2. Of the stages of writing a poem that Beard Whitlow presents here, which one do you think would be most difficult to endure? Why?
3. One of the more interesting details appears in paragraph 9, where Beard Whitlow explains that she retypes a poem each time she makes any change. How do you think revising in this manner helps her?
4. In paragraph 14, Beard Whitlow explains the reasons that poems may be rejected. Summarize the advice implied in this paragraph.

Examining the Writer's Method

1. In what ways does Beard Whitlow's introduction engage the reader?
2. How does the order Beard Whitlow sets enable her reader to understand the process she follows?
3. In which section has she best conveyed the struggles inherent in her work? Why?
4. Beard Whitlow ends her essay with an ellipsis. Explain what you feel she is trying to say by allowing her essay to taper off in this way.

Considering Style and Language

1. Beard Whitlow might have chosen to explain how to develop a poem by writing a set of instructions. Instead, she chose to use process narrative, that is, to tell how she her-

self writes a poem. What benefit does she gain as a result
of presenting the process in this way?

2. Beard Whitlow divides the process of writing a poem into
   five stages, each of which contains a number of steps.
   What advantage did she gain in presenting the steps this
   way rather than in one long series of steps?

3. In paragraphs 3 and 4, she uses a number of images having to do with fire. Why is this choice of imagery effective
   in relation to the subject of poetry?

4. What do the following words mean in the context of the
   writing? Repel (para. 1); ecstasy, apprehension, machinations, endeavors, fruition (para. 2); tentatively, revelations,
   jottings, rarity, muse, conjured, saturated, kindle (para. 3);
   inflames, agitation (para. 4); cull, gestation (para. 5); roost
   (para. 8); coerced (para. 11); indicative, waffling (para. 12);
   sheaf, solicited (para. 13); dejected, mourn, thematic
   (para. 14); mentor, exhilarating, debilitating (para. 16); co-
   alesce (para. 17); voraciously (para. 18).

Your Turn: Responding to the Subject

a. In this essay, Beard Whitlow explains in full detail the
   process she follows when she writes a poem. For this assignment, write an essay in which you explain the process
   you follow when you do one of the following: write an
   essay, term paper, or letter; write or master a song; paint a
   painting; make a sketch; and so on.

b. Observe someone else at work writing, rehearsing, painting, drawing, and so forth, and record the stages that person goes through.

Other Possibilities for Using Process

Here are additional subjects that could be developed into papers featuring process. If you choose one of these topics, remember to develop it fully and provide plenty of supporting details to guide your reader through the steps.

- how to insert a contact lens
- how earthquakes occur
- how to apply makeup
- how to perform a simple magic trick
- how a microwave cooks food
- how to write a check
- how a movie special effect was created
- how to housebreak a dog
- how to perform a simple experiment
- how a serious accident occurred
- how to snorkel
- how the human liver functions
- how thunderstorms occur
- how to erect a tent
- how fossils were created

Practical Application: Process

When you are working toward your degree, you have the opportunity to intern with your town's largest commercial bank. The officers of the bank are so impressed with the quality of your work that the director of human relations offers you a position when you finish school. Three days after graduation, you begin work in the customer relations division.

After a two-week orientation, you attend your first weekly staff meeting. The subject under discussion is the use — or lack of use — of the Automatic Teller Machines (ATMs) in the downtown branch. Because customers aren't taking advantage of the ATMs, they often face long lines to meet with tellers for such basic banking services as deposits and withdrawals, leading to numerous complaints.

The problem appears to be a matter of demographics. A survey conducted in response to the complaints indicates that the average age of patrons of this branch is 55, an older group that has comparatively little experience with and therefore less confidence in anything computerized, especially when it concerns their hard-earned money. The bank's goal, then, is to find a way to make using the ATMs less intimidating.

After some discussion, one of the vice presidents suggests sending a one-page mailer to all patrons that explains in simple, clear terms how to use an ATM and the advantages patrons gain with the ATM in terms of saving time and gaining flexibility in scheduling. The vice president looks around the table, recognizes you from your work during your internship, and assigns you the task of preparing the *one-page mailer,* emphasizing the importance of maintaining an upbeat and encouraging tone. As you begin your work, he supplies a guideline, a set of instructions he has received about registering for college courses by phone, to be an example of *approach* and *format.*

PhoneSelect **Registration at Taylor College**

INTRODUCTION

Welcome to *PhoneSelect*, Taylor College's register-by-phone system. For years, registering for classes at Taylor meant actually coming to campus and waiting in long lines as staffers from the Registrar's Office filled out your schedule by hand, the paper and pencil method. But all that changed last year with the advent of *PhoneSelect*. Now the only line you need to think about is the phone line.

THE STEPS INVOLVED

The process itself couldn't be simpler. During the last month, you had the opportunity to visit the campus advisement center and pick up the list of courses available for next semester, your personal identification number (PIN), and the designated day and time between 8 a.m. and 6 p.m. for you to register. Now all you need is a touch tone phone and you're all set to begin.

1. Before you call, list on a piece of paper your social security number and your PIN. Next, write the names and the five-digit code numbers for all the courses you are interested in, for example, *College English, 10763*. When you have completed your list, double check to make sure there are no time conflicts in your proposed schedule. *PhoneSelect* will automatically reject any courses with conflicting times.
2. On your designated day and time, dial 1-800-555-2531 to connect to *PhoneSelect*. You will be directed to enter your social security number and then your PIN, using the keypad of the phone. Once *PhoneSelect* verifies this information, you are ready to begin registration.
3. Press the "∗" key, enter the five-digit code for your first course, and then press the "#" key. If the course is closed or your selection invalid for any reason, you will be told to try again or to make another selection.
4. Repeat step 3 for each course you plan to take.

5. After your final selection, press the "1" key to verify your entire schedule. If your schedule is correct, press the "#" key.
6. If you find it necessary to change your schedule after verifying it, press the "5" key, enter the five-digit number of the course to be dropped, and press the "#" key. If a course is to be added, repeat step 3. To verify your new schedule, repeat step 5.

Should you encounter difficulty with any step, press the "0" key and an operator will assist you.

That's all there is to it. For most students, the entire process takes less than five minutes.

FINAL WORDS

We at Taylor College's Registrar's Office are interested in what you think. If there are ways for us to improve the *PhoneSelect* system, stop by or give us a call at 1-800-555-2531. Thanks and good luck with your courses.

7

Definition

The Technique

Writing successfully on any subject depends greatly on whether your reader understands what you mean. For this reason alone, you will find definition invaluable in your writing. If you were writing an essay about the strength of a family grieving over the loss of a child, the definition of strength would be important. By strength, do you mean a stoic denial of emotions, a willingness to seek counseling, the courage to break down in public and show emotions, or something else entirely? Clearly, the effectiveness of your essay would depend on how well you communicated the meaning of strength to your reader.

To take full advantage of definition when you write, you should make sure to

- recognize *the elements of an effective definition;*
- consider *denotation, connotation, and etymology;* and
- use *limited and extended definition and negation.*

THE ELEMENTS OF AN EFFECTIVE DEFINITION

A dictionary is the logical place to begin for any writer dealing with definition. With many terms, formal dictionary definitions follow a simple formula: a word is presented, placed in its appropriate class, and then differentiated from other items in the same classification. With many words, ensuring clarity is relatively simple because they are *concrete;* that is, they have identifiable physical characteristics. Other words are *abstract;* they name ideas, concepts, and situations that are intangible or lack consistent characteristics. Abstract words present more of a problem for you as a writer.

The secret to providing clear definitions of abstract words is to provide effective support through concrete words and specific examples. Consider an abstract term such as *fear.* You might define fear by delineating what happens physically when one experiences fear, giving examples of things that trigger fear, listing things that people are afraid of, and so on.

The late Dr. Martin Luther King clearly considered these elements when he wrote this passage defining *just law* and *unjust law* while composing his powerful "Letter from Birmingham Jail," written in 1963 during his imprisonment for activities advancing civil rights:

> A just law is a man-made code that squares with the moral law or the law of God. An unjust law is a code that is out of harmony with the moral law. To put it in terms of St. Thomas Aquinas: an unjust law is the human law that is not rooted in eternal law and natural law. Any law that uplifts human personality is just. Any law that degrades human personality is unjust. All segregation statutes are unjust because segregation distorts the soul and damages the personality. It gives the segregator a false sense of superiority and the segregated a false sense of inferiority.

DENOTATION, CONNOTATION, AND ETYMOLOGY

Preparing an effective definition also means taking into account the literal meaning of the word — *denotation* — and the additional subjective meanings the word suggests or implies — *connotation.* The denotation of the word *clever,* for example, is to be mentally quick and capable. But your sense of clever when you think of a clever child is far different than when you think of a clever politician. In short, by considering the denotation and connotation of the words you use, you focus on shades of meaning that may help you better communicate your point to your reader.

You may also occasionally find a word's origin and historical development — its *etymology* — useful. The etymology of a word is generally available in any collegiate dictionary, although an unabridged dictionary such as *Oxford English Dictionary (OED)* is the best place to find extensive etymological information. If you've ever wondered, for example, whether the world is slanted against left-handed people, consider the etymology of two words, *gauche* and *adroit. Gauche* is defined as "lacking tact or social graces." It comes from a French word, *gauche,* which means *left. Adroit* is defined as "deft and skillful," and it too is derived from a French word, *droit,* which means *right.* What is gained by an examination of the etymology of these two words is the implication that left-handed people are somehow awkward or unrefined whereas right-handed people are capable and proficient.

In this brief passage from *Why Do We Say . . . ?: Words and Sayings and Where They Come From,* Nigel Rees focuses on these aspects of definition to give a fuller understanding of the word commonly used to identify a second year U.S. high-school or college student, *sophomore:*

> The Greek *sophos* means "wise" and *moros* means "foolish." So a second-year student is half-way between ignorance and wisdom. Well, that is more or less the idea. *The Shorter Oxford English Dictionary* clings to an obscure definition relating the word to "sophism" plus "or."
>
> Sophomoric means "pretentious, bombastic, foolish."

LIMITED AND EXTENDED DEFINITION AND NEGATION

Definition takes many forms in a writing, depending on the specific purpose of an essay. Sometimes a paper will call for one or more limited definitions, a sentence or two to specify a point or subject under discussion. In other cases, however, a particular assignment will call for a more thorough explanation of some term or concept. With these assignments, an extended definition is the proper choice. This type of definition is a multiparagraph presentation, which often includes a limited definition supported with a series of specific details and examples.

Think of a term such as *charisma,* for instance. If you relied on a limited definition of charisma, explaining it as a quality possessed by those who are able to attract the admiration and devotion of many others, you wouldn't paint a clear enough picture of the word for your reader. You'd be better off providing an extended definition discussing the ways that people have been affected by specific charismatic individuals. Such a definition would do a far better job of illustrating the power wielded by famous (or infamous) religious and political leaders; actors and musicians; media personalities, and so forth.

Incidentally, at times the best way to define something is to explain what it *isn't,* a technique called *negation.* When you write that intelligence isn't merely the knowledge of a great volume of facts, you also suggest that being intelligent involves not only knowing the facts but also the significance of and connections among these facts.

Look at how novelist Kaye Gibbons uses all these elements in her 1993 novel *Charms for the Easy Life* to explain the behavior of Charlie Kate, the narrator's grandmother:

> She wasn't *abnormal.* That word described the old man who roamed about downtown, grabbing people by the sleeve, telling them the time, temperature, and current world news that had no connection to reality. Or the little girl we had just read about in the paper who wasn't sure of her age or name but could do fantastically long sums in her head. They were abnormal. My grandmother was certainly nothing like these two, but she wasn't normal in the sense of being like other people who worked in banks or stores, women with permanent waves and moisturized skin. But all the same, in the strangest sort of way, I considered her normal for herself. It was normal for her to eat two cloves of raw garlic every morning, wear her late mother's seventy-five-year-old shoes, preserve the laces in linseed oil, and sit up all night laughing uproariously over *Tristram Shandy.*

AN ANNOTATED EXAMPLE

Ellen Goodman

The Workaholic

In the United States, the legend goes, work hard and you will suc-
ceed. But some people step far beyond merely working hard and lose
themselves in the process. These individuals are the workaholics. In
this piece Ellen Goodman, nationally syndicated Boston Globe
columnist, defines the term workaholic *by discussing the life — and*
death — of Phil, the ultimate company man. Widely recognized for
her insightful writing, Goodman, whose columns regularly appear in
the Washington Post *and other newspapers across the United*
States, was awarded the Pulitzer Prize for commentary in 1980.
Goodman, who began her career in 1963 as a researcher and reporter
for Newsweek, *has seen her work collected in several volumes, in-*
cluding At Large *(1981),* Keeping in Touch *(1985),* Making Sense
(1989), and Value Judgments *(1993).*

Why is it that Phil never sees where his attitude and lifestyle
are taking him?

The opening
paragraphs identify
the characteristics
that typify a
workaholic.

He worked himself to death <u>finally</u> and 1
<u>precisely</u> at 3 A.M. Sunday morning.

The obituary didn't say that, of 2
course. It said that he died of a coro-
nary thrombosis — I think that was it
— but everyone of his friends and acquaintances knew it instantly. <u>He was</u>
<u>a perfect Type A, a workaholic, a clas-</u>
<u>sic,</u> they said to each other and shook
their heads — and thought for five or
ten minutes about the way they lived.

This man who worked himself to 3
death <u>finally</u> and <u>precisely</u> at 3 A.M.
Sunday morning — on his day off —

His background and status are part of the definition of workaholic.

was 51 years old and he was a vice-president. He was, however, one of the six vice-presidents, and one of the three who might conceivably — if the president died or retired soon enough — have moved to the top spot. Phil knew that.

He worked six days a week, five of   4
them until 8 or 9 at night, during a time when his own company had begun the four-day week for everyone but the executives. He worked like the Important People. He had no outside

She includes additional parts of the definition.

"extracurricular interests," unless, of course, you think about a monthly golf game that way. To Phil, it was work. He always ate egg-salad sandwiches at his desk. He was, of course, overweight, by 20 or 25 pounds. He thought it was okay though, because he didn't smoke.

Note the irony.

On Saturdays, Phil wore a sports   5
jacket to the office instead of a suit, be-cause it was the weekend.

He had a lot of people working for   6
him, maybe 60, and most of them liked him most of the time. Three of them will be seriously considered for his job. The obituary didn't mention that.

But it did list his "survivors" quite   7
accurately. He is survived by his wife,

She shifts to others affected — this is also a part of the extended definition.

Helen, 48, a good woman of no particu-lar marketable skills, who worked in an office before marrying and mothering.

She had, according to her daugh-   8
ter, given up trying to compete with his work years ago, when the children were small. A company friend said, "I know how much you will miss him." And she answered, "I already have."

"Missing him all these years," she   9
must have given up part of herself

which had cared too much for the man. She would be "well taken care of."

She includes other consequences — part of the definition.

His eldest of the "dearly beloved" children is a hard-working executive in a manufacturing firm down South. In the day and a half before the funeral, he went around the neighborhood researching his father, asking the neighbors what he was like. They were embarrassed. 10

His second child was a girl, who is 24 and newly married. She lives near her mother and they are close, but whenever she was alone with her father, in a car driving somewhere, they had nothing to say to each other. 11

Others in the family are affected by Phil's workaholism.

The youngest is 20, a boy, a high-school graduate who has spent the last couple of years, like a lot of his friends, doing enough odd jobs to stay in grass and food. He was the one who tried to grab at his father, and tried to mean enough to him to keep the man at home. 12

He was his father's favorite. Over the last two years, Phil stayed up nights worrying about the boy. 13

The boy once said, "My father and I only board here." 14

At the funeral, the 60-year-old company president told the 48-year-old widow that the 51-year-old deceased had meant much to the company and would be missed and would be hard to replace. The widow didn't look him in the eye. She was afraid he would read her bitterness and, after all, she would need him to straighten out the finances — the stock options and all that. 15

She includes additional ramifications of Phil's workaholism.

Phil was overweight and nervous and worked too hard. If he wasn't at 16 the office, he was worried about it. Phil was a Type A, a heart-attack natural. You could have picked him out in a minute from a lineup.

She repeats these words from the first paragraph to signal the conclusion and the moral of the story.

So when he <u>finally</u> worked himself   17
to death, at <u>precisely</u> 3 A.M. Sunday morning, no one was really surprised.

By 5 P.M. the afternoon of the fu-   18
neral, the company president had begun, discreetly of course, with care and taste, to make inquiries about his replacement. One of three men. He asked around: "Who's been working the hardest?"

Your Turn: Responding to the Subject

a. In many ways, Ellen Goodman has supplied the portrait of the perfect worker, a man so devoted to the company that he dies on his own time. For this assignment, choose a subject — for instance, a politician, coach, public servant, or parent — and provide an extended definition of its ideal.

b. Following Goodman's lead, focus on the hazards associated with being the perfect example of anything.

Francine Prose

Gossip

Accuse someone of spreading gossip and watch the sparks fly. Yet, as essayist and novelist Francine Prose illustrates, gossiping is a common activity that doesn't necessarily deserve the bad reputation it has. Prose's novels include The Glorious Ones, Household Saints, Judah the Pious, Hungry Hearts, *and* Bigfoot Dreams, *and her articles have appeared in such periodicals as* Mademoiselle, *the* Atlantic Monthly, *and the* New York Times. *In this essay, Prose provides an extended definition of gossip that illustrates points that most of us don't think of.*

How can something that has such a bad reputation be defined as something worthwhile?

Once I met a woman who grew up in the small North Carolina   1
town to which Chang and Eng, the original Siamese twins, retired after their circus careers. When I asked her how the town reacted to the twins marrying local girls and setting up adjacent households, she laughed and said: "Honey, that was *nothing* compared to what happened *before* the twins got there. Get the good gossip on any little mountain town, scratch the surface and you'll find a snake pit!"

Surely she was exaggerating; one assumes the domestic   2
arrangements of a pair of Siamese twins and their families would cause a few ripples anywhere. And yet the truth of what she said seemed less important than the glee with which she said it, her pride in the snake pit she'd come from, in its history, its scandals, its legacy of "good gossip." Gossip, the juicier the better, was her heritage, her birthright; that town, with its social life freakish enough to make Chang and Eng's seem mundane, was part of who she was.

Gossip must be nearly as old as language itself. It was, I   3
imagine, the earliest recreational use of the spoken word. First the cave man learned to describe the location of the plumpest

193

bison, then he began to report and speculate on the doings of his neighbors in the cave next door. And yet, for all its antiquity, gossip has rarely received its due; its very name connotes idleness, time-wasting, frivolity and worse. Gossip is the unacknowledged poor relative of civilized conversation: Almost everyone does it but hardly anyone will admit to or defend it; and of these only the smallest and most shameless fraction will own up to enjoying it.

My mother and her friends are eloquent on the subject and 4 on the distinction between gossiping and exchanging information: "John got a new job," is, they say, information. "Hey, did you hear John got fired?" is gossip; which is, they agree, predominantly scurrilous, mean-spirited. That's the conventional wisdom on gossip and why it's so tempting to disown. Not long ago I heard myself describe a friend, half-jokingly, as "a much better person than I am, that is, she doesn't gossip so much." I heard my voice distorted by that same false note that sometimes creeps into it when social strain and some misguided notion of amiability make me assent to opinions I don't really share. What in the world was I talking about?

I don't, of course, mean rumor-mongering, outright slan- 5 der, willful fabrication meant to damage and undermine. But rather, ordinary gossip, incidents from and analyses of the lives of our heroes and heroines, our relatives, acquaintances and friends. The fact is, I love gossip, and beyond that, I believe in it — in its purposes, its human uses.

I'm even fond of the word, its etymology, its origins in 6 the Anglo-Saxon term "godsibbe" for god-parent, relative, its meaning widening by the Renaissance to include friends, cronies and later what one *does* with one's cronies. One gossips. Paring away its less flattering modern connotations, we discover a kind of synonym for connection, for community, and this, it seems to me, is the primary function of gossip. It maps our ties, reminds us of what sort of people we know and what manner of lives they lead, confirms our sense of who we are, how we live and where we have come from. The roots of the grapevine are inextricably entwined with our own. Who knows how much of our sense of the world has reached us on its branches, how often, as babies, we dropped off to sleep to the rhythms of family gossip? I've often thought that gossip's bad name might be cleared by calling it "oral tradition"; for what, after all, is an oral tradition but the stories of other lives, other eras, legends from a time when human traffic with spirits and gods was considered fit material for gossipy speculation?

Older children gossip; adolescents certainly do. Except in 7 the case of those rare toddler-fabulists, enchanting parents and siblings with fairy tales made up on the spot, gossip may be the way that most of us learn to tell stories. And though, as Gertrude Stein is supposed to have told Hemingway, gossip is not literature, some similar criteria may apply to both. Pacing, tone, clarity and authenticity are as essential for the reportage of neighborhood news as they are for well-made fiction.

Perhaps more important is gossip's analytical component. 8 Most people — I'm leaving out writers, psychologists and probably some large proportion of the academic and service professions — are, at least in theory, free to go about their lives without feeling the compulsion to endlessly dissect the minutiae of human motivation. They can indulge in this at their leisure, for pleasure, in their gossip. And while there are those who clearly believe that the sole aim of gossip is to criticize, to condemn (or, frequently, to titillate, to bask in the aura of scandal as if it were one's own), I prefer to see gossip as a tool of understanding. It only takes a moment to tell what someone did. Far more mileage — and more enjoyment — can be extracted from debating why he did it. Such questions, impossible to discuss without touching on matters of choice and consequence, responsibility and will, are, one might argue, the beginnings of moral inquiry, first steps toward a moral education. It has always seemed peculiar that a pastime so conducive to the moral life should be considered faintly immoral.

I don't mean to deny the role of plain nosiness in all this, 9 of unadorned curiosity about our neighbors' secrets. And curiosity (where would we be without it?) has, like gossip, come in for some negative press. Still, it's understandable, everyone wants to gossip, hardly anyone wants to be gossiped about. What rankles is the fear that our secrets will be revealed, some essential privacy stripped away and, of course, the lack of control over what others say. Still, such talk is unavoidable; it's part of human nature, of the human community. When one asks, "What's the gossip?" it's that community that is being affirmed.

So I continue to ask, mostly without apology and espe-   *10*
cially when I'm talking to friends who still live in places I've
moved away from. And when they answer — recalling the personalities, telling the stories, the news — I feel as close as I ever
will to the lives we shared, to what we know and remember in
common, to those much-missed, familiar and essentially
beneficent snake pits I've lived in and left behind.

Understanding the Significance

1. What point is Francine Prose making with her opening
   anecdote about Chang and Eng?
2. In paragraph 3, Prose suggests that gossip was perhaps
   "the earliest recreational use of the spoken word," and she
   devotes most of her essay to showing that gossiping is a
   natural activity that is usually harmless. But in arguing
   this point of view, isn't she conveniently ignoring the
   harm that often occurs when people gossip? Explain.
3. In paragraph 5, Prose notes that she loves the "human
   uses" of gossip. What are the "human uses" as she explains
   them?
4. In paragraph 9, Prose states that gossip is simply "unavoidable." Do you agree with her, or is this attitude really
   just an excuse to do something that one delights in regardless of whether it hurts someone else?

Discovering the Writer's Purpose

1. Which of the connotations of gossip provided by Prose do
   you feel best makes her case that gossip can be good?
2. In paragraph 4, Prose explains the distinction drawn between gossiping and exchanging information. Do you
   agree that one method is not gossiping but the second is,
   or are they both examples of gossip?

3. In paragraph 6, Prose says, "Paring away its less flattering modern connotations, we discover a kind of synonym for connection, for community, and this, it seems to me, is the primary function of gossip." If she hadn't pared away these less flattering connotations of gossip, how would her essay have been different?

4. In paragraph 9 Prose states, "When one asks, 'What's the gossip?' it's that community that is being affirmed." What do you think Prose means here? Do you agree? Explain.

Examining the Writer's Method

1. Prose uses the story of the local people's reaction to the marriage of Chang and Eng to set up her reader for her essay. Do you think beginning her paper in this way is an effective choice? Why?

2. Prose devotes paragraph 6 to the etymology of *gossip*. How does this material help her make her case that we should reexamine the value of gossip?

3. In paragraph 8, Prose states that gossip is "a tool of understanding." What does she mean by this? How does the material in her essay support her case?

4. In this essay, Prose relies on connotation, etymology, and negation to define gossip. Which technique do you find most effective? Why?

Considering Style and Language

1. In your judgment, what is the tone of Prose's essay? How does this tone help Prose make her case?

2. When it comes to a subject like gossip, it would seem reasonable to say that writing an essay condemning it would be far easier than writing one supporting it. Why, then, do you think Prose chose to write an essay advocating greater understanding of this dubious activity?

3. How does Prose use her concluding paragraph to emphasize the connection between her thesis and the material she uses to support and illustrate it?

4. What do the following words mean in the context of the writing? Adjacent (para. 1); domestic, legacy, mundane (para. 2); speculate, antiquity, connotes, frivolity (para. 3); eloquent, scurrilous, amiability, assent (para. 4); mongering, slander, fabrication (para. 5); Renaissance, cronies, inextricably, entwined (para. 6); fabulists, reportage (para. 7); compulsion, dissect, minutiae, titillate, bask, aura (para. 8); unadorned, rankles (para. 9); beneficent (para. 10).

Your Turn: Responding to the Subject

a. Although one might argue that she is merely attempting to justify her own love of gossip by claiming that such a desire is a natural tendency, Prose mounts a good case for reconsidering the way we view gossip. It is, after all, something we all do and not always for malicious purposes. For this assignment, take another activity that all people do — for example, worrying, nagging, daydreaming, crowd-watching, and so on — and attempt to justify why participating in such an activity is good for us.

b. Some might argue that Prose is merely rationalizing her own behavior. Define and illustrate the term *rationalizing*.

Roger Rosenblatt
The Man in the Water

When Air Florida's Flight 90 hit a bridge and crashed into the Po-
tomac River on January 14, 1982, shortly after takeoff from Wash-
ington National Airport, television cameras brought the aftermath of
the tragedy right into the living rooms of America. Writer Roger
Rosenblatt, whose work has appeared in Time, Life, *and the* Washington Post, *was one of the millions of television witnesses who*
watched as victims struggled to survive in the icy waters and rescuers
risked their own lives to try to save them. In this essay, which ap-
peared in Time *shortly after the crash, Rosenblatt discusses the be-*
havior and fate of one of the victims, a man who chose to help others
rather than to save himself. Through this focus, Rosenblatt, who has
also served as literary editor for the New Republic; *director of edu-*
cation for the National Endowment for the Humanities; author of
several books, including Children of War *(1983) and* The Man in
the Water *(1994); and essayist and commentator for the* Mac-
Neil/Lehrer Newshour, *provides a moving definition of heroism.*

Amid the actions of many people who acted heroically, what
makes this man in the water so special?

As disasters go, this one was terrible, but not unique, certainly   *1*
not among the worst on the roster of U.S. air crashes. There
was the unusual element of the bridge, of course, and the fact
that the plane clipped it at a moment of high traffic, one routine thus intersecting another and disrupting both. Then, too,
there was the location of the event. Washington, the city of
form and regulations, turned chaotic, deregulated, by a blast
of real winter and a single slap of metal on metal. The jets
from Washington National Airport that normally swoop
around the presidential monuments like rushed gulls are, for
the moment, emblemized by the one that fell; so there is that
detail. And there was the aesthetic clash as well — blue-and-
green Air Florida, the name a flying garden, sunk down among

199

gray chunks in a black river. All that was worth noticing, to be sure. Still, there was nothing very special in any of it, except death, which, while always special, does not necessarily bring millions to tears or to attention. Why, then, the shock here?

Perhaps because the nation saw in this disaster something 2
more than a mechanical failure. Perhaps because people saw in it no failure at all, but rather something successful about their makeup. Here, after all, were two forms of nature in collision: the elements and human character. Last Wednesday, the elements, indifferent as ever, brought down Flight 90. And on that same afternoon, human nature — groping and flailing in mysteries of its own — rose to the occasion.

Of the four acknowledged heroes of the event, three are 3
able to account for their behavior. Donald Usher and Eugene Windsor, a park police helicopter team, risked their lives every time they clipped the skids into the water to pick up survivors. On television, side by side in bright blue jumpsuits, they described their courage as all in the line of duty. Lenny Skutnik, a 28-year-old employee of the Congressional Budget Office, said: "It's something I never thought I would do" — referring to his jumping into the water to drag an injured woman to shore. Skutnik added that "somebody had to go in the water," delivering every hero's line that is no less admirable for its repetitions. In fact, nobody had to go into the water. That somebody actually did so is part of the reason this particular tragedy sticks in the mind.

But the person most responsible for the emotional impact 4
of the disaster is the one known at first simply as "the man in the water." (Balding, probably in his 50s, an extravagant mustache.) He was seen clinging with five other survivors to the tail section of the airplane. This man was described by Usher and Windsor as appearing alert and in control. Every time they lowered a lifeline and flotation ring to him, he passed it on to another of the passengers. "In a mass casualty, you'll find people like him," said Windsor. "But I've never seen one with that commitment." When the helicopter came back for him, the man had gone under. His selflessness was one reason the story held national attention, his anonymity another. The fact that he went unidentified invested him with a universal character.

For a while he was Everyman, and thus proof (as if one needed it) that no man is ordinary.

Still, he could never have imagined such a capacity in   5
himself. Only minutes before his character was tested, he was sitting in the ordinary plane among the ordinary passengers, dutifully listening to the stewardess telling him to fasten his seat belt and saying something about the "no smoking sign." So our man relaxed with the others, some of whom would owe their lives to him. Perhaps he started to read, or to doze, or to regret some harsh remark made in the office that morning. Then suddenly he knew that the trip would not be ordinary. Like every other person on that flight, he was desperate to live, which makes his final act so stunning.

For at some moment in the water he must have realized   6
that he would not live if he continued to hand over the rope and ring to others. He *had* to know it, no matter how gradual the effect of the cold. In his judgment he had no choice. When the helicopter took off with what was to be the last survivor, he watched everything in the world move away from him, and he deliberately let it happen.

Yet there was something else about the man that kept our   7
thoughts on him, and which keeps our thoughts on him still. He was *there,* in the essential, classic circumstance. Man in nature. The man in the water. For its part, nature cared nothing about the five passengers. Our man, on the other hand, cared totally. So the timeless battle commenced in the Potomac. For as long as that man could last, they went at each other, nature and man; the one making no distinctions of good and evil, acting on no principles, offering no lifelines; the other acting wholly on distinctions, principles and, one supposes, on faith.

Since it was he who lost the fight, we ought to come again   8
to the conclusion that people are powerless in the world. In reality, we believe the reverse, and it takes the act of the man in the water to remind us of our true feelings in this matter. It is not to say that everyone would have acted as he did, or as Usher, Windsor and Skutnik. Yet whatever moved these men to challenge death on behalf of their fellows is not peculiar to them. Everyone feels the possibility in himself. That is the abiding wonder of the story. That is why we would not let go of it.

If the man in the water gave a lifeline to the people gasping for survival, he was likewise giving a lifeline to those who observed him.

The odd thing is that we do not even really believe that 9 the man in the water lost his fight. "Everything in Nature contains all the powers of Nature," said Emerson. Exactly. So the man in the water had his own natural powers. He could not make ice storms, or freeze the water until it froze the blood. But he could hand life over to a stranger, and that is a power of nature too. The man in the water pitted himself against an implacable, impersonal enemy; he fought it with charity; and he held it to a standoff. He was the best we can do.

Understanding the Significance

1. The people that Roger Rosenblatt identifies — Donald Usher, Eugene Windsor, Lenny Skutnik, and the man in the water — are all heroes. In paragraph 3, he says the first three can "account for their behavior." What does he mean by this statement? Does this factor make their actions somehow less heroic?

2. Certainly most people would agree that the man in the water acted heroically. But isn't there a fine line between heroism and self-destruction? As Rosenblatt points out in paragraph 6, "at some moment in the water he must have realized that he would not live if he continued to hand over the rope and ring to others." Why do you think he ultimately refused to save himself?

3. At the end of paragraph 8, Rosenblatt states that "[i]f the man in the water gave a lifeline to the people gasping for survival, he was likewise giving a lifeline to those who observed him." What does Rosenblatt mean? Explain.

4. In the final paragraph, Rosenblatt makes this statement: "The odd thing is that we do not even really believe that the man in the water lost his fight." The man in the water

perishes, so what do you think Rosenblatt means? Do you agree with his reasoning? Why or why not?

Discovering the Writer's Purpose

1. In his introduction to this essay, Rosenblatt provides a number of striking details. In your judgment, which phrase or image does the most to bring the scene to life?
2. In paragraph 2, Rosenblatt suggests that people didn't see the crash as a failure but as an event that showed "something successful" in our makeup. What element of the human character is he talking about? In what way did the actions of people after the crash, especially the man in the water, display this successful aspect?
3. Part of Rosenblatt's definition, as he notes in paragraph 8, is that "[e]veryone feels the possibility in himself" to perform heroically. Do you agree? Why or why not?
4. In the final paragraph, what is Rosenblatt trying to say about the relationship between man and nature?

Examining the Writer's Method

1. Rosenblatt doesn't establish his main focus until paragraph 4, when he first mentions the man in the water. Do you feel his essay would have been more effective if he had indicated this focus in the opening paragraph? Explain.
2. In paragraph 4, Rosenblatt notes that one thing that makes this situation unique is that the hero was anonymous. How might Rosenblatt's definition have been different if he knew the name of the man in the water?
3. In paragraph 5, Rosenblatt suggests what the man in the water might have been thinking and experiencing before the crash. How does this material tie into Rosenblatt's definition of heroism?

4. If you were going to reduce Rosenblatt's extended definition of heroism (as illustrated by the story of the man in the water) to a limited definition, what characteristics or elements would you include in that definition?

Considering Style and Language

1. Some readers might point out that in his opening paragraph Rosenblatt seems almost to undercut this tragedy. Why do you think he chose to discuss it in this way?
2. In paragraph 7, Rosenblatt sums up the struggle of the man in the water as "the essential, classic circumstance. Man in nature." What point does he make through this comparison?
3. From paragraph 5 on, Rosenblatt uses the first-person plural (*we, our,* and *us*) as he discusses the man in the water. What point is Rosenblatt making by using the plural forms rather than the singular ones?
4. What do the following words mean in the context of the writing? Chaotic, aesthetic, clash (para. 1); indifferent, groping, flailing (para. 2); extravagant, commitment, self-lessness, invested, universal (para. 4); capacity, dutifully (para. 5); classic (para. 7); abiding (para. 8); pitted, implacable (para. 9).

Your Turn: Responding to the Subject

a. The concrete actions of the man in the water enable Rosenblatt to define the abstract concept of heroism. For this assignment, choose another abstract concept, such as charity, fear, apathy, and so on, and use the actions of some person or persons to define the term.
b. The crash of Air Florida's Flight 90 certainly qualifies as a tragedy, but why exactly? In other words, what constitutes a tragedy? For this assignment, define tragedy.

Anna Quindlen
Homeless

A 1974 graduate of Barnard College, Anna Quindlen began her journalistic career as a part-time reporter for the New York Post *while still a college student. In 1977, she joined the* New York Times *as a general assignment reporter. Following stints writing the Times' "About New York" and "Hers" columns and serving as the deputy metropolitan editor, Quindlen took a brief sabbatical from journalism to concentrate on raising her family and to work on her fiction. (Her first novel,* Object Lessons, *was published in 1991; her most recent,* Black and Blue, *was published in 1998.) In 1986, she returned to the* New York Times, *this time to write columns entitled "Life in the 30's," a collection of which were published in 1987 under the title of* Living Out Loud. *The following writing is taken from that collection. In 1990, she moved to the op–ed page of the* New York Times, *writing a column entitled "Public and Private" that covered a wide variety of topics, including social issues, politics, abortion, and so on, and for which she was awarded the Pulitzer Prize for commentary in 1992. A collection of "Public and Private" pieces was published in 1993 under the title* Thinking Out Loud. *In this essay, Quindlen focuses on the issue of homelessness, examining what this apparently simple term actually means.*

Is homelessness more than merely being without a place to live?

Her name was Ann, and we met in the Port Authority Bus Terminal several Januarys ago. I was doing a story on homeless people. She said I was wasting my time talking to her; she was just passing through, although she'd been passing through for more than two weeks. To prove to me that this was true, she rummaged through a tote bag and a manila envelope and finally unfolded a sheet of typing paper and brought out her photographs. 1

They were not pictures of family, or friends, or even a dog or cat, its eyes brown-red in the flashbulb's light. They were 2 pictures of a house. It was like a thousand houses in a hundred towns, not suburb, not city, but somewhere in between, with aluminum siding and a chain-link fence, a narrow driveway running up to a one-car garage and a patch of backyard. The house was yellow. I looked on the back for a date or a name, but neither was there. There was no need for discussion. I knew what she was trying to tell me, for it was something I had often felt. She was not adrift, alone, anonymous, although her bags and her raincoat with the grime shadowing its creases had made me believe she was. She had a house, or at least once upon a time had had one. Inside were curtains, a couch, a stove, pot-holders. You are where you live. She was somebody.

I've never been very good at looking at the big picture, tak- 3
ing the global view, and I've always been a person with an overactive sense of place, the legacy of an Irish grandfather. So it is natural that the thing that seems most wrong with the world to me right now is that there are so many people with no homes. I'm not simply talking about shelter from the elements, or three square meals a day or a mailing address to which the welfare people can send the check — although I know that all these are important for survival. I'm talking about a home, about precisely those kinds of feelings that have wound up in cross-stitch and French knots on samplers over the years.

Home is where the heart is. There's no place like it. I love 4
my home with a ferocity totally out of proportion to its ap-pearance or location. I love dumb things about: the hot-water heater, the plastic rack you drain dishes in, the roof over my head, which occasionally leaks. And yet it is precisely those dumb things that make it what it is — a place of certainty, sta-bility, predictability, privacy, for me and for my family. It is where I live. What more can you say about a place than that? That is everything.

Yet it is something that we have been edging away from 5
gradually during my lifetime and the lifetimes of my parents and grandparents. There was a time when where you lived often was where you worked and where you grew the food you ate and even where you were buried. When that era passed, where you lived at least was where your parents had lived and where you would live with your children when you became

enfeebled. Then, suddenly where you lived was where you lived for three years, until you could move on to something else and something else again.

And so we have come to something else again, to children 6 who do not understand what it means to go to their rooms because they have never had a room, to men and women whose fantasy is a wall they can paint a color of their own choosing, to old people reduced to sitting on molded plastic chairs, their skin blue-white in the lights of a bus station, who pull pictures of houses out of their bags. Homes have stopped being homes. Now they are real estate.

People find it curious that those without homes would 7 rather sleep sitting up on benches or huddled in doorways than go to shelters. Certainly some prefer to do so because they are emotionally ill, because they have been locked in before and they are damned if they will be locked in again. Others are afraid of the violence and trouble they may find there. But some seem to want something that is not available in shelters, and they will not compromise, not for a cot, or oatmeal, or a shower with special soap that kills the bugs. "One room," a woman with a baby who was sleeping on her sister's floor, once told me, "painted blue." That was the crux of it; not size or location, but pride of ownership. Painted blue.

This is a difficult problem, and some wise and compas- 8 sionate people are working hard at it. But in the main I think we work around it, just as we walk around it when it is lying on the sidewalk or sitting in the bus terminal — the problem, that is. It has been customary to take people's pain and lessen our own participation in it by turning it into an issue, not a collection of human beings. We turn an adjective into a noun: the poor, not poor people; the homeless, not Ann or the man who lives in the box or the woman who sleeps on the subway grate.

Sometimes I think we would be better off if we forgot 9 about the broad strokes and concentrated on the details. Here is a woman without a bureau. There is a man with no mirror, no wall to hang it on. They are not the homeless. They are people who have no homes. No drawer that holds the spoons. No window to look out upon the world. My God. That is everything.

Understanding the Significance

1. In the first two paragraphs, Anna Quindlen introduces the reader to Ann. What does Ann do to demonstrate to Quindlen that she is not homeless?
2. From the description Quindlen provides, what kind of life do you think Ann had once enjoyed?
3. According to Quindlen, why do some people prefer living on the street instead of living in a shelter?
4. As Quindlen sees it, what is the difference between someone who is homeless and someone who has no home?

Discovering the Writer's Purpose

1. In the opening paragraph, Anna Quindlen notes that Ann keeps her photographs wrapped in a sheet of typing paper. What point is Quindlen trying to make by mentioning this detail?
2. About herself, Quindlen states that she has "an overactive sense of place" (paragraph 3). What do you think she means?
3. In paragraph 8, Quindlen states that to keep ourselves from becoming too involved in the problems of others we "turn an adjective into a noun." What point is she making?
4. Quindlen uses the brief sentence, "That is everything" twice, once in paragraph 4 and again in paragraph 9. In your view, does the sentence have the same meaning each time? Explain.

Examining the Writer's Method

1. In the introduction, Quindlen makes it a point to identify the homeless woman by name. Why do you think she chooses to discuss the woman in this way?
2. In your view, where in her essay does Quindlen provide the most thorough definition of homelessness?

3. What does Quindlen mean in the sixth paragraph when she discusses a home versus real estate?
4. How does the concluding paragraph help Quindlen reiterate her point about the homeless?

Considering Style and Language

1. Quindlen uses negation in the third paragraph as a way to expand her definition of homelessness. Why do you think she chooses to state what homelessness *isn't* rather than to concentrate on what homelessness *is?*
2. Quindlen makes it a point in paragraph 7 to say that one homeless woman with a baby had once told her that what she wanted was a single room, "painted blue." What is the significance of the woman's aspiration? Why does Quindlen repeat the words?
3. In the concluding paragraph, Quindlen first uses some specific details ("a woman without a bureau," "a man with no mirror, no wall to hang it on") to reiterate what she feels is the difference between being homeless and lacking a home. But then, rather than ending her essay, she provides a few other specific details. Why does she structure the paragraph in this way? Why doesn't she provide all the specific details before emphasizing the distinction between the two states of existence?
4. What do the following words mean in the context of the writing? Rummaged (para. 1); adrift, anonymous, grime (para. 2); legacy, cross-stitch, French knots, samplers (para. 3); ferocity, certainty, stability, predictability (para. 4); enfeebled (para. 5); huddled, crux (para. 7); 9, bureau (para. 9).

Your Turn: Responding to the Subject

a. Anna Quindlen makes it abundantly clear in this essay that a home is far more than simple shelter from the elements.

But what makes a home a home? For this assignment, examine in detail your view of the elements that constitute a home.

b. In the third paragraph, Quindlen notes that she has "never been good at looking at the big picture, taking the global view. . . ." *The big picture* and *the global view* are both common expressions, but what do they mean? For this assignment, choose one of these terms and define it as you understand it.

Other Possibilities for Using Definition

Here are some additional subjects for a paper that features definition. Feel free to adapt these topics until you feel more comfortable with them. Then concentrate on explaining your main idea in detail and providing plenty of support in the form of specific details and examples.

- faith
- a masterpiece of literature, music, or art
- freedom
- tabloid journalism
- success
- beauty
- conscience
- sexual harassment
- etiquette
- humor
- an effective teacher
- fear
- date rape
- family values
- depression

Practical Application: Definition

"I like my job as administrative assistant to the chair of the Chamber of Commerce," you were just telling a friend the other day. "The best part is that I never know from one day to the next what I'll be asked to do." So you shouldn't really have been surprised when your boss approached you this afternoon, looking uncharacteristically flustered.

The problem, she explains, is tomorrow evening's annual Chamber banquet and the five-minute speech she is supposed to make about the award winner. Each year the selection committee chooses a theme and then selects the nominee whose qualities and actions match the theme. This year's theme is *heroism,* and the recipient is Miss Lucretia Salinger, a retired legal secretary in her late 70s who has devoted her energies to the cause of adult literacy. Three afternoons a week since her retirement fifteen years ago, she has worked with adults who desperately want to learn to read and write, tutoring them one-on-one in a small room in the back of the public library.

Your boss knows how deserving Miss Salinger is of the award; so far she has not been able to express her admiration effectively, however, and she has four other tasks on her desk that must be done by the end of the day. "You had a course in speech in college — would you write it up for me, about *three hundred words or so?* And would you also list the main ideas in a rough outline to make it easier for me to keep things straight? Thanks!" After swallowing nervously, you agree. To make your job easier, she gives you a copy of the speech "Courage: A Hero in Our Midst" — with a brief outline — prepared for last year's presentation by staffer Stephen M. Haugh on the theme of *courage.* Use it to guide you in terms of *approach* and *format* as you prepare your speech and outline about Miss Salinger.

Courage: A Hero in Our Midst

Good evening, ladies and gentlemen, and welcome to our annual banquet. It's great to see such a big turnout, and I know we're all going to enjoy ourselves tonight.

As you know, the theme of this year's banquet is courage. We are so very proud to honor our nominee this year. In fact, this is not the only award he has received this month. Our guest of honor, Mr. John Slovack, recently was awarded one of our nation's top military honors — the Silver Star Medal.

John Slovack grew up in this town. He has raised a fine family and is a respected member of the community. Like many of our young men, he enlisted in the army in the late '60s and served in Vietnam. Now, I knew that John saw plenty of action on the front lines and was wounded in battle himself. What I certainly did not know about was the exceptional courage and bravery that he exhibited in that terrible war.

During a fierce battle, according to his fellow soldiers, John's unit was pinned down by artillery fire and was in a very bad way. A few members of his squad had already been killed or wounded.

Well, apparently, that's when our John took matters into his own hands. Crawling on his belly, he worked his way around and behind the enemy fire and knocked out their stronghold single-handedly, probably saving the lives of his entire unit.

Now John should have received his Silver Star more than 25 years ago, but the paperwork somehow got lost. So that's why we're finally hearing about all this now. A group of his buddies petitioned Washington and got it all straightened out. Lord knows, we never heard a word about it from the man himself.

In addition to your courage, John, we ought to honor you for your modesty as well. Honestly, a war hero in our midst all these years, and we never knew. Well it's out now, John.

Now I know this little award of ours is nothing compared to the Silver Star, but we had to let you know just how proud we are of you.

Ladies and gentlemen, it is indeed our privilege and honor to award to John Slovack this humble award for courage above and beyond the call of duty.

I. Welcome

II. This year's theme: Courage; John Slovack — Silver Star

III. Slovack — local boy — Vietnam

IV. Fierce battle — pinned down

V. Bravery in action

VI. Should have received medal 25 years ago — finally straightened out

VII. A hero in our midst all these years

VIII. Our award versus Silver Star

IX. Our privilege and honor — humble award

8

Comparison and Contrast

The Technique

In writing, the analytical method used to examine similarities or differences is called *comparison and contrast,* with *comparison* referring to an examination of similarities and *contrast* referring to an examination of differences. You'll probably find that you use comparison and contrast frequently when you write, both in a supporting role and as the dominant mode in an essay.

Although you'll rely on comparison and contrast in a variety of writing situations, you'll find this mode especially helpful in the academic writing you'll be expected to complete. In a literature class, for instance, you might be asked to discuss the similarities of characters in a novel or the imagery in some poems. In a history class, you might be asked to examine one civilization or political system in relation to another. In a psychology class, you might be asked to note the differences between behavioral disorders. To gain the most from your use of comparison and contrast, regardless of your purpose, you need to

- establish *a clear basis for comparison;*
- make *a thorough and specific presentation;* and
- provide *an effective arrangement* for the material.

A CLEAR BASIS FOR COMPARISON

Whenever you use comparison and contrast, you need to establish a clear basis for comparison. In other words, once you have your subjects, you need to decide whether you are going to examine the similarities, the differences, or both. Then you choose the aspects, characteristics, or elements of each that you are going to present.

Of course, before doing this you need to focus on your subjects. Dealing with two subjects is often an ideal strategy because it enables you to examine the subjects in detail with a minimum of complications for you and your reader. Of course, it is possible to examine three or more subjects in the same essay; magazines such as *Consumer Reports* regularly include articles that study several brands of the same product. Keep in mind, however, that the more subjects you compare or contrast, the greater the chances that you may confuse your reader as you switch from subject to subject. For example, a reader is unlikely to become sidetracked or confused reading a paper about which computer system, the Macintosh or the IBM PC, would be better for a college student. Add one or more computer systems to the discussion, and suddenly there is a good deal more information for your reader to keep track of.

Once you've zeroed in on your subjects, you need to decide which elements to examine. With the essay about computer systems, you would identify several aspects that potential buyers would need to know, such as price, portability, types and availability of software, ease of operation, and warranty. With a clear basis of comparison established, you're prepared to develop the essay, discussing each element in relation to each subject.

The following is a brief excerpt from "Listening to Khakis," Malcolm Gladwell's essay on Levi Strauss & Company's successful marketing strategy to sell Docker pants. As he refers to Professor Joan Meyers-Levy's research on this subject, Gladwell sets up his basis of comparison for his discussion of the different ways that women and men process information:

This idea — men eliminate and women integrate — is called by Meyers-Levy the "selectivity hypothesis." Men are looking for a way to simplify the route to a conclusion, so they seize on the most obvious evidence and ignore the rest, while women, by contrast, try to process information comprehensively. So-called bandwidth research, for example, has consistently shown that if you ask a group of people to sort a series of objects or ideas into categories, the men will create fewer and larger categories than the women will. They use bigger mental bandwidths. Why? Because the bigger the bandwidth the less time and attention you have to pay to each individual object.

A THOROUGH AND SPECIFIC PRESENTATION

As is true anytime you write, when you write an essay in which you compare or contrast subjects, you need to examine the subjects fully. Of course, there is no rule that sets an automatic number of points of comparison you should establish, but common sense indicates that subjects striking you as similar or dissimilar do so because of more than one or two aspects. Therefore, as you work through the writing process, shoot for a basis of comparison that contains at least three points and then add any additional points that you develop as you write.

For example, imagine you were going to write a paper contrasting downhill skiing with cross-country skiing. Certainly, these two winter sports are different in terms of the expense involved and specialized equipment required. But these activities also differ in terms of terrain required (steep mountain slopes for downhill versus rolling country for cross-country); degree of danger involved (considerable danger in downhill, especially to legs because of speed and strain from sharp turns, versus minimal danger in cross-country); and amount of training involved (several hours of lessons and practice for downhill skiing versus a brief lesson and an hour or so of practice for cross-country skiing). A paper dealing with only the first two points of comparison would be inadequate; an essay that features these five points of comparison would clearly do a better job of showing that these two sports are indeed vastly different.

In this brief passage on macroeconomics, note how author Stephen L. Slavin sets up his discussion of the two different economic systems:

> The big difference between the old Soviet economy and our own is what consumer goods and services are produced. In our economy, the market forces of supply and demand dictate what gets produced and how much of it gets produced. But a government planning agency in the Soviet Union dictated what and how much was made. In effect, central planning attempted to direct a production and distribution process that works automatically in a market economy.

With this focus identified, Slavin is then able to discuss in detail the various characteristics that typify the two different economic systems.

AN EFFECTIVE ARRANGEMENT

How you present the material constituting an essay is always important because an effective arrangement makes it easier for your reader to follow your line of reasoning. In writing that features comparison and contrast, organization is especially important because the focus is on an examination of more than one subject.

With an essay comparing or contrasting two subjects, you have three possible methods of arrangement: the *block method,* the *alternating method,* and the *mixed method.* Imagine, for example, that you were doing a paper concerning whether parents should use conventional cloth diapers or disposable diapers, and you had established this basis of comparison: cost, degree of convenience, baby's comfort, and overall environmental impact.

With the block method, you would first discuss — paragraph by paragraph — cost, degree of convenience, comfort, and environmental impact for cloth diapers; and then cost, degree of convenience, comfort, and environmental impact for disposable diapers. With the alternating method, you would first discuss cost for conventional diapers and then cost for disposable diapers. Next you would talk about degree of convenience for conventional diapers and then degree of convenience for disposable diapers, and so on. Brief outlines for these two methods would look like this:

Block method:	*Alternating method:*
Conventional diapers	**Cost**
cost	conventional diapers
degree of convenience	disposable diapers
comfort	**Degree of convenience**
environmental impact	conventional diapers
Disposable diapers	disposable diapers
cost	**Comfort**
degree of convenience	conventional diapers
comfort	disposable diapers
environmental impact	**Environmental impact**
	conventional diapers
	disposable diapers

This paragraph on the differences between softball and baseball illustrates the alternating pattern:

> Even though the rules for both games are the same, baseball and slow-pitch softball are definitely different games. Baseball is played on a large diamond. Softball, however, is played on a smaller field, more like a little league field. A baseball is pitched fast, up to ninety miles per hour in the major leagues, and overhand. In contrast, a slow-pitch softball is lobbed underhand. Because of the speed of the pitching and the variety of pitches, a .300 batting average for a baseball player is good. Because a softball is pitched more slowly, though, batting averages of .500 or more are common. Also, in baseball, players are allowed to steal bases. In softball, though, a runner can't leave the base until the ball is hit.

And this paragraph from Jay M. Pasachoff's discussion of Earth and its nearest neighbor, Venus, illustrates the block pattern:

> Venus and the Earth are sister planets: their sizes, masses, and densities are about the same. But they are as different from each other as the wicked sisters were from Cinderella.

The Earth is lush; it has oceans and rainstorms of water, an atmosphere containing oxygen, and creatures swimming in the sea, flying in the air, and walking on the ground. On the other hand, Venus is a hot, foreboding planet with temperatures constantly over 750 K (900°F), a planet on which life seems unlikely to develop. Why is Venus like that? How did these harsh conditions come about? Can it happen to us here on Earth?

Of course with the mixed method, as the name suggests, you set up the information in some other way. In the paper about diapers, using the block format to present the first three points and then switching to the alternating format for the final point would enable you to emphasize the efforts by manufacturers of disposable diapers to make their product more biodegradable, leading your reader to the conclusion that overall, disposable diapers are the better choice.

AN ANNOTATED EXAMPLE

S. I. Hayakawa
Snarl-Words and Purr-Words

Although you probably aren't accustomed to thinking about what you do when you communicate, the process always involves choosing words to fulfill some specific purpose. Semantics is the name given to the study of the ways people use language, and it is a field that fascinated the late S. I. Hayakawa. In addition to being an accomplished writer, Hayakawa was a teacher, administrator, politician, and activist; during his lifetime, he served as a professor of English, the president of San Francisco State College, a U.S. senator, and in the latter years of his life, an advocate for the movement to make English the official language of the United States. In this passage from the fifth edition of his landmark text Language in Thought and Action, *Hayakawa uses comparison and contrast to differentiate between two types of words that express what a speaker believes about a subject.*

How does language that expresses your feelings differ from language that expresses what is known or observed?

He uses the introduction to establish his subject of discussion.

Language is not an isolated phenomenon. Our concern is with language in action — in the full context of nonlinguistic events which are its setting. The making of noises, like other muscle activities, is sometimes involuntary. Our responses to powerful stimuli, such as to things that make us very angry, are a complex of muscular and physiological events: the contracting of fighting muscles, the increase of blood pressure, a change in body chemistry, *and* the making of noises such as growls and snarls. We are a little too dignified, perhaps, to growl like dogs, but we do the next best thing and substitute series of words such as "You dirty sneak!" "The filthy scum!" Similarly, if we are pleasurably agitated, we may, instead of purring or wagging the tail, say things like "She's the sweetest little girl in all the world!" 1

He specifies by subjects — the contrasting categories of expressions.

Such statements have less to do with reporting the outside world than they do with our inadvertently reporting the state of our internal world; they are the human equivalents of snarling and purring. On hearing "She's the sweetest girl in the whole world," the listener would be wise to allocate the meaning correctly — as a revelation of the speaker's state of mind and not as a revelation about the girl. 2

He offers explanations of the two types, focusing on the differences.

Although this observation may seem obvious, it is surprising how often, when such a statement is made, both the speaker and the hearer feel that something has been said about the girl. This error is especially common in the interpretation of utterances of orators and editorialists in some of their more excited denunciations of "leftists," "facists," "Wall Street," "right-wingers," and in their glowing support of "our way of life." Constantly, because of the impressive sound of the words, the elaborate structure of the sentences, and the appearance of intellectual progression, we get the feeling that something is being said about something. On closer examination, however, we discover that these utterances really say "What I hate ('liberals,' 'Wall Street,') I hate very, very much," and "What I like ('our way of life') I like very, very much." We may call such utterances *snarl-words* and *purr-words*. 3

He follows a mixed method of arrangement and notes similarities.

On the other hand, if the snarl-words and purr-words are accompanied by verifiable reports (which would also mean that we have previously agreed as to what specifically is meant by the terms used), we might find reason to accept the emotional position of the speaker or writer. But snarl-words and purr-words as such, unaccompanied by verifiable reports, offer nothing further to discuss, except possibly the question "Why do you feel as you do?" 4

Issues like gun control, abortion, capital punishment, and elections often lead us to resort to the equivalent of snarl-words and purr-words. It is usually 5 fruitless to argue such statements as "Reagan was the great Teflon president — nothing stuck," "She is anti-life," "Wagner's music is just a cacophony of hysterical screeching," "People who don't want to control the purchase of handguns are nuts." To take sides on such issues phrased in such judgmental ways is to reduce communication to a level of stubborn imbecility. But to ask questions relating to the statements (Why do you like or dislike President Reagan? Why are you for or against gun control?) is to learn something about the beliefs of others. After listening to their opinions and the reasons for them, we may leave the discussion slightly wiser, slightly better informed, and perhaps less one-sided than we were before the discussion began.

The final sentence serves as the conclusion, restating the significance of the writing.

Your Turn: Responding to the Subject

a. In this excerpt, S. I. Hayakawa discusses two types of expression used in everyday discourse. His intent is to make us more aware of how complex a process spoken communication is. For this assignment, discuss two types of language you use or have observed — for example, talking at school versus talking at home, conversing with a boss versus conversing with coworkers, discussion on a first date versus discussion after a relationship has been established, and so on.

b. Do we say what we mean? For this assignment, think of an argument or heated discussion you've witnessed or had yourself. Then interpret those passages that you feel had hidden meaning, contrasting what was said with what was implied.

Steven Doloff

The Opposite Sex

Steven Doloff is an associate professor of English and humanities at Pratt Institute in New York City. His essays on culture and education have appeared in a number of publications including the New York Times, *the* Philadelphia Inquirer, *the* Boston Globe, *and the* Chronicle of Higher Education. *In this essay, which was originally published in the* Washington Post, *Doloff recounts what happened when he gave several of his writing classes a simple assignment: Imagine what your life would be like if you were of the opposite sex. The resulting papers offered Doloff an interesting view of the perceptions some people have about gender roles.*

What stereotypes does the average person hold about the life the opposite sex leads?

Having seen Dustin Hoffman's female impersonation in the 1 movie, *Tootsie,* I decided to give myself some reading over the Christmas recess by assigning in-class essays to my English composition students on how each would spend a day as a member of his or her respective opposite sex. From four classes I received approximately 100 essays. The sample, perhaps like the movie, proved both entertaining and annoying in its predictability.

The female students, as a group, took to the subject imme- 2 diately and with obvious gusto, while the male students tended to wait a while (in several cases half the period), in something of a dare, before starting. The activities hypothetically engaged in by the women, whose ages averaged about 20, generally reflected two areas: envy of men's physical and social privileges, and curiosity regarding men's true feelings concerning women.

In their essays, women jauntily went places *alone,* and 3 sometimes stayed out *all night.* They threw their clothes on the floor and left dishes in the sink. They hung out on the street and sweated happily in a variety of sports from football to weightlifting.

More than a third of them went out to cruise for dates. Ap-   *4*
pointing themselves in brand names of men's clothing and
dousing themselves in men's cologne I have never heard of (I
was instructed to read Gentleman's Quarterly magazine), they
deliberately and aggressively accosted women, *many* women,
on the street, in discos, in supermarkets. Others sought out the
proverbial locker room for the kinds of bull sessions they
hoped would reveal the real nitty-gritty masculine mind at
work (on the subject of women).

At least two female students in each class spent chunks of   *5*
their essays under the sheets with imaginary girlfriends, wives
or strangers, finding out with a kind of scientific zeal what sex
is like as a man.

Some, but not all of the women ended their essays with a   *6*
formal, almost obligatory sounding statement of preference to
be a female, and of gratitude in returning to their correct gender after a day as Mr. Hyde.

The male students, after their initial paralysis wore off, did   *7*
not write as much as the females. They seemed envious of very
little that was female, and curious about nothing. Three or
four spent their day as women frantically seeking medical help
to turn back into men more quickly. Those who accepted the
assignment more seriously, if unenthusiastically, either stayed
home and apathetically checked off a list of domestic chores
or, more evasively, went off to work in an office and engaged
in totally asexual business office routines.

A small percentage of the men ventured into the more   *8*
feminine pursuits of putting on makeup and going to the
beauty parlor. They agreed looking good was important.

If they stayed home as housewives, when their hypothet-   *9*
ical husbands returned from work they ate dinner, watched
some television and then went right to sleep. If they were busi-
nesswomen, they came directly home after work, ate some
dinner, watched TV and went right to sleep. A handful actually went out on dates, had dinner in the most expensive
restaurants they could cajole their escorts into taking them to,
and then, after being taken home, very politely slammed the
doors in their escorts faces and went right to sleep. Not one
male student let anybody lay a finger on him/her.

Finally, the sense of heartfelt relief at the end of the male   *10*
students' essays, underscored by the much-repeated fervent

anticipation of masculinity returning with the dawn, seemed equivalent to that of jumping up after having been forced to sit on a lit stove.

Granted, my flimsy statistical sample is nothing to go to the   *11*
Ford Foundation with for research money. But on the other hand, do I really need to prove that young people even now are still burdened with sexist stereotypes and sexist self-images not nearly as vestigial as we would like to think? (One male student rhetorically crumpled up his paper after 10 minutes and growled, "You can't make me write this!") What does that imply about the rest of us? What would *you* do as a member of the opposite sex for a day? This last question is your essay assignment.

Understanding the Significance

1. According to the papers Steven Doloff received, what two areas about males most interested his female students?
2. How did the female students who wrote about going out alone behave on their fictional evenings?
3. In general, how did Doloff's male students react to and deal with the assignment?
4. From the examples Doloff provides, why did the male students generally write less than the female students?

Discovering the Writer's Purpose

1. In the final sentence of the introduction, Doloff states that the result of his exercise was "both entertaining and annoying in its predictability." What do you think he means?
2. In the fourth paragraph, Doloff makes it clear that his female students knew a lot about the habits and rituals of males, in one case more than Doloff himself knew. What point is he making about the curiosity and insight of women versus men?
3. When Doloff discusses his male students' thoughts on dating, he notes that while the men were willing to enjoy a

fancy dinner, they all very definitively rejected any possibility of further contact or intimacy. What conclusion could you draw from this behavior?

4. Why do you think Doloff ends his essay with a rhetorical question?

Examining the Writer's Method

1. In the introduction to his essay, Doloff refers to *Tootsie,* a movie in which renowned actor Dustin Hoffman experiences life as a female soap-opera star. What effect does Doloff create by making reference to this movie?

2. What method of arrangement does Doloff predominately rely on: block, alternating, or mixed? Explain your answer.

3. Would Doloff's essay have been more — or less — effective if he had discussed the responses of his male students *before* the responses of his female students?

4. In the conclusion, Doloff includes in parentheses the response one of his male students had to the assignment. Why do you think he included these comments? Do you think the parentheses are necessary? Why or why not?

Considering Style and Language

1. The paragraphs in which Doloff discusses the responses of his female students contain far more specific details and examples than the corresponding paragraphs covering his male students' responses. What idea does he communicate as a result?

2. In the third paragraph, Doloff uses italics twice — for *alone* and *all night.* Why do you think he sets these particular words off in this way?

3. The tone of Doloff's final paragraph is markedly different from the tone in the rest of the essay. In what way is it different? What is the overall effect of the change?

4. What do the following words mean in the context of the writing? Respective, predictability (para. 1); gusto,

hypothetically (para. 2); jauntily (para. 3); cruise, appointing, dousing, accosted, proverbial, nitty-gritty (para. 4); zeal (para. 5); obligatory (para. 6); apathetically, asexual (para. 7); cajole (para. 9); fervent (para. 10); flimsy, vestigial, rhetorically (para. 11).

Your Turn Responding to the Subject

a. In this essay Steven Doloff discusses his students' ideas about the lives experienced by people of the opposite sex. How about you? What do you think your life would be like if you were a member of the opposite sex? For this assignment contrast the life you think you would lead as a member of the opposite sex with the life you actually lead.

b. Doloff's female and male students responded quite differently to his assignment. In your experience, do men and women respond to situations in similar ways or in different ways? Focus on several typical situations, for instance, shopping, selecting movies, arranging a party, and so on, and compare or contrast how men and women react.

Patrice Gaines-Carter

Is My "Post-Integration" Daughter Black Enough?

Common wisdom holds that when people are given something, they don't appreciate it as much as if they had earned it themselves. In this essay, newspaper reporter Patrice Gaines-Carter discusses this wisdom in relation to civil rights advances. Because of the suffering and sacrifices made by Gaines-Carter's generation and those who came before her, life is better for today's African American children. Yet, because things are better, these children may not fully understand how precious these gains are and what must be done to maintain them. In this essay, which appeared first in the Washington Post *and was then reprinted in* Ebony, *Gaines-Carter uses comparison and contrast to illustrate the differences between the world as she knew it and the world her daughter knows today.*

Is it possible for a generation of people to fully understand the sacrifices that earlier generations made so that life today could be better for them?

My dearest Daughter:

Something's been troubling me for the past two years. I 1
jokingly call it the "Post-Integration Blues." Actually, it's no
laughing matter.

I get it every time something happens like last month 2
when I said to you, "Martin Luther King's birthday is coming
up and we're going to do something special like attend a
memorial service." You looked at me with total disdain and
said, "Momma, that's the only day I'll get to sleep late."

When you say things like that, I take them personally. I 3
know that I shouldn't, but I hurt. I take it as rejection of all
that my generation of Blacks fought for, yet I know that is not
how you intended it.

I don't want you to let King's birthday go by without re- 4
membering what he stood for. Although you are 16, I want

229

you to fight racism. I want you to march at the South African Embassy, and even if you can't, I want you to be aware that someone else is marching.

We've discussed this. You told me just recently, "Just be- 5 cause we don't march doesn't mean we don't know it's Dr. King's birthday." Still, I hurt, and wonder; What happened to my little girl who could barely print, but wrote the governor of North Carolina to ask him to "free the Wilmington 10?"

See, at 35, I come from a generation of marchers. I do not 6 understand inaction. In fact, it frightens me. I do not trust it. You think my distrust is paranoia; I understand. It is because you have not seen what I have seen. At my segregated school in Beaufort, S.C., everything — our buses, books, desks — was hand-me-downs from the White school. On cold days we wore our coats in class because the heat didn't always work. The White children passed us in their new buses, on their way to their new school.

You have never known such. You ride a shiny school bus to 7 a nine-year-old school that is thoroughly integrated. "Momma, we just don't put the emphasis on Black and White that you do," you told me the other day, adding, "But when we are in school, I do end up hanging with my friends, who just happen to be Black. Everybody does the same thing, so that Black people end up on one side and White people on another."

That wasn't exactly what I wanted to hear either, believe 8 it or not. I was part of a busing plan that helped integrate DuVal Senior High School in Greenbelt, just a couple of miles from your school. I suffered at that school. I felt like a stranger in a foreign land because I was one of 50 Black students out of about 2,000 pupils. Some of the Black students adapted well; I did not. I pacified myself by imagining I was a sacrificial lamb, being used so that generations of Blacks after me would receive benefits I had been denied.

My payback, I figured, would be the lives of those Black 9 children who came after me. They would ride new buses and go to new schools. They would not sit in unheated classrooms. They would do all of this because of integration. They would do all of this without assimilating, without becoming like the people we were fighting or, in other words, "They would never act White."

You would probably say I am overreacting. I wonder if *10* what I want isn't impossible. You think that you don't "act White," and mostly you're right. But changes can creep up so slowly and in such small ways.

For instance, you watch music videos for hours at a time *11* and seem pleased at what you see. When I look at them, what I notice is that the Black women who are featured as lovers are light-skinned Black women with long, straight hair — women who look like they're White.

My generation watched television shows that seldom *12* showed Blacks. We fought hard to get Blacks on television; then we fought harder to get all shades of Black people shown: dark chocolate, saffron, cinnamon, blue-black and ginger. I don't see these colors in your videos — certainly not the ones meant to be physically attractive.

What bothers me is that you don't seem to miss the shades *13* of color. To me, to not miss them is, in a way, to not act Black. It is like returning to the days when only Lena Horne, with her light skin and narrow nose, was considered a beautiful Black woman — by Blacks and Whites. It is like returning to days when women like Cicely Tyson, your grandmother and your great-grandmother, with their ebony skin and wide noses, were considered ugly because their features were different from those of White women. To not accept all of the shades of Black beauty is one step from "acting White."

I don't know when I first caught this Post-Integration *14* Blues. It was around the first time I heard strange music coming from your room. The door was closed, but I knocked and you allowed me to peep in.

"What is it?" I asked, pointing to the stereo. *15*

"I like that song," you said, hardly looking up from your *16* book.

"Who is it? Sounds like somebody White." *17*

"It's Cyndi Lauper," you replied, explaining that she was a *18* new rock 'n' roll star.

"Cyndi who?" I asked. *19*

You mumbled something, but by that time I was blue *20* again. I was thinking about a time when Black people listened to music that had what I call a definite beat, a time when you could really tell a Black recording artist from a White one. I left the room floating on memories of songs by Frankie Lyman and the Teenagers, Ben E. King and James Brown. Soul Music.

While music and marching and television seem insignifi- 21
cant, they are not. It is the tiny threads of life that weave a whole history of a people. As far as I am concerned we are dealing with the continued existence of Black people. I want you to know this without knowing the pain. I wish I could push history into your consciousness simply by pressing the palm of my hand against your chest.

Every time I think I might suffer a total breakdown from 22
the Post-Integration Blues, something happens to give me strength. This strength comes in ironic ways, too, like last November when you got called "nigger" for the first time.

You should have seen your face when you told me about 23
it. You said you were working at the drive-in window at McDonald's and this man was at the window, waiting for his food and staring at you in a strange way. You asked if you could help him and he said, "No, I'm just looking at a nigger about to give me my food."

You threw the food in his car and the young Black woman 24
working with you, who had not heard the man, screamed, "You're going to lose your job!"

"Momma," you told me, "I didn't care about the job. But 25
I was too stunned to say anything to him."

In the old days I would have been ready to find the man 26
and shoot him, but here I was thankful and slightly amused. "I am just amazed that it took 16 years," I said. "The first time somebody called me nigger I was too young to understand what they meant."

Sure, the fact that it took 16 years for you to be called a "nig- 27
ger" was a sign of how some things have changed for the better. But it gave me strength for another reason: I also couldn't help feeling that it won't hurt your generation to get called "nigger" at least once to your face.

Every time somebody called me "nigger," I became more 28
determined to not let up, to keep on coming, to march, to fight, to succeed. In your generation, I don't see that determination to march or fight. I think you need some reminders of what this country could easily return to unless we all fight daily.

I thought about the difference in our worlds on the night   29
in July 1984 when your cousin Christopher was born. He
struggled to come into this world on the very night that Jesse
Jackson spoke at the Democratic National Convention.

I was in the delivery room with his mother and I went   30
back and forth from wiping her brow and telling her, "Okay
now, breathe, 1-2-3; that's good," to crying over the fact that
I had lived long enough to see a Black man considered a serious presidential candidate.

When I think of Christopher now, I wonder: What will life   31
be like for a young Black boy born into a world where a Black
man has already run for president?

I first assumed Christopher's life would be better, then the   32
Post-Integration Blues set in, and I looked at my blue self, who
has marched and picketed, and said, "Do not assume anything." That is what frightens me about your own generation.
I sometimes think you take too much for granted.

I am torn. I don't want you to live on the razor's edge as I   33
did in South Carolina, when I couldn't enter certain doors,
drink from certain water fountains or eat a meal sitting down
at any restaurant downtown. But I don't want you to forget either. I'm afraid if you haven't lived on the razor's edge you forget you can bleed.

I am encouraged by incidents like the one when you came   34
home a couple of weeks ago and in a disgusted voice said, "My
history teacher didn't even know who Louis Farrakhan is,
momma."

Maybe my words aren't just flying around your head. You   35
have caught some of what I've been saying. Anyway, it's not
just you who triggers my blues, but a lot of Black children.

For instance, remember when I took my friend's 12-year-   36
old son, David-Askia, to the movie? Well, while we were sitting there waiting for the film to begin, I started telling him
about how when I lived in Beaufort, S.C., in 1962, Black people could only sit in the balcony of the theater.

"We used to throw popcorn and ice from our sodas down   37
on the White kids," I said.

"There would always be two empty rows just under the   38
edge of the balcony, since none of the White kids wanted to
sit there and have to duck all the time."

"That was dumb, to throw things down on people," 39
David-Askia said.

"It seems dumb now but it wasn't dumb if that was the 40
only way you could get back at them," I said.

"Anyway," he said, turning to give me a puzzled look, 41
"You can see better in the balcony."

"True," I told him. "But you only know that if you have 42
had the chance to sit everywhere in the theater." He's so young,
I'm not sure he understood what I was saying.

I hope you do. 43

> With Love,
> Momma

Understanding the Significance

1. What does Patrice Gaines-Carter mean by the "Post-
   Integration Blues"?
2. How have Gaines-Carter's life experiences influenced the
   way she views life?
3. What is Gaines-Carter afraid will happen to her daughter
   and her daughter's entire generation?
4. In paragraph 27, Gaines-Carter states that she "couldn't
   help feeling that it won't hurt your generation to get
   called 'nigger' at least once to your face." What does she
   mean?

Discovering the Writer's Purpose

1. In paragraph 2, Gaines-Carter presents the first in a series
   of examples illustrating the differences between herself
   and her daughter. What point do you think she is making
   with this example?
2. In paragraphs 11–21, Gaines-Carter takes issue with her
   daughter's taste in music videos and music, remembering
   a time when "you could really tell a Black recording artist

from a White one." Do you feel that Gaines-Carter's concern is legitimate, or is she overreacting? Explain.

3. In your judgment, what is it that Gaines-Carter would like her daughter to do?

4. In paragraph 21, Gaines-Carter states that she would like her daughter to understand the struggle of those who came before her, "without knowing the pain. I wish I could push history into your consciousness simply by pressing the palm of my hand against your chest." In your judgment, can such things ever happen? In other words, can people ever truly appreciate the suffering of others without having suffered the same way themselves?

Examining the Writer's Method

1. Gaines-Carter sets her writing up as a letter. Why? Would it have been less effective presented as a straight essay rather than as a personal letter? Why or why not?

2. Gaines-Carter includes a number of powerful details and examples of the prejudice she has faced. In your judgment, which one has the most impact? Why?

3. Gaines-Carter ends her essay with a single sentence. Why do you think she chose to close her paper this way?

4. For most of her essay, Gaines-Carter relies on the alternating pattern to organize the material in her essay. If she had chosen to use the block method, would her essay have been any less effective? Why or why not?

Considering Style and Language

1. Do you think the tone in her essay indicates that Gaines-Carter is hopeful or pessimistic? Explain.

2. At several points in paragraphs 22–28, Gaines-Carter uses the highly offensive, highly inflammatory term *nigger*. Why do you think she repeats the derogatory term rather

than substituting the expression "a racial slur" or some other euphemism?

3. How does the anecdote of David-Askia, related in paragraphs 36–43, help Gaines-Carter make her point?

4. What do the following words mean in the context of the writing? Disdain (para. 2); paranoia, segregated (para. 6); pacified, sacrificial (para. 8); assimilating (para. 9); saffron, ginger (para. 12); insignificant, consciousness (para. 21); ironic (para. 22).

Your Turn: Responding to the Subject

a. Gaines-Carter's essay expresses her deep concern that people have failed to learn from the events of the past; the specter of bigotry that lingers in our country is sad proof that she has reason to be concerned. For this assignment, take another issue — the environment, the economy, education, sexual abuse, homelessness, politics — and answer this question: are people dealing better with this situation now than twenty-five years ago? Worse? The same?

b. How does the life that your generation enjoys differ from the life that your parents' generation has experienced? For this assignment, discuss the differences.

Richard Rodriguez

Aria

Language connects people — if the people involved share the same language. Those who don't share the language are forced to retreat to the safety of their own tongues, to the comfort of familiar words and sounds. There is indeed comfort in this retreat, but there is also isolation and a great sense of loss. Such is the message that Richard Rodriguez makes in this excerpt from his 1981 award-winning book Hunger of Memory: The Education of Richard Rodriguez, *which deals with his life as the child of Mexican immigrants. Rodriguez has also published a number of articles in such periodicals as* Harper's, *the* New Republic, *and the* Saturday Review, *and a 1992 book* Days of Obligation.

Is the way people view themselves influenced by whether they are in the mainstream?

I remember to start with that day in Sacramento — a California now nearly thirty years past — when I first entered a classroom, able to understand some fifty stray English words. 1

The third of four children, I had been preceded to a neighborhood Roman Catholic school by an older brother and sister. But neither of them had revealed very much about their classroom experiences. Each afternoon they returned, as they left in the morning, always together, speaking in Spanish as they climbed the five steps of the porch. And their mysterious books, wrapped in shopping-bag paper, remained on the table next to the door, closed firmly behind them. 2

An accident of geography sent me to a school where all my classmates were white, many the children of doctors and lawyers and business executives. All my classmates certainly must have been uneasy on that first day of school — as most children are uneasy — to find themselves apart from their families in the first institution of their lives. But I was astonished. 3

The nun said, in a friendly but oddly impersonal voice, "Boys and girls, this is Richard Rodriguez." (I heard her sound 4 out: *Rich-heard Road-ree-guess.*) It was the first time I had heard anyone name me in English. "Richard," the nun repeated more slowly, writing my name down in her black leather book. Quickly I turned to see my mother's face dissolve in a watery blur behind the pebbled glass door.

Many years later there is something called bilingual 5
education — a scheme proposed in the late 1960s by Hispanic-American social activists, later endorsed by a congressional vote. It is a program that seeks to permit non-English-speaking children, many from lower-class homes, to use their family language as the language of school. (Such is the goal its supporters announce.) I hear them and am forced to say no: It is not possible for a child — any child — ever to use his family's language in school. Not to understand this is to misunderstand the public uses of schooling and to trivialize the nature of intimate life — a family's "language."

Memory teaches me what I know of these matters; the boy 6
reminds the adult. I was a bilingual child, a certain kind — socially disadvantaged — the son of working-class parents, both Mexican immigrants.

In the early years of my boyhood, my parents coped very 7
well in America. My father had steady work. My mother managed at home. They were nobody's victims. Optimism and ambition led them to a house (our home) many blocks from the Mexican south side of town. We lived among *gringos* and only a block from the biggest, whitest houses. It never occurred to my parents that they couldn't live wherever they chose. Nor was the Sacramento of the fifties bent on teaching them a contrary lesson. My mother and father were more annoyed than intimidated by those two or three neighbors who tried initially to make us unwelcome. ("Keep your brats away from my sidewalk!") But despite all they achieved, perhaps because they had so much to achieve, any deep feeling of ease, the confidence of "belonging" in public was withheld from them both. They regarded the people at work, the faces in crowds, as very distant from us. They were the others, *los gringos*. That term was interchangeable in their speech with another, even more telling, *los americanos*.

I grew up in a house where the only regular guests were my 8
relations. For one day, enormous families of relatives would visit

and there would be so many people that the noise and the bodies would spill out to the backyard and front porch. Then, for weeks, no one came by. (It was usually a salesman who rang the doorbell.) Our house stood apart. A gaudy yellow in a row of white bungalows. We were the people with the noisy dog. The people who raised pigeons and chickens. We were the foreigners on the block. A few neighbors smiled and waved. We waved back. But no one in the family knew the names of the old couple who lived next door; until I was seven years old, I did not know the names of the kids who lived across the street.

In public, my father and mother spoke a hesitant, accented, not always grammatical English. And they would have to strain — their bodies tense — to catch the sense of what was rapidly said by *los gringos*. At home they spoke Spanish. The language of their Mexican past sounded in counterpoint to the English of public society. The words would come quickly, with ease. Conveyed through those sounds was the pleasing, soothing, consoling reminder of being at home.   9

During those years when I was first conscious of hearing, my mother and father addressed me only in Spanish; in Spanish I learned to reply. By contrast, English (*inglés*), rarely heard in the house, was the language I came to associate with *gringos*. I learned my first words of English overhearing my parents speak to strangers. At five years of age, I knew just enough English for my mother to trust me on errands to stores one block away. No more.   10

I was a listening child, careful to hear the very different sounds of Spanish and English. Wide-eyed with hearing, I'd listen to sounds more than words. First, there were English (*gringo*) sounds. So many words were still unknown that when the butcher or the lady at the drugstore said something to me, exotic polysyllabic sounds would bloom in the midst of their sentences. Often, the speech of people in public seemed to me very loud, booming with confidence. The man behind the counter would literally ask, "What can I do for you?" But by being so firm and so clear, the sound of his voice said that he was a *gringo;* he belonged in public society.   11

I would also hear then the high nasal notes of middle-class American speech. The air stirred with sound. Sometimes, even now, when I have been traveling abroad for several weeks, I will   12 hear what I heard as a boy. In hotel lobbies or airports, in Turkey or Brazil, some Americans will pass, and suddenly I will hear it again — the high sound of American voices. For a few seconds I will hear it with pleasure, for it is now the sound of *my* society — a reminder of home. But inevitably — already on the flight headed for home — the sound fades with repetition. I will be unable to hear it anymore.

When I was a boy, things were different. The accent of *los gringos* was never pleasing nor was it hard to hear. Crowds at Safeway or at bus stops would be noisy with sound. And I would be forced to edge away from the chirping chatter above me.   13

I was unable to hear my own sounds, but I knew very well that I spoke English poorly. My words could not stretch far enough to form complete thoughts. And the words I did speak I didn't know well enough to make into distinct sounds. (Listeners would usually lower their heads, better to hear what I was trying to say.) But it was one thing for *me* to speak English with difficulty. It was more troubling for me to hear my parents speak in public: their high-whining vowels and guttural consonants; their sentences that got stuck with "eh" and "ah" sounds; the confused syntax; the hesitant rhythm of sounds so different from the way *gringos* spoke. I'd notice, moreover, that my parents' voices were softer than those of *gringos* we'd meet.   14

I am tempted now to say that none of this mattered. In adulthood I am embarrassed by childhood fears. And, in a way, it didn't matter very much that my parents could not speak English with ease. Their linguistic difficulties had no serious consequences. My mother and father made themselves understood at the county hospital clinic and at government offices. And yet, in another way, it mattered very much — it was unsettling to hear my parents struggle with English. Hearing them, I'd grow nervous, my clutching trust in their protection and power weakened.   15

There were many times like the night at a brightly lit gasoline station (a blaring white memory) when I stood uneasily, hearing my father. He was talking to a teenaged attendant. I do not recall what they were saying, but I cannot forget the sounds my father made as he spoke. At one point his words slid together to form one word — sounds as confused as the threads of blue and green oil in the puddle next to my shoes.   16

His voice rushed through what he had left to say. And, toward the end, reached falsetto notes, appealing to his listener's understanding. I looked away to the lights of passing automobiles. I tried not to hear anymore. But I heard only too well the calm, easy tones in the attendant's reply. Shortly afterward, walking toward home with my father, I shivered when he put his hand on my shoulder. The very first chance that I got, I evaded his grasp and ran on ahead into the dark, skipping with feigned boyish exuberance.

But then there was Spanish. *Español:* my family's language. *17* *Español:* the language that seemed to me a private language. I'd hear strangers on the radio and in the Mexican Catholic church across town speaking in Spanish, but I couldn't really believe that Spanish was a public language, like English. Spanish speakers, rather, seemed related to me, for I sensed that we shared — through our language — the experience of feeling apart from *los gringos*. It was thus a ghetto Spanish that I heard and I spoke. Like those whose lives are bound by a barrio, I was reminded by Spanish of my separateness from *los otros, los gringos* in power. But more intensely than for most barrio children — because I did not live in a barrio — Spanish seemed to me the language of home. (Most days it was only at home that I'd hear it.) It became the language of joyful return.

A family member would say something to me and I would *18* feel myself specially recognized. My parents would say something to me and I would feel embraced by the sounds of their words. Those sounds said: *I am speaking with ease in Spanish. I am addressing you in words I never use with* los gringos. *I recognize you as someone special, close, like no one outside. You belong with us. In the family.*

(*Ricardo.*) *19*

At the age of five, six, well past the time when most other *20* children no longer easily notice the difference between sounds uttered at home and words spoken in public, I had a different experience. I lived in a world magically compounded of sounds. I remained a child longer than most; I lingered too long, poised at the edge of language — often frightened by the sounds of *los gringos*, delighted by the sounds of Spanish at home. I shared with my family a language that was startlingly different from that used in the great city around us.

For me there were none of the gradations between public   *21*
and private society so normal to a maturing child. Outside the
house was public society; inside the house was private. Just
opening or closing the screen door behind me was an important experience. I'd rarely leave home all alone or without reluctance. Walking down the sidewalk, under the canopy of tall
trees, I'd warily notice the — suddenly — silent neighborhood
kids who stood warily watching me. Nervously, I'd arrive at the
grocery store to hear there the sounds of the *gringo* — foreign
to me — reminding me that in this world so big, I was a for-
eigner. But then I'd return. Walking back toward our house,
climbing the steps from the sidewalk, when the front door was
open in summer, I'd hear voices beyond the screen door talking in Spanish. For a second or two, I'd stay, linger there, listening. Smiling, I'd hear my mother call out, saying in Spanish
(words): "Is that you, Richard?" All the while her sounds would
assure me: *You are home now; come closer; inside. With us.*

"*Sí,*" I'd reply.   *22*

Once more inside the house I would resume (assume) my   *23*
place in the family. The sounds would dim, grow harder to hear.
Once more at home, I would grow less aware of that fact. It required, however, no more than the blurt of the doorbell to alert
me to listen to sounds all over again. The house would turn instantly still while my mother went to the door. I'd hear her hard
English sounds. I'd wait to hear her voice return to soft-sound-
ing Spanish, which assured me, as surely as did the clicking
tongue of the lock on the door, that the stranger was gone.

Plainly, it is not healthy to hear such sounds so often. It is   *24*
not healthy to distinguish public words from private sounds
so easily. I remained cloistered by sounds, timid and shy in
public, too dependent on voices at home. And yet it needs to
be emphasized: I was an extremely happy child at home. I remember many nights when my father would come back from
work, and I'd hear him call out to my mother in Spanish,
sounding relieved. In Spanish, he'd sound light and free notes
he never could manage in English. Some nights I'd jump up
just at hearing his voice. With *mis hermanos* I would come running into the room where he was with my mother. Our laughing (so deep was the pleasure!) became screaming. Like others
who know the pain of public alienation, we transformed the

knowledge of our public separateness and made it consoling — the reminder of intimacy. Excited, we joined our voices in a celebration of sounds. *We are speaking now the way we never speak out in public. We are alone — together,* voices sounded, surrounded to tell me. Some nights, no one seemed willing to loosen the hold sounds had on us. At dinner, we invented new words. (Ours sounded Spanish, but made sense only to us.) We pieced together new words by taking, say, an English verb and giving it Spanish endings. My mother's instructions at bedtime would be lacquered with mock-urgent tones. Or a word like *sí* would become, in several notes, able to convey added measures of feeling. Tongues explored the edges of words, especially the fat vowels. And we happily sounded that military drum roll, the twirling roar of the Spanish *r*. Family language: my family's sounds. The voices of my parents and sisters and brother. Their voices insisting: *You belong here. We are family members. Related. Special to one another. Listen!* Voices singing and sighing, rising, straining, then surging, teeming with pleasure that burst syllables into fragments of laughter. At times it seemed there was steady quiet only when, from another room, the rustling whispers of my parents faded and I moved closer to sleep.

Understanding the Significance

1. What made Richard Rodriguez's experience on the first day of school so different from his classmates'?
2. In paragraph 9, Rodriguez mentions the different sounds of Spanish and English, a point he discusses in several other spots in his essay. In what ways do the two languages sound different to Rodriguez?
3. What was the major difference between the two worlds Richard Rodriguez faced daily as a child?
4. At the beginning of the final paragraph, Rodriguez writes, "Plainly, it is not healthy to hear such sounds so often. It is not healthy to distinguish public words from private sounds so easily." What does he mean?

Discovering the Writer's Purpose

1. Throughout this excerpt Rodriguez supplies a number of moving images from both of his worlds. Which image do you feel has the most impact? Why?

2. Throughout this excerpt Rodriguez makes it clear that he felt very much lost in the English-speaking world. Yet, in paragraph 7, Rodriguez says this of his parents: "They were nobody's victims." How would you explain the difference between Rodriguez's feelings and the attitude his parents held?

3. In paragraph 16, Rodriguez relates the story of his father's talking with the teenaged gas station attendant. What was it that so troubled Rodriguez about the exchange? And why, when his father put his hand on his shoulder, did Rodriguez brush away his father's touch, "skipping with feigned boyish exuberance"?

4. Rodriguez was obviously shy and sensitive as a child. He would therefore probably have felt intimidated by the outside world and more comfortable at home even if he and his parents knew the language. How do you think his story would have differed if English had been Rodriguez's primary language?

Examining the Writer's Method

1. Rodriguez begins paragraph 4 this way: "The nun said, in a friendly but oddly impersonal voice, 'Boys and girls, this is Richard Rodriguez.' (I heard her sound out: *Rich-heard Road-ree-guess*)." What point do you feel he is making by including a phonetic pronunciation of his name?

2. In this excerpt, Rodriguez illustrates the pain he felt at not knowing English. Yet in paragraph 5 Rodriguez talks about bilingual education and then states, "It is not possible for a child — any child — ever to use his family's language in school." Does this mean he is against programs that teach a child English while being educated in their own languages? Explain.

3. The beginning of paragraph 17 makes a powerful transition: "But then there was Spanish. *Español*: my family's language." How does it connect the final section of the essay with the material that has already gone before?
4. The final paragraph is quite long, and there are several points at which Rodriguez might have broken it into multiple paragraphs. How might the overall effect of the conclusion have been different if Rodriguez had divided the paragraph?

Considering Style and Language

1. In a number of spots throughout this writing, Rodriguez uses Spanish words rather than their English equivalents. What point is he making through this use?
2. What details help Rodriguez convey the sense that although they lived in the neighborhood, they were never quite part of it?
3. Why does Rodriguez save his discussion of his Spanish-speaking world until the end of the excerpt rather than presenting it first?
4. What do the following words mean in the context of the writing? Institution (para. 3); dissolve (para. 4); scheme, trivialize, intimate (para. 5); gaudy, bungalows (para. 8); counterpoint, conveyed (para. 9); exotic, bloom (para. 11); guttural, syntax, rhythm (para. 14); blaring, falsetto, evaded, feigned, exuberance (para. 16); barrio (para. 17); compounded, poised (para. 20); gradations, canopy, warily (para. 21); blurt (para. 23); cloistered, timid, alienation, intimacy, lacquered, mock (para. 24).

Your Turn: Responding to the Subject

a. In this excerpt Rodriguez shows his reader how very different the two worlds were in which he simultaneously lived. For this assignment, consider two different environments or levels you have experienced — for example, two schools, country living versus city living, two different countries, two different age levels, or two different cultures — and discuss what made these so different.

b. Rodriguez gives a good view of what his early life was like. How do his experiences compare with yours? For this assignment, examine your household and upbringing in relation to Rodriguez's.

Other Possibilities for Using Comparison and Contrast

Here are some additional subjects from which you might develop a paper focusing on comparison and contrast. As always, adapt the topic as you write your paper. For instance, if you feel the two subjects that are ordinarily seen as different are actually quite similar, feel free to follow that line of reasoning.

- two methods of exercise or athletic activity — aerobics and jogging, raquetball and tennis, and so on
- renting a video compared with seeing the movie in a theater
- an older TV show or movie and a more recent version of it
- living at college versus commuting
- anorexia and bulimia
- two professional athletes, musicians, or politicians
- the typical family today versus the typical family twenty-five years ago
- public versus private schools or colleges
- two teachers, bosses, dates, partners, or siblings
- two civilizations
- two different types of investments
- two religions
- love versus an infatuation
- two types of video or board games
- two writers of horror, satire, romance, intrigue, and so on

Practical Application:
Comparison and Contrast

Just as you are about to save the document you have been working on for the last half an hour, your computer screen goes blank. At the same moment, you hear the angry exclamations of your supervisor and the other computer operator at the end of the room. Your blank screen and their screams can mean only one thing: the office computer system has crashed again, the third time in the last two weeks.

In many ways, it's no wonder the system keeps going down. The components are over ten years old, ancient by computer standards. For the last year, you and your coworker have been urging your supervisor to replace the system. He has been resistant, citing the expense involved. Your argument has been that he should be considering the cost to the business in terms of loss or delayed work every time the system crashes, an expense that is sure to increase as the system ages further and breaks down more often.

This last crash has convinced your supervisor to change his mind. As a result, you have a new assignment. Right now, the company can absorb a $9,000 expenditure, and that translates to three computer systems at $3,000 each. Your job is to check the large national electronics retailers, computer magazines, mail-order houses, the Internet, and so on, and identify the two best systems (including ink jet printers and color monitors) available for that price. Once you finish this research, prepare a *one- to two-page memo* outlining the characteristics and capabilities of the two best systems to help him decide which system to buy. To assist you in terms of *approach* and *format* he gives you a copy of the following memo, prepared by your coworker Allen E. Brickhill, that examines two different brands of fax machines.

Memorandum

To: Doug Mackenzie, Vice President of Operations
From: Allen E. Brickhill, Information Services Manager
Date: November 11, 1997
Subject: <u>Results of Office Technology Study</u>

As part of the company-wide campaign to increase efficiency, the Information Services department has conducted an evaluation of the equipment and technology available to office personnel. The study's purpose was to determine: 1) if the existing office equipment is adequate for our level of business, and 2) how time spent waiting for service or to use a particular piece of equipment affects overall employee performance.

To simplify the data-collection process, department heads were asked to

- provide a comprehensive list of hardware and software in their areas;
- complete a questionnaire, rating their equipment on a scale of one to ten; and
- estimate monthly "down time" for their departments, caused by unreliable and/or outdated equipment.

The results of the study indicate that the majority of department heads and employees are comfortable with the equipment in their areas, with one exception: fax machines. Most of the machines were purchased over eleven years ago, and while they have served their purpose faithfully, they are hopelessly outdated. Many machines have been deemed as "not repairable" by our maintenance staff, since spare parts have been out of production for years. The consensus is that replacement machines are in order.

In an effort to determine which fax machines are best for our business, we contracted the services of LCSC Technologies, Inc., of Dundee, New York. LCSC Technologies is a highly-respected consulting firm that specializes in providing office solutions for small-to-medium sized companies such as ours. They stay abreast of the latest innovations in office technology, and regularly publish test results in the major trade and consumer magazines. Their research and experience indicate that the two best machines available are GCI's Fax Master and Highline Inc.'s Fast Fax.

LCSC compared these two brands on the following basis:

- Price — The brands tested ranged from $595 to $1499, depending upon equipment levels. At $999, Highline's Fast Fax was the choice over GCI's Fax Master at $1200.
- Sending Speed — Newer machines are capable of sending information at higher speeds (14,000 bits per second versus 9,600 on our current machine). This is an important consideration, since one of the frequently overlooked costs of a fax machine is phone time. Fast Fax wins here, too, sending at a maximum of 14,400 compared to Fax Master at 12,400.
- Memory — While it adds about $200 to the cost of a machine, most companies simply cannot afford to ignore this feature. Memory allows the user to scan documents and send them later (when long-distance rates are lower). It also permits broadcasting to multiple locations without having to feed the document in each time. Fast Fax has a larger memory than Fax Master making Fast Fax superior in this area as well.

This last point is of major concern to our sales department, as customers require us to fax specifications and proposals to them in a timely fashion. Since our fax machines are not equipped with memory, our sales staff is losing valuable time waiting to fax documents, and critical programs are falling behind schedule.

Clearly, fax technology has advanced significantly in the past 11 years. Let me emphasize that while all brands of fax machines examined are obviously superior to our current machine, the purchase price and per-page costs are actually lower. This translates into a more efficient (and less frustrated) office staff and lower operating costs. With that in mind, I recommend that we include the purchase of new machines in next year's office budget, and that our choice be Highline Inc.'s Fast Fax.

9

Cause and Effect

The Technique

Appreciating the full significance of a subject involves recognizing what has led up to it and what has resulted or may result from it. When you write, the technique that enables you to handle such subjects, to establish what led to an event or what resulted from it, is known as *cause and effect. Cause* refers to what led to an event, and *effect* refers to what resulted from it. A writing examining the work of civil rights leaders Malcolm X and Martin Luther King, Jr. might point out the *effects* that their personal sacrifices and ultimate deaths had on the struggle for equality. It might also include background information explaining what *caused* each of the two to become so deeply involved in the struggle for equal rights for all people. In addition to serving as a supporting mode, cause and effect is often called upon to be the dominant mode in an essay. A paper examining the possible reasons for the rise in crimes such as carjacking would be an example. Regardless of the subject, to use cause and effect properly you must make sure to

- distinguish between *direct and related causes and effects;*
- acknowledge *multiple cause-and-effect situations;*
- choose *an appropriate focus;* and
- provide *an effective arrangement* of the material.

251

DIRECT AND RELATED CAUSES AND EFFECTS

All events and situations have both direct and related causes and effects, and it's important to distinguish between them to avoid overstating the relationships between what has led up to something and what has occurred as a result. Consider what happened to the U.S. Midwest during the 1930s, a phenomenon that became known as the "Dust Bowl." After several years of drought, the topsoil became so parched that it literally turned to dust and blew away.

Clearly, the *direct* cause of this disaster was the weather. But *related* causes include the farmers' ignorance about such farming techniques as proper crop rotation, fertilization, and irrigation, and the marketplace demands, which encouraged farmers to grow the same crops year after year, even though doing so would eventually strip the soil of its vitality. The *direct* effect of the calamity was widespread crop failure. Two *related* effects were the permanent displacement of thousands of farming families, whose heavily mortgaged farms were taken by the banks, and an increase in the population of migrant workers in agriculturally rich California.

Regardless of the subject, you can avoid overstating your case by using qualifying language — words such as *might be, seems, appears, rarely, often, sometimes, maybe, perhaps, probably,* and *seldom.* By using these kinds of words, you will avoid making a claim that can't be supported.

In this brief excerpt from *Tuesdays with Morrie: An Old Man, a Young Man, and Life's Greatest Lesson,* writer Mitch Albom spells out the direct effects of the amyotrophic lateral sclerosis (ALS), commonly called Lou Gehrig's disease, that is destroying Professor Morrie Schwartz's entire neurological system:

> ALS is like a lit candle: it melts your nerves and leaves your body a pile of wax. Often, it begins with the legs and works its way up. You lose control of your thigh muscles, so that you cannot support yourself standing. You lose control of your trunk muscles, so that you cannot sit up straight. By the end, if you are still alive, you are breathing through a tube in a hole in your throat, while your soul, perfectly awake, is

imprisoned inside a limp husk, perhaps able to blink, or cluck a tongue, like something from a science fiction movie, the man frozen inside his own flesh. This takes no more than five years from the day you contract the disease.

Incidentally, one potential hazard when using cause and effect is confusing actual cause-and-effect relationships with coincidence. This error in logic is referred to as *post hoc,* short for *post hoc, ergo prompter hoc,* a Latin phrase meaning "after this, therefore because of this." Concluding that the release on Monday of a film about a serial killer was the cause of murders Tuesday in several major American cities would be an example of this type of error; unfortunately, murders occur in major urban areas every day. It's also important to distinguish between correlative events — that is, events that occur at about the same time — and actual cause-and-effect relationships.

Imagine, for example, that a year-long study of high-school students shows a decline in college-board scores statewide, and another study of the same population of students shows a decline in the use of alcohol and illegal drugs over the same period of time. Surely no reasonable person would suggest that a reduction in the use of alcohol and drugs would result in lower test scores; the two findings are simply matters of correlation, not cause and effect.

MULTIPLE CAUSE-AND-EFFECT SITUATIONS

Most situations and conditions have multiple causes and multiple effects. Take a subject such as the popularity of such supermarket tabloids as the *Star* and the *National Enquirer.* To conclude that millions buy these tabloids simply because they are gullible overlooks other causes. Many buyers purchase these periodicals on impulse or out of curiosity, others buy them for pure amusement, and still others buy them because they believe there is a small kernel of truth in even the most outrageous story.

And concluding that harmless skepticism is the only effect of publishing such dubious information is also too simplistic.

For one thing, merely because they have appeared in print, the stories in these tabloids — no matter how absurd or untrue — gain credence with some people. In addition, when prominent daily newspapers publish stories that have first appeared in the tabloids, the public's confidence in the legitimacy of traditional newspapers may be undermined. Also, the consistent popularity of the tabloids has led to an entirely new industry, tabloid television shows; these shows, like their print counterparts, sensationalize lurid crimes and the lives of people in the public eye.

In this excerpt from "The Words that Remade America: Lincoln at Gettysburg," his examination of how Lincoln's "Gettysburg Address" dramatically changed the form of political speeches, scholar and writer Garry Wills outlines several changes that appeared in Lincoln's writing style during his political career:

> It would be wrong to think that Lincoln moved toward the plain style of the Gettysburg Address just by writing shorter, simpler sentences. Actually, that address ends with a very long sentence — eighty-two words, almost a third of the whole talk's length. So does the Second Inaugural Address, Lincoln's second most famous piece of eloquence: its final sentence runs to seventy-five words. Because of his early experiments, Lincoln's prose acquired a flexibility of structure, a rhythmic pacing, a variation in length of words and phrases and clauses and sentences, that make his sentences move "naturally," for all their density and scope.

AN APPROPRIATE FOCUS

Although causes and effects are clearly related, there is no requirement that you deal with both in the same essay. In fact, some subjects clearly call for an emphasis on one rather than the other, so you need to evaluate the subject thoroughly to see which direction you should follow.

With a topic such as the legal and personal difficulties so many young entertainment figures experience, you could focus on such causes as the pressure of being under public scrutiny at all times, the availability of enormous amounts of cash with no accountability, the mistaken belief that fame gives one the power to do anything without consequence, and the loss of personal freedom. On the other hand, with a subject such as the influence that television has on children, you could focus on such effects as a distorted view of reality, increased exposure to stereotypes and violence, and decreased physical activity, all of which children experience as a result of watching television.

In this brief passage from his essay dealing with the medical amputation of a finger, "Losing Touch," A. John Roche focuses on cause — in this case, what led to the need for the amputation:

> It had started about 25 years before, when, working for a gardener one summer, I cut the end of my finger with an electric hedge trimmer. The finger healed, but a piece of it was missing; a scar ran from the first knuckle up under the fingernail, and because some of the nerves were damaged, the pad of my finger didn't have much feeling.

And in this excerpt from his article "The Warming of the World," dealing with global warming, scientist and writer Carl Sagan deals with effect — in this case, what would happen should the sun cease to shine on our planet:

> It is warm down here on Earth because the Sun shines. If the Sun were somehow turned off, the Earth would rapidly cool. The oceans would freeze, eventually the atmosphere itself would condense out and our planet would be covered everywhere by snowbanks of solid oxygen and nitrogen 10 meters (about 30 feet) high. Only the tiny trickle of heat from the Earth's interior and the faint starlight would save our world from a temperature of absolute zero.

Sometimes, of course, an examination of both cause and effect is necessary in order for the reader to gain a full understanding of the significance of a subject. With a topic like the destruction of the Brazilian rain forest, for instance, you could easily discuss both the economic needs of the residents and the consequences of these needs.

AN EFFECTIVE ARRANGEMENT

Regardless of whether you focus on causes, effects, or both, you should also consider the best way to arrange the information you include. In some cases, you may find chronological order useful. A paper that discusses causes or consequences occurring over a period of time such as the effects of acid rain, which are both gradual and cumulative, would be a good example.

With many subjects, however, you will probably find that emphatic order is useful. With the paper about the effects of television on children, for instance, it's important to keep in mind that some of the effects are more potentially dangerous than others. Therefore, it would make sense to use emphatic order, beginning with a strong example such as decreased physical activity and then building up to the most serious effect, the prolonged exposure to stereotypes and violence. (For a more detailed discussion of chronological and emphatic order, see pp. 27–29).

In this brief passage from the second edition of his textbook *Concepts of Chemical Dependency,* notice how Harold E. Doweiko uses emphatic order to arrange some of the effects of addiction:

> At this point in the continuum, the person demonstrates the classic addiction syndrome. Multiple social, legal, financial, occupational, and personal problems become increasingly worse. The person also will demonstrate various medical complications associated with chemical abuse and may be near death as a result of chronic addiction. This individual is clearly addicted beyond any shadow of a doubt in the mind of an outside observer. It should be noted, however, that the addicted individual may try to rationalize away or deny problems associated with his or her alcohol or drug use even at this late stage. More than one elderly alcoholic, for example, has tried to explain away an abnormal liver function as being the aftermath of a childhood illness.

AN ANNOTATED EXAMPLE

Susan Jacoby

When Bright Girls Decide that Math Is "A Waste of Time"

Despite the advances that women have made in many areas, those fields in which mathematics plays a major role continue to attract few females and, as a result, are dominated by men. In Susan Jacoby's view, girls' aversion to math is less a matter of genetic abilities than it is a matter of socialization. In other words, girls are generally no more or less capable than boys in mathematics, but girls are discouraged in many ways from pursuing math courses. Jacoby has served as the education writer for the Washington Post *and a columnist for the* New York Times. *She is the author of two books on Russian life, including* Moscow Conversations *and* Inside Soviet Schools. *In addition, her essays have been collected in* The Possible She *and* Money, Manners, and Morals. *In this essay Jacoby relies on cause and effect to show the incentives girls have to abandon math as well as some of the consequences.*

How do a society's sexist beliefs limit the potential of its children?

She uses this anecdote of Susannah to give her reader a sense of focus in the essay.	Susannah, a 16-year-old who has always been an A student in every subject from algebra to English, recently informed her parents that she intended to drop physics and calculus in her senior year of high school and replace them with a drama seminar and a work-study program. She expects to

1

major in art or history in college, she explained, and "any more science or math will just be a waste of my time."

Her parents were neither con-   2
cerned by nor opposed to her decision. "Fine, dear," they said. Their daughter is, after all, an outstanding student. What does it matter if, at age 16, she has taken a step that may limit her understanding of both machines and the natural world for the rest of her life?

She explicitly states her thesis, indicating that her primary emphasis is cause.

This kind of decision, in which   3
girls turn away from studies that would give them a sure footing in the world of science and technology, is a self-inflicted female disability that is, regrettably, almost as common today as it was when I was in high school. If Susannah had announced that she had decided to stop taking English in her senior year, her mother and father would have been horrified. I also think they would have been a good deal less sanguine about her decision if she were a boy.

She notes a related cause — that females and males are treated differently.

In saying that scientific and math-   4
ematical ignorance is a self-inflicted female wound, I do not, obviously, mean that cultural expectations play no role in the process. But the world does not conspire to deprive modern women of access to science as it did in the 1930's, when Rosalyn S. Yalow, the Nobel Prize-winning physicist, graduated from Hunter College and was advised to go to work as a secretary because no graduate school would admit her to its physics department. The current generation of adolescent girls — and their parents, bred on old

She notes another related cause.

She points out an effect of discrimination.

She reiterates the primary cause.

expectations about women's interests — are active conspirators in limiting their own intellectual development.

It is true that the proportion of young women in science-related graduate and professional schools, most notably medical schools, has increased significantly in the past decade. It is also true that so few women were studying advanced science and mathematics before the early 1970's that the percentage increase in female enrollment does not yet translate into large numbers of women actually working in science. 5

She repeats the primary cause again.

The real problem is that so many girls eliminate themselves from any serious possibility of studying science as a result of decisions made during the vulnerable period of mid-adolescence, when they are most likely to be influenced — on both conscious and subconscious levels — by the traditional belief that math and science are "masculine" subjects. 6

She notes another related cause.

During the teen-age years the well-documented phenomenon of "math anxiety" strikes girls who never had any problem handling numbers during earlier schooling. Some men, too, experience this syndrome—a form of panic, akin to a phobia, at any task involving numbers — but women constitute the overwhelming majority of sufferers. 7

She reiterates her thesis.

The onset of acute math anxiety during the teen-age years is, as Stalin was fond of saying, "not by accident."

She explains why girls make the choice to avoid math and science.

In adolescence girls begin to fear that they will be unattractive to boys if they are typed as "brains." Science and math epitomize unfeminine braininess 8 in a way that, say, foreign languages do not. High-school girls who pursue an advanced interest in science and math (unless they are students at special institutions like the Bronx High School of Science where everyone is a brain) usually find that they are greatly outnumbered by boys in their classes. They are, therefore, intruding on male turf at a time when their sexual confidence, as well as that of the boys, is most fragile.

A 1981 assessment of female achievement in mathematics, based on research conducted under a National Institute for Education grant, found significant differences in the mathematical achievements of 9th and 12th graders. At age 13 girls were equal to or slightly better than boys in tests involving algebra, problem solving and spatial ability; four years later the boys had outstripped the girls. *9*

She repeats the primary cause, supporting it with a personal anecdote.

It is not mysterious that some very bright high-school girls suddenly decide that math is "too hard" and "a waste of time." In my experience, self-sabotage of mathematical and scientific ability is often a conscious process. I remember deliberately pretending to be puzzled by geometry problems in my sophomore year in high school. A male teacher called me in after class and said, in a baffled tone, "I don't see how you can be having so much trouble when you got straight A's last year in my algebra class." *10*

She notes a direct effect of the choice to avoid math and science.

The decision to avoid advanced biology, chemistry, physics and calculus in high school automatically restricts *11* academic and professional choices that ought to be wide open to anyone beginning college. At all coeducational universities women are overwhelmingly concentrated in the fine arts, social sciences and traditionally female departments like education. Courses leading to degrees in science- and technology-related fields are filled mainly by men.

She lists other specific effects of the decision.

In my generation, the practical consequences of mathematical and scientific illiteracy are visible in the large number of special programs to help professional women overcome the anxiety they feel when they are promoted into jobs that require them to handle statistics.

12

The consequences of this syndrome should not, however, be viewed in narrowly professional terms. Competence in science and math does not mean one is going to become a scientist or mathematician any more than competence in writing English means one is going to become a professional writer. Scientific and mathematical illiteracy — which has been cited in several recent critiques by panels studying American education from kindergarten through college — produces an incalculably impoverished vision of human experience.

13

Scientific illiteracy is not, of course, the exclusive province of women. In certain intellectual circles it has become fashionable to proclaim a willed, aggressive ignorance about science and technology. Some female writers specialize in ominous, uninformed diatribes against genetic research as a plot

14

to remove control of childbearing from women, while some well-known men of letters proudly announce that they understand absolutely nothing about computers, or, for that matter, about electricity. This lack of understanding is nothing in which women or men ought to take pride.

She notes an effect of the lack of scientific and mathematicel background plus the cause of the helplessness.

Failure to comprehend either com-   15
puters or chromosomes leads to a terrible sense of helplessness, because the profound impact of science on everyday life is evident even to those who insist they don't, won't, can't understand why the changes are taking place. At this stage of history women are more prone to such feelings of helplessness than men because the culture judges their ignorance less harshly and because women themselves acquiesce in that indulgence.

She uses her conclusion to reiterate the cause of the problem as well as to state the solution to the problem.

Since there is ample evidence of   16
such feelings in adolescence, it is up to parents to see that their daughters do not accede to the old stereotypes about "masculine" and "feminine" knowledge. Unless we want our daughters to share our intellectual handicaps, we had better tell them no, they can't stop taking mathematics and science at the ripe old age of 16.

Your Turn: Responding to the Subject

a. Jacoby's concern in this essay is that too many young women deny themselves a full range of career options because they avoid taking higher-level mathematics courses. Jacoby knows that with the proper encouragement, many of these students would be able to handle this course work and would thus broaden their possibilities for the future. Follow a similar line of reasoning for this assignment: what field have you been encouraged to pursue — or discouraged from pursuing? Why? And how has this encouragement — or lack of it — affected your life?

b. Some elements of Jacoby's article concern peer pressure. For this assignment, discuss the power of peer pressure, dealing with why people are so willing to conform regardless of potential consequences or how going along with the crowd affects the life of the follower.

Richard Wright

The Ethics of Living Jim Crow

Originally the title of a nineteenth-century song, Jim Crow *is the term used to describe the overt systematic discrimination and seg-regation against African Americans that continued well into the latter half of the twentieth century. Richard Wright endured life in the Jim Crow South, and his struggles became the theme woven through his writings. His first collection of stories,* Uncle Tom's Children *(1936), was followed in 1940 by the novel* Native Son, *the work for which he is best known. His powerful autobiograph-ical account of his early years,* Black Boy: A Record of Child-hood and Youth, *was published in 1937. Racism in the United States eventually led Wright to move to France where he lived out his life continuing to write. In this excerpt, which is taken from* Uncle Tom's Children *(a slightly different version of the incident also appears in* Black Boy), *cause-and-effect reasoning is used to crystallize what happened to any African Americans when they failed to "stay in their place" as the strictures of the Jim Crow world demanded.*

What can a person do when the two alternatives facing him both lead to the same result?

It was a long time before I came in close contact with white   *1*
folks again. We moved from Arkansas to Mississippi. Here we
had the good fortune not to live behind the railroad tracks,
or close to white neighborhoods. We lived in the very heart
of the local Black Belt. There were black churches and black
preachers; there were black schools and black teachers; black
groceries and black clerks. In fact, everything was so solidly
black that for a long time I did not even think of white folks,
save in remote and vague terms. But this could not last for-

ever. As one grows older one eats more. One's clothing costs more. When I finished grammar school I had to go to work. My mother could no longer feed and clothe me on her cooking job.

There is but one place where a black boy who knows no   *2*
trade can get a job, and that's where the houses and faces are white, where the trees, lawns, and hedges are green. My first job was with an optical company in Jackson, Mississippi. The morning I applied I stood straight and neat before the boss, answering all his questions with sharp yessirs and nosirs. I was very careful to pronounce my *sirs* distinctly, in order that he might know that I was polite, that I knew where I was, and that I knew he was a *white* man. I wanted that job badly.

He looked me over as though he were examining a prize   *3*
poodle. He questioned me closely about my schooling, being particularly insistent about how much mathematics I had had. He seemed very pleased when I told him I had had two years of algebra.

"Boy, how would you like to try to learn something   *4*
around here?" he asked me.

"I'd like it fine, sir," I said, happy. I had visions of "work-   *5*
ing my way up." Even Negroes have those visions.

"All right," he said. "Come on."   *6*

I followed him to the small factory.   *7*

"Pease," he said to a white man of about thirty-five, "this   *8*
is Richard. He's going to work for us."

Pease looked at me and nodded.   *9*

I was then taken to a white boy of about seventeen.   *10*

"Morrie, this is Richard, who's going to work for us."   *11*

"Whut yuh sayin' there, boy!" Morrie boomed at me.   *12*

"Fine!" I answered.   *13*

The boss instructed these two to help me, teach me, give   *14*
me jobs to do, and let me learn what I could in my spare time.

My wages were five dollars a week.   *15*

I worked hard, trying to please. For the first month I got   *16*
along O.K. Both Pease and Morrie seemed to like me. But one thing was missing. And I kept thinking about it. I was not learning anything and nobody was volunteering to help me.

Thinking they had forgotten that I was to learn something about the mechanics of grinding lenses, I asked Morrie one day to tell me about the work. He grew red.

"Whut yuh tryin' t' do, nigger, get smart?" he asked.   17

"Naw; I ain' tryin' t' git smart," I said.   18

"Well, don't, if yuh know whut's good for yuh!"   19

I was puzzled. Maybe he just doesn't want to help me, I   20
thought. I went to Pease.

"Say, are yuh crazy, you black bastard?" Pease asked me.   21
His gray eyes growing hard.

I spoke out, reminding him that the boss had said I was to   22
be given a chance to learn something.

"Nigger, you think you're *white,* don't you?"   23

"Naw, sir!"   24

"Well, you're acting mighty like it!"   25

"But, Mr. Pease, the boss said . . ."   26

Pease shook his fist in my face.   27

"This is a *white* man's work around here, and you better   28
watch yourself!"

From then on they changed toward me. They said good-   29
morning no more. When I was just a bit slow in performing
some duty, I was called a lazy black son-of-a-bitch.

Once I thought of reporting all this to the boss. But the   30
mere idea of what would happen to me if Pease and Morrie
should learn that I had "snitched" stopped me. And after all
the boss was a white man, too. What was the use?

The climax came at noon one summer day. Pease called   31
me to his work-bench. To get to him I had to go between two
narrow benches and stand with my back against a wall.

"Yes, sir," I said.   32

"Richard, I want to ask you something," Pease began   33
pleasantly, not looking up from his work.

"Yes, sir," I said again.   34

Morrie came over, blocking the narrow passage between   35
the benches. He folded his arms, staring at me solemnly.

I looked from one to the other, sensing that something   36
was coming.

"Yes, sir," I said for the third time.   37

Pease looked up and spoke very slowly.   38

"Richard, *Mr.* Morrie here tells me you called me *Pease.*"   39

I stiffened. A void seemed to open up in me. I knew this was the show-down. 40

He meant that I had failed to call him Mr. Pease. I looked at Morrie. He was gripping a steel bar in his hands. I opened my mouth to speak, to protest, to assure Pease that I had never called him simply *Pease,* and that I had never had any intentions of doing so, when Morrie grabbed me by the collar, ramming my head against the wall. 41

"Now, be careful, nigger!" snarled Morrie, baring his teeth. "*I* heard yuh call 'im *Pease!* 'N' if yuh say yuh didn't, yuh're callin' me a *lie,* see?" He waved the steel bar threateningly. 42

If I had said: No, sir, Mr. Pease, I never called you *Pease,* I would have been automatically calling Morrie a liar. And if I had said: Yes, sir, Mr. Pease, I called you *Pease,* I would have been pleading guilty to having uttered the worst insult that a Negro can utter to a southern white man. I stood hesitating, trying to frame a neutral reply. 43

"Richard, I asked you a question!" said Pease. Anger was creeping into his voice. 44

"I don't remember calling you *Pease,* Mr. Pease," I said cautiously. "And if I did, I sure didn't mean . . ." 45

"You black son-of-a-bitch! You called me *Pease,* then!" he spat, slapping me till I bent sideways over a bench. Morrie was on top of me, demanding: 46

"Didn't yuh call 'im *Pease?* If yuh say yuh didn't, I'll rip yo' gut string loose with this bar, yuh black granny dodger! Yuh can't call a white man a lie 'n' git erway with it, you black son-of-a-bitch!" 47

I wilted. I begged them not to bother me. I knew what they wanted. They wanted me to leave. 48

"I'll leave," I promised. "I'll leave right *now.*" 49

They gave me a minute to get out of the factory. I was warned not to show up again, or tell the boss. 50

I went. 51

When I told the folks at home what had happened, they called me a fool. They told me that I must never again attempt to exceed my boundaries. When you are working for white folks, they said, you got to "stay in your place" if you want to keep working. 52

Understanding the Significance

1. What was Richard Wright's life like before he sought out the job with the optical company?
2. Initially, Wright's working relationship with coworkers Pease and Morrie was good. What caused his coworkers' change in attitude?
3. In paragraph 30, Wright explains how he dismissed the prospect of informing his boss of the abuse he was suffering because "after all the boss was a white man, too. What was the use?" What does Wright mean by this statement?
4. Why doesn't Wright's answer, presented in paragraph 45, satisfy Pease?

Discovering the Writer's Purpose

1. In paragraph 2, after he outlines how he presented himself at the first meeting with his employer, Wright concludes the paragraph with this sentence: "I wanted that job badly." What do you think he is saying here about the way he behaved during the interview?
2. In paragraph 3, Wright states that the boss "looked me over as though he were examining a prize poodle." What point do you feel Wright is trying to make about his employer?
3. Why doesn't Wright go to the boss and ask him to ensure that he receives the training he was promised?
4. In the final paragraph, Wright explains how his family chastised him for exceeding his "boundaries" and warned him that he must learn to "stay in your place." What are those boundaries? What must Wright endure to stay in his place?

Examining the Writer's Method

1. In the first two paragraphs, Wright compares the two worlds, the "white neighborhoods" and the "local Black

Belt," that existed side by side. Explain the elements that made the black community so different from the white community next door.

2. Wright chooses to use extensive passages of dialogue rather than standard prose. What advantage does he gain as a result?

3. Paragraph 51 consists of two words: "I went." Is this paragraph effective? Why or why not?

4. Overall, this excerpt is deeply disturbing for a variety of reasons. Which aspect of it do you find most upsetting? The unfulfilled promise? The insults? The beating he endures? His decision to quit? The response at home where, as the victim, he is blamed for the incident? Explain.

Considering Style and Language

1. "There is but one place where a black boy who knows no trade can get a job, and that's where the houses and faces are white, where the trees, lawns, and hedges are green." Wright asserts this at the beginning of paragraph 2, but he doesn't explain why this is so. Why doesn't he offer an explanation?

2. In paragraph 43, Wright presents the actual words he might have said in answer to Morrie's accusation rather than simply paraphrasing. How does this technique affect his writing?

3. Generally speaking, it's a good idea to use exclamation points sparingly so that you don't dilute their power to show excitement or emotion. In this writing, however, Wright uses a total of twelve exclamation points, all of them within the dialogue. What sense does he create for the reader by using so many exclamation points?

4. What do the following words mean in the context of the writing? Remote, vague (para. 1); distinctly (para. 2); insistent (para. 3); snitched (para. 30); solemnly (para. 35); void (para. 40); frame (para. 43); wilted (para. 48); boundaries (para. 52).

Your Turn: Responding to the Subject

a. In this excerpt, Wright captures in horrifying detail the frustration, hopelessness, and sheer anger felt by a victim of racism. For this assignment, think of a traumatic incident concerning race, religion, ethnicity, sexual orientation, and so forth that you were involved in or that you witnessed (either in person or through a news account). Write a paper in which you focus on what might have caused the incident or what happened as a result of it.

b. For this assignment, consider the situation that Richard Wright records in this excerpt. Then, on the basis of the information Wright supplies, discuss the causes that ultimately led to the confrontation at the optical company and the effects that you think the entire incident had for all the people involved.

Adrienne Rich

The Anger of a Child

Adrienne Rich saw her first book of poetry, A Change of World, *published in 1951, the year she graduated from Radcliffe College. She has been a powerful force on the literary scene since, publishing a number of collections of poetry, including* The Diamond Cutters and Other Poems *(1955),* The Will to Change: Poems 1968–1970 *(1971),* Diving into the Wreck: Poems 1971–1972 *(1973) and* Dark Fields of the Republic: 1991–1995 *(1995). She is also the author of the 1993 book* What I Found There: Notebooks on Poetry and Politics. *Over the last two decades, she has focused her attention on a number of issues associated with her interest in feminism and related concerns, including motherhood and lesbianism. In this essay from her 1976 book* Of Woman Born: Motherhood As Experience and Institution, *Rich uses cause and effect to illustrate how her attitudes about herself, her parents, and parenting have evolved.*

What happens to a child when he or she sees one parent being unjustly denied an opportunity for a full life?

It is hard to write about my mother. Whatever I do write, it is my story I am telling, my version of the past. If she were to tell her own story other landscapes would be revealed. But in my landscape or hers, there would be old, smoldering patches of deep-burning anger. Before her marriage, she had trained seriously for years both as a concert pianist and a composer. Born in a southern town, mothered by a strong, frustrated woman, she had won a scholarship to study with the director at the Peabody Conservatory in Baltimore, and by teaching at girls' schools had earned her way to further study in New York, Paris, and Vienna. From the age of sixteen, she had been a young belle, who could have married at any time, but she also possessed unusual talent, determination, and independence for her time and place. She read — and reads — widely and wrote — as her journals from my childhood and her letters of today reveal — with grace and pungency.

271

She married my father after a ten years' engagement dur-   2
ing which he finished his medical training and began to establish himself in academic medicine. Once married, she gave
up the possibility of a concert career, though for some years
she went on composing, and she is still a skilled and dedicated
pianist. My father, brilliant, ambitious, possessed by his own
drive, assumed that she would give her life over to the enhancement of his. She would manage his household with the
formality and grace becoming to a medical professor's wife,
though on a limited budget; she would "keep up" her music,
though there was no question of letting her composing and
practice conflict with her duties as a wife and mother. She was
supposed to bear him two children, a boy and a girl. She had
to keep her household books to the last penny — I still can see
the big blue gray ledgers, inscribed in her clear, strong hand;
she marketed by streetcar, and later, when they could afford a
car, she drove my father to and from his laboratory or lectures,
often awaiting him for hours. She raised two children, and
taught us all our lessons, including music. (Neither of us was
sent to school until the fourth grade.) I am sure that she was
made to feel responsible for all our imperfections.

My father, like the transcendentalist Bronson Alcott, be-   3
lieved that he (or rather, his wife) could raise children according to his unique moral and intellectual plan, thus proving to
the world the values of enlightened, unorthodox child-rearing.
I believe that my mother, like Abigail Alcott, at first genuinely
and enthusiastically embraced the experiment, and only later
found that in carrying out my father's intense, perfectionist program, she was in conflict with her deep instincts as a mother.
Like Abigail Alcott, too, she must have found that while ideas
might be unfolded by her husband, their daily, hourly practice
was going to be up to her. (" 'Mr. A. aids me in general principles, but nobody can aid me in the details,' she mourned. . . .
Moreover her husband's views kept her constantly wondering if
she were doing a good job. 'Am I doing what is right? Am I
doing enough? Am I doing too much?' " The appearance of
"temper" and "will" in Louisa, the second Alcott daughter, was
blamed by her father on her inheritance from her mother.)
Under the institution of motherhood, the mother is the first to
blame if theory proves unworkable in practice, or if anything

whatsoever goes wrong. But even earlier, my mother had failed at one part of the plan: she had not produced a son.

For years, I felt my mother had chosen my father over me,   4 had sacrificed me to his needs and theories. When my first child was born, I was barely in communication with my parents. I had been fighting my father for my right to an emotional life and a selfhood beyond his needs and theories. We were all at a draw. Emerging from the fear, exhaustion, and alienation of my first childbirth, I could not admit even to myself that I wanted my mother, let alone tell her how much I wanted her. When she visited me in the hospital neither of us could uncoil the obscure lashings of feeling that darkened the room, the tangled thread running backward to where she had labored for three days to give birth to me, and I was not a son. Now, twenty-six years later, I lay in a contagious hospital with my allergy, my skin covered with a mysterious rash, my lips and eyelids swollen, my body bruised and sutured, and, in a cot beside my bed, slept the perfect, golden, male child I had brought forth. How could I have interpreted her feelings when I could not begin to decipher my own? My body had spoken all too eloquently, but it was, medically, just my body. I wanted her to mother me again, to hold my baby in her arms as she had once held me; but that baby was also a gauntlet flung down: *my son.* Part of me longed to offer him for her blessing; part of me wanted to hold him up as a badge of victory in our tragic, unnecessary rivalry as women.

But I was only at the beginning. I know now as I could not   5 possibly know then, that among the tangle of feelings between us, in that crucial yet unreal meeting, was her guilt. Soon I would begin to understand the full weight and burden of maternal guilt, that daily, nightly, hourly, *Am I doing what is right? Am I doing enough? Am I doing too much?* The institution of motherhood finds all mothers more or less guilty of having failed their children; and my mother, in particular, had been expected to help create, according to my father's plan, a perfect daughter. This "perfect" daughter, though gratifyingly precocious, had early been given to tics and tantrums, had become permanently lame from arthritis at twenty-two; she had finally resisted her father's Victorian paternalism, his seductive charm and controlling cruelty, had married a divorced graduate student, had begun to write "modern," "obscure," "pessimistic" poetry, lacking the fluent sweetness of Tennyson, had had the final temerity to get pregnant and bring a living baby into the world. She had ceased to be the demure and precocious child or the poetic, seducible adolescent. Something, in my father's view, had gone terribly wrong. I can imagine that whatever else my mother felt (and I know that part of her *was* mutely on my side) she also was made to feel blame. Beneath the "numbness" that she has since told me she experienced at that time, I can imagine the guilt of Everymother, because I have known it myself.

But I did not know it yet. And it is difficult for me to write   6
of my mother now, because I have known it too well. I struggle to describe what it felt like to be her daughter, but I find myself divided, slipping under her skin; a part of me identifies too much with her. I know deep reservoirs of anger toward her still exist: the anger of a four-year-old locked in the closet (my father's orders, but my mother carried them out) for childish misbehavior; the anger of a six-year-old kept too long at piano practice (again, at his insistence, but it was she who gave the lessons) till I developed a series of facial tics. (As a mother I know what a child's facial tic is — a lancet of guilt and pain running through one's own body.) And I still feel the anger of a daughter, pregnant, wanting my mother desperately and feeling she had gone over to the enemy.

And I know there must be deep reservoirs of anger in her;   7
every mother has known overwhelming, unacceptable anger at her children. When I think of the conditions under which my mother became a mother, the impossible expectations, my father's distaste for pregnant women, his hatred of all that he could not control, my anger at her dissolves into grief and anger *for* her, and then dissolves back again into anger at her: the ancient, unpurged anger of the child.

My mother lives today as an independent woman, which   8
she was always meant to be. She is a much-loved, much-admired grandmother, an explorer in new realms; she lives in the present and future, not the past. I no longer have fantasies — they are the unhealed child's fantasies, I think — of some infinitely healing conversation with her, in which we could show all our wounds, transcend the pain we have shared as

mother and daughter, say everything at last. But in writing
these pages, I am admitting, at least, how important her existence is and has been for me.

Understanding the Significance

1. As Adrienne Rich explains it in this selection, what had
   her mother given up when she married?
2. What was the source of the anger that Rich felt toward her
   mother?
3. In what ways did Rich rebel against her father?
4. In paragraph 6, Rich tells of some of the discipline she endured on her father's orders. Yet her anger is directed more
   at her mother than her father. Why?

Discovering the Writer's Purpose

1. In the first paragraph, Rich states that no matter whether
   one hears her version of the story or her mother's, it would
   contain "old, smoldering patches of deep-burning anger."
   Rich devotes her essay to explaining her own anger, and although she suggests in paragraph 7 what her mother's
   anger entails, she never deals with it in detail. What do you
   think her mother would feel anger about? Is she angry with
   her daughter, her husband, life, or some combination?
2. Who do you think Rich feels more anger toward, her
   mother or her father? Explain.
3. In paragraph 4, Rich talks about the birth of her son and
   the feelings it evoked concerning her relationship with her
   mother. Why does she feel that having had a son was both
   a connection to and a separation from her mother?
4. Rich concludes her piece with a paragraph explaining
   what she and her mother have come to be. What point do
   you think Rich is trying to make here?

Examining the Writer's Method

1. "It is hard to write about my mother." This is the way that Rich opens this piece. Then in the second sentence of paragraph 6, she repeats the same idea: "And it is difficult for me to write of my mother now, because I have known it too well." Does the idea have more impact the second time? Why or why not?
2. Rich devotes much of this essay to providing a portrait of her mother. On the basis of the information she provides, what kind of woman do you feel Rich's mother is?
3. Evaluate the tone in the essay. Does Rich maintain the same tone throughout the essay or does she vary it? Explain.
4. Rich fills her paper with a number of powerful examples and images. Which one affected you most? Why?

Considering Style and Language

1. Rich's essay has two threads of development: one dealing with her mother and the other with herself. Why does she tell these two stories together rather than devoting her efforts to one or the other?
2. In paragraph 5, in relation to her own sense of motherhood, Rich repeats the passage from Abigail Alcott she had provided in paragraph 3, this time putting it in italics: *"Am I doing what is right? Am I doing enough? Am I doing too much?"* What point is she trying to make by repeating the words but setting them up differently this time?
3. How does Rich's choice to relate the events in chronological order help her communicate the deep emotions she feels over her parents and upbringing?
4. What do the following words mean in the context of the writing? Belle, grace, pungency (para. 1); enhancement, formality, inscribed (para. 2); transcendentalist, unorthodox, unfolded (para. 3); uncoil, obscure, decipher, eloquently, gauntlet (para. 4); precocious, tics, fluent, temerity, demure, mutely (para. 5); lancet (para. 6); unpurged (para. 7).

Your Turn: Responding to the Subject

a. Rich's essay makes it clear that the emotional pain endured as a child can remain long after the end of childhood. For this assignment, write an essay in which you recount your own anger or resentment from some childhood or adolescent experience. What brought about the incident? What happened as a result?

b. What happens to you when you experience a strong emotion? For this assignment, detail the physical and emotional effects that accompany that emotion.

Frederick Douglass
The Right to Write

Among the most famous figures associated with slavery in the United States is Frederick Douglass, the son of a white man and slave woman, who escaped from slavery and settled in the North as a free man. Before long, he became actively involved in the abolitionist movement, spending several years lecturing on the evils of slavery. In 1845 the self-taught Douglass completed Narrative of the Life of Frederick Douglass, An American Slave, *his personal account of the horrors of slavery, from which this excerpt is taken. Douglass later served as a newspaper publisher, United States marshall and recorder of deeds, and consul-general to the Republic of Haiti. In this writing, cause and effect help Douglass recount his struggle to achieve literacy.*

What happens when a person is denied the opportunity to learn?

I lived in Master Hugh's family about seven years. During this   1
time, I succeeded in learning to read and write. In accomplishing this, I was compelled to resort to various stratagems. I had no regular teacher. My mistress, who had kindly commenced to instruct me, had, in compliance with the advice and direction of her husband, not only ceased to instruct, but had set her face against my being instructed by any one else. It is due, however, to my mistress to say of her, that she did not adopt this course of treatment immediately. She at first lacked the depravity indispensable to shutting me up in mental darkness. It was at least necessary for her to have some training in the exercise of irresponsible power, to make her equal to the task of treating me as though I were a brute.

My mistress was, as I have said, a kind and tender-hearted   2
woman; and in the simplicity of her soul she commenced, when I first went to live with her, to treat me as she supposed one human being ought to treat another. In entering upon the duties of a slaveholder, she did not seem to perceive that I sus-

tained to her the relation of a mere chattel, and that for her to treat me as a human being was not only wrong, but dangerously so. Slavery proved as injurious to her as it did to me. When I went there, she was a pious, warm, and tender-hearted woman. There was no sorrow or suffering for which she had not a tear. She had bread for the hungry, clothes for the naked, and comfort for every mourner that came within her reach. Slavery soon proved its ability to divest her of these heavenly qualities. Under its influence, the tender heart became stone, and the lamblike disposition gave way to one of tiger-like fierceness. The first step in her downward course was in her ceasing to instruct me. She now commenced to practise her husband's precepts. She finally became even more violent in her opposition than her husband himself. She was not satisfied with simply doing as well as he had commanded; she seemed anxious to do better. Nothing seemed to make her more angry than to see me with a newspaper. She seemed to think that here lay the danger. I have had her rush at me with a face made all up of fury, and snatch from me a newspaper, in a manner that fully revealed her apprehension. She was an apt woman; and a little experience soon demonstrated, to her satisfaction, that education and slavery were incompatible with each other.

From this time I was most narrowly watched. If I was in a   *3* separate room any considerable length of time, I was sure to be suspected of having a book, and was at once called to give an account of myself. All this, however, was too late. The first step had been taken. Mistress, in teaching me the alphabet, had given me the *inch,* and no precaution could prevent me from taking the *ell.*

The plan which I adopted, and the one by which I was   *4* most successful, was that of making friends of all the little white boys whom I met in the street. As many of these as I could, I converted into teachers. With their kindly aid, obtained at different times and in different places, I finally succeeded in learning to read. When I was sent of errands, I always took my book with me, and by going one part of my errand quickly, I found time to get a lesson before my return. I used also to carry bread with me, enough of which was always in the house, and to which I was always welcome; for I was much better off in this regard than many of the poor white children in our neighborhood. This bread I used to bestow upon the hungry little urchins, who, in return, would give me that more valuable bread of knowledge. I am strongly tempted to give the names of two or three of those little boys, as a testimonial of the gratitude and affection I bear them; but prudence forbids; — not that it would injure me, but it might embarrass them; for it is almost an unpardonable offence to teach slaves to read in this Christian country. It is enough to say of the dear little fellows, that they lived on Philpot Street, very near Durgin and Bailey's ship-yard. I used to talk this matter of slavery over with them. I would sometimes say to them, I wished I could be as free as they would be when they got to be men. "You will be free as soon as you are twenty-one, *but I am a slave for life!* Have not I as good a right to be free as you have?" These words used to trouble them, they would express for me the liveliest sympathy, and console me with the hope that something would occur by which I might be free.

I was now about twelve years old, and the thought of being   5 *a slave for life* began to bear heavily upon my heart. Just about this time, I got hold of a book entitled "The Columbian Orator." Every opportunity I got, I used to read this book. Among much of other interesting matter, I found in it a dialogue between a master and his slave. The slave was represented as having run away from his master three times. The dialogue represented the conversation which took place between them, when the slave was retaken the third time. In this dialogue, the whole argument in behalf of slavery was brought forward by the master, all of which was disposed of by the slave. The slave was made to say some very smart as well as impressive things in reply to his master — things which had the desired though unexpected effect; for the conversation resulted in the voluntary emancipation of the slave on the part of the master.

In the same book, I met with one of Sheridan's mighty   6 speeches on and in behalf of Catholic emancipation. These were choice documents to me. I read them over and over again with unabated interest. They gave tongue to interesting thoughts of my own soul, which had frequently flashed through my mind, and died away for want of utterance. The moral which I gained from the dialogue was the power of truth over the conscience of even a slaveholder. What I got from Sheridan was a bold denunciation of slavery, and a powerful vindication of human rights. The reading of these documents enabled me to utter my thoughts, and to meet the arguments brought forward to sustain slavery; but while they relieved me of one difficulty, they brought on another even more painful than the one of which I was relieved. The more I read, the more I was led to abhor and detest my enslavers. I could regard them in no other light than a band of successful robbers, who had left their homes, and gone to Africa, and stolen from our homes, and in a strange land reduced us to slavery. I loathed them as being the meanest as well as the most wicked of men. As I read and contemplated the subject, behold! that very discontentment which Master Hugh had predicted would follow my learning to read had already come, to torment and sting my soul to unutterable anguish. As I writhed under it, I would at times feel that learning to read had been a curse rather than a blessing. It had given me a view of my wretched condition, without the remedy. It opened my eyes to the horrible pit, but to no ladder upon which to get out. In moments of agony, I envied my fellow-slaves for their stupidity. I have often wished myself a beast. I preferred the condition of the meanest reptile to my own. Any thing, no matter what, to get rid of thinking! It was this everlasting thinking of my condition that tormented me. There was no getting rid of it. It was pressed upon me by every object within sight or hearing, animate or inanimate. The silver trump of freedom had roused my soul to eternal wakefulness. Freedom now appeared, to disappear no more forever. It was heard in every sound, and seen in every thing. It was ever present to torment me with a sense of my wretched condition. I saw nothing without seeing it, I heard nothing without hearing it, and felt nothing without feeling it. It looked from every star, it smiled in every calm, breathed in every wind, and moved in every storm.

I often found myself regretting my own existence, and 7 wishing myself dead; and but for the hope of being free, I have no doubt but that I should have killed myself, or done something for which I should have been killed. While in this state of mind, I was eager to hear any one speak of slavery. I was a ready listener. Every little while, I could hear something about the abolitionists. It was some time before I found what the word meant. It was always used in such connections as to make it an interesting word to me. If a slave ran away and succeeded in getting clear, or if a slave killed his master, set fire to a barn, or did any thing very wrong in the mind of a slaveholder, it was spoken of as the fruit of *abolition.* Hearing the word in this connection very often, I set about learning what it meant. The dictionary afforded me little or no help. I found it was "the act of abolishing;" but then I did not know what was to be abolished. Here I was perplexed. I did not dare to ask any one about its meaning, for I was satisfied that it was something they wanted me to know very little about. After a patient waiting, I got one of our city papers, containing an account of the number of petitions from the north, praying for the abolition of slavery in the District of Columbia, and of the slave trade between the States. From this time I understood the words *abolition* and *abolitionist,* and always drew near when that word was spoken, expecting to hear something of importance to myself and fellow-slaves. The light broke in upon me by degrees. I went one day down on the wharf of Mr. Waters; and seeing two Irish-men unloading a scow of stone, I went, unasked, and helped them. When we had finished, one of them came to me and asked me if I were a slave. I told him I was. He asked, "Are ye a slave for life?" I told him that I was. The good Irishman seemed to be deeply affected by the statement. He said to the other that it was a pity so fine a little fellow as myself should be a slave for life. He said it was a shame to hold me. They both advised me to run away to the north; that I should find friends there, and that I should be free. I pretended not to be interested in what they said, and treated them as if I did not understand them; for I feared they might be treacherous. White men have been known to encourage slaves to escape, and then, to get the reward, catch them and return them to their masters. I was afraid that these seemingly good men might use me so; but I nevertheless remembered their advice, and from that time I resolved to run away. I looked forward to a time at which it would be safe for me to escape. I was too young to think of doing so immediately; besides, I wished to learn how to write, as I might have occasion to write my own pass. I consoled myself with the hope that I should one day find a good chance. Meanwhile, I would learn to write.

The idea as to how I might learn to write was suggested to me by being in Durgin and Bailey's ship-yard, and frequently seeing the ship carpenters, after hewing, and getting a piece of timber ready for use, write on the timber the name of that part of the ship for which it was intended. When a piece of timber was intended for the larboard side, it would be marked thus — "L." When a piece was for the starboard side, it would be marked thus — "S." A piece for the larboard side forward, would be marked thus — "L. F." When a piece was for starboard side forward, it would be marked thus — "S. F." For larboard aft, it would be marked thus — "L. A." For starboard aft, it would be marked thus — "S. A." I soon learned the names of these letters, and for what they were intended when placed upon a piece of timber in the ship-yard. I immediately commenced copying them, and in a short time was able to make the four letters named. After that, when I met with any boy who I knew could write, I would tell him I could write as well as he. The next word would be, "I don't believe you. Let me see you try it." I would then make the letters which I had been so fortunate as to learn, and ask him to beat that. In this way I got a good many lessons in writing, which it is quite possible I should never have gotten in any other way. During this time, my copy-book was the board fence, brick wall, and pavement; my pen and ink was a lump of chalk. With these, I learned mainly how to write. I then commenced and continued copying the Italics in Webster's Spelling Book, until I could make them all without looking on the book. By this time, my little Master Thomas had gone to school, and learned how to write, and had written over a number of copy-books. These had been brought home, and shown to some of our near neighbors, and then laid aside. My mistress used to go to class meeting at the Wilk Street meeting-house every Monday afternoon, and leave me to take care of the house. When left thus, I used to spend the time in writing in the spaces left in Master Thomas's copy-book, copying what he had written. I continued to do this until I could write a hand very similar to that of Master Thomas. Thus, after a long, tedious effort for years, I finally succeeded in learning how to write.

Understanding the Significance

1. In paragraph 2, Frederick Douglass states that slavery "proved as injurious to her [his mistress] as it did to me." What does he mean — in what ways was his mistress affected by slavery?
2. What effects did his mistress' decision to stop teaching him have on Douglass? What strategies did he adopt as a result?
3. In paragraph 5, Douglass tells of reading *The Columbian Orator*. What did he learn from this book? How did this knowledge affect him?
4. In paragraph 6, Douglass states, "I would at times feel that learning to read had been a curse rather than a blessing." What caused him to feel this way? What happened as a result?

Discovering the Writer's Purpose

1. In the introduction, Douglass indicates that his master had ordered that Douglass not be taught to read and write, after his mistress had already begun teaching him. Had she not begun her lessons, do you feel that Douglass's desire to learn would have been so great? Explain.
2. In paragraph 4, Douglass notes that he would publicly thank the young white boys who helped him learn to read, but he feared that such a revelation "might embarrass them; for it is almost an unpardonable offence [*sic*] to teach slaves to read in this Christian country." Why was this so, and how could it have been a "Christian" country if it were a terrible offense to teach another human being to read?
3. In paragraph 7, Douglass discusses his discovery of the abolitionist movement. What effect did the knowledge of this movement have on him? On the slaveholders?

4. Douglass's excerpt contains several powerful examples of cause and effect. Which one did you find the most moving or disturbing? Why?

Examining the Writer's Method

1. How does Douglass's use of chronological order emphasize the horrors of being a slave?
2. In paragraphs 5 and 6, Douglass relates two stories having to do with reading he had done about persecution and emancipation. How does the material in these paragraphs help the reader understand Douglass's despair more fully?
3. Why has Douglass included the conversation with the Irish laborers, related in paragraph 7?
4. In the final paragraph, Douglass describes the lengths he went to in order to learn how to write. Why has Douglass used this episode to end the writing?

Considering Style and Language

1. While Douglass declares that his mistress eventually became more committed to embracing the "precepts" of slavery, he still has kind words for her. What point is Douglass making about slavery with this portrait?
2. In paragraph 3, Douglass offers a version of a popular saying: "Mistress, in teaching me the alphabet, had given me the *inch,* and no precaution could prevent me from taking the *ell.*" What point is he making through his adaptation of this proverb?
3. In paragraph 6, Douglass relates how reading enabled him to understand the full, terrible significance of his "wretched condition." Yet, in the same paragraph he states that "[f]reedom now appeared, to disappear no more forever." What is he trying to say by using these contrasting ideas?

4. What do the following words mean in the context of the writing? Stratagems, compliance, depravity, indispensable (para. 1); chattel, pious, divest, precepts, apt (para. 2); ell (para. 3); urchins, prudence (para. 4); emancipation (para. 5); unabated, denunciation, vindication, abhor, loathed, writhed, trump (para. 6); abolitionists, perplexed, wharf, scow, treacherous (para. 7); hewing, larboard, starboard, aft (para. 8).

Your Turn: Responding to the Subject

a. In many ways, Douglass's excerpt is all about denied opportunity. As a slave Douglass was denied that most basic of opportunities — to experience life as a human being rather than as a piece of property. In addition, he was denied the opportunity to learn to read and write, a denial that actually drove him with greater fervor to master these abilities. For this assignment, consider some experiences or situations involving denied opportunities that you have encountered or witnessed at work, in school, in your neighborhood, on campus, and so forth. You might focus on why the opportunity was denied, what has happened because of the denial, or some combination of both.

b. Douglass's struggle against almost insurmountable obstacles to educate himself and eventually escape from slavery is an example of the human ability to carry on toward a goal when there is little hope. For this assignment, explain what you feel motivates people to struggle even when the fight seems hopeless.

Other Possibilities for Using Cause and Effect

The following list contains a number of topics that could be developed into essays employing cause and effect. Remember, how you approach the topic is up to you. Feel free to focus on causes, on effects, or on both causes and effects.

- the breakup of a relationship
- a famous health epidemic
- negative attitudes about the media
- a flood, hurricane, tornado, or other natural disaster
- strict or lenient upbringing
- a learning disability
- city, town, or campus violence
- belief in religious, ethnic, sexual, or racial stereotypes
- your choice of college or major
- cheating in the college classroom
- sudden prosperity or poverty
- water or air pollution
- failure in a course
- popularity of plastic surgery
- loss of consumer confidence in a product or company

Practical Application: Cause and Effect

As you sit at the battered desk in the Student Public Interest Research Group's office in the student union building, you smile, thinking how glad you are to have seen the notice for the group's initial meeting. Social and consumer issues have always been important to you, and after this first meeting you know that this organization will give you the opportunity to pursue these interests.

This year the group has decided to devote its efforts to issues involving children. So far, your organization has published two position papers, one pointing out the need for improved nutrition programs in public schools and the second calling for increased screening of preschool youngsters for vision and hearing problems. Because you are new to the group, your role with each of these position papers has been minor — you have read and commented on each paper in draft form and then have distributed the final versions on campus and in various places around the city.

Now you understand the way things work within the organization, so the chairperson has assigned you to prepare the group's next position paper — *three hundred to five hundred words* — on the potential television has for negatively influencing children. If you need to get some background information, the chair of the group suggests that you conduct a little research first (for example, consult textbooks, newspapers, the Internet, etc.). To guide you in terms of *approach* and *format,* she gives you the following position paper from last year's files: Edward Angell's "Gambling Away the Future?," which discusses a proposed gambling casino's potential dangers to the community.

Gambling Away the Future?

Industries that want to bring in casinos are generous with their promises. But as is often the case in these situations, the touted benefits of such propositions — jobs, schools, infrastructure improvements, and new avenues of revenue — overshadow the

288

drawbacks, from hidden social costs to increases in crime. A closer look needs to be taken at the situation before irreparable damage is done.

REVENUE

Gambling was legalized as a means of raising revenue without increasing taxes. However, according to a recent study by the University of Nevada, the lower class spends eight times more annually on gambling than their upper class counterparts. Gambling is not only legal in many communities — it's encouraged as a way to solve economic shortfalls. While no one forces those who can't afford it to gamble, most low income people see it as their only opportunity for transforming their lives.

Studies by the Business Department of the State of Illinois estimate that for every $1 of gambling revenue brought into the state, between $3 and $7 in hidden costs will be passed on to its residents. These costs arise from increases in crime prevention to costs related to the treatment of social problems like treatment for compulsive gamblers.

JOBS

Dangled like a carrot in front of a starving horse, the promise of jobs to an economically depressed community blinds them from seeing the potential dangers down the road. While the advent of new employment opportunities is seen as a bonus in the short run, the long-term effects on employment and local economies can be devastating. Experts estimate that for every job created by a casino, one to two jobs will be lost from the surrounding community. The jobs shift to the casino as local restaurants, theaters, and businesses lose sales and close.

ATLANTIC CITY

Nowhere are these statistics better illustrated than in the case of Atlantic City. Legalization of casino gambling in 1978 promised to virtually eliminate the poverty in this once-rich city, but it did not happen. Poverty has not diminished, and problems with gambling addiction are up. Since the advent of the casinos, 40 percent of the restaurants not associated with the gambling enterprises have closed, and one-third of the city's retail businesses have folded. Unemployment in Atlantic City is now the state's highest. Crime is up significantly — almost tripled — and the population has fallen by over 25 percent.

CONCLUSION

Gambling is not the great panacea it was first envisioned to be by many communities. Other areas of economic development need to be explored and investigated. It's no coincidence that Utah, which has no form of legalized gambling, also has one of the healthiest growing economies in the nation. Businesses prefer locating in gambling-free areas because of lower taxes, better communities, and more attractive business environments. If we are going to have anything to leave future generations, we need to invest in economic growth rather than gambling on a solution to our fiscal problems.

10

Division and Classification

The Technique

Writing often entails dealing with complex subjects that must be broken down or somehow simplified in order to communicate them clearly to a reader. With these subjects you will frequently rely on *division and classification*. For example, division and classification would be useful in a paper detailing the headaches involved in protesting a speeding ticket. *Division* would enable you to show the enormous bureaucracy in the judicial system. *Classification* would allow you to illustrate the various types of people who spend their days in the courthouse, from the uniformed court officers to the conservatively dressed attorneys to the agitated defendants.

In addition to using division and classification to support other modes, you will also face writing tasks that call for a use of division and classification as the dominant writing technique. An example of this would be an assignment concerning the types of business opportunities available for today's entrepreneur willing to invest a great deal of time but only a moderate amount of money. Regardless of whether you use division and classification to support other modes or as the main technique in an essay, you need to

- establish *a logical method of analysis*;
- maintain *a consistent presentation*;

291

- use *distinct and complete elements of analysis*; and
- provide *an effective arrangement* for the elements of the analysis.

A LOGICAL METHOD OF ANALYSIS

When you focus on division and classification, effectively structuring the analysis means establishing a logical method of presentation so that your reader is able to view the concept piece by piece. As a result, the whole concept becomes easier to understand.

One subject can of course be presented in a variety of ways. If your intent is to explain the workings of a local hospital, for example, you might divide the topic on the basis of the hospital's role as a full health care center, discussing its emergency department, its inpatient treatment area, its diagnostic testing center, and its rehabilitation clinic. But you might also divide the hospital on the basis of its role as a business, focusing on its administrative division, customer-service area, treasurer's department, fund-raising center, and so on.

You have the same variety of approaches available when you classify. If you were writing about the various sports that high-school and college athletes can participate in, you could classify these sports on the basis of the potential for injury involved, with football, hockey, and basketball ranking as *high-risk sports;* gymnastics, softball, and baseball as *moderate-risk sports;* and track and cross-country, tennis, golf, and swimming as *low-risk sports.* But you could also arrange the sports on the basis of how popular they are with student athletes, how expensive they are to operate, and so forth.

In this short passage from his book *What to Listen for in Music,* composer Aaron Copland sets forth a logical method of classification for what people focus on when listening to music:

> We all listen to music according to our separate capacities. But, for the sake of analysis, the whole listening process may become clearer if we break it up into its component parts, so to speak. In a certain sense we all listen to music on three separate planes. For lack of a better ter-

minology, one might name these: (1) the sensuous plane, (2) the expressive plane, (3) the sheerly musical plane. The only advantage to be gained from mechanically splitting up the listening process into these hypothetical planes is the clearer view to be had of the way in which we listen.

A CONSISTENT PRESENTATION

As you establish the method of analysis for your essay, it is important that you maintain consistency in the sections or classes you establish. Otherwise you run the risk of making your subject even more confusing or difficult for your reader to understand because your discussion is no longer unified. (See pp. 26–27 for a more complete discussion of *unity.*)

For instance, you would be likely to use division in a paper in which you explain how you handle your personal finances. The essay might include sections on budgeting for such things as *clothing, food, laundry and dry cleaning, savings, entertainment,* and *miscellaneous expenses.* But if you added a section on *additional sources of income,* the paper would no longer be consistent because this section would deal with a source of income rather than with expenditures.

If you were writing a paper about types of child abuse, it would make sense to provide categories such as *physical abuse, emotional abuse,* and *sexual abuse.* But adding additional classifications such as *reasons that parents abuse* or *highly publicized cases of child abuse* would be inconsistent because neither of these additional categories fits the method of analysis. The first three classifications deal with types of child abuse, but the two proposed categories deal with explanations for and illustrations of child abuse.

In the following excerpt, note how Zick Rubin, Letitia Anne Peplau, and Peter Salovey maintain consistency as they first divide *reinforcement* into two main categories and then classify the examples of both types:

Reinforcement is the process of using rewards — or reinforcers — to strengthen particular responses. A *reinforcer* is any event that strengthens the response it follows — that is, that increases the likelihood of that response occurring again. One of the most important challenges for anyone trying to teach something to an animal or person is to figure out just what things are reinforcing to that individual. Some things, such as food, water, and affection, seem to be naturally reinforcing; these are called **primary reinforcers**. Other things or events become reinforcing as a result of their association with primary reinforcers; these are called **secondary reinforcers**. Secondary reinforcers play a big part in shaping our behavior. Think of all the behaviors we engage in to earn awards, pats on the back, and grades. We have learned that the awards, pats, and grades are rewarding because they tend to go along with other more basic rewards, such as affection and esteem.

DISTINCT AND COMPLETE ELEMENTS OF ANALYSIS

Dividing a complex device such as a telephone into the outside casing and the inside works wouldn't do much to make the way a phone functions accessible to the reader. Likewise, classifying the people who attend community theater productions as either family members of the cast or other people from the community would provide a far too general view of the second group. Therefore, as you develop the method of analysis for a paper featuring division and classification, it's important to supply a sufficient number of sections or categories.

A fuller explanation of a phone, for example, would contain sections about several exterior parts — the casing, the panel of push buttons, and the connecting cord — as well as several interior parts — the receiver, the internal wiring, and the transmitter. And a more thorough discussion of the people who attend community theaters might include such groups as senior citizens looking for a night out, civic and community leaders seeking to support the arts, students looking for their first theater experience, and so on.

In this passage from his book *I Can Sell You Anything*, Carl Wrighter makes his presentation complete but still manages to keep the elements distinct in this discussion of "weasel words," advertising slogans and expressions designed to mislead the consumer:

> A weasel word is a word that's used to imply a meaning that cannot be truthfully stated. Some weasels imply meanings that are not the same as their actual definition, such as "help," "like," or "fortified." They can act as qualifiers and/or comparatives. Other weasels, such as "taste" and "flavor," have no definite meanings, and are simply subjective opinions offered by a manufacturer. A weasel of omission is one that implies a claim so strongly that it forces you to supply the bogus fact. Adjectives are weasels used to convey feelings and emotions to a greater extent than the product itself.

Of course, it's important to remember that the classes you establish may overlap a bit and that some subjects don't quite fit into any of your categories. That a community theater ticket holder might be a senior citizen *and* a community leader *and* related to a cast member doesn't affect the main idea of the paper, nor does the fact that a handful of people attend the shows for reasons other than those you've noted. As long as you don't claim that your groupings represent the only possible classifications or that all subjects must fit into one of the categories, you'll be all set.

AN EFFECTIVE ARRANGEMENT

It isn't enough for an essay to have a clear purpose and a series of solid examples. The examples must also be effectively arranged. Consider a paper in which division is used to explain the way a solar water-heating system functions. In this case, spatial order would be an appropriate choice. With the material arranged this way, the reader would be able to see where the various elements of the system — such as the solar collectors, the control panel, the pump, and the storage tanks — are in relation to each other.

But emphatic order would be the logical choice for a paper using division to show how the federal government spends the tax money it collects. Ranking the divisions from smallest to largest — or largest to smallest — would illustrate critics' claims that the government spends too much money on defense — more than twenty percent of the budget — and too little on social programs — a combined nine percent on such programs as food stamps, aid to families with dependent children, and supplemental security income; and only a combined five percent for social services, assisted housing, public health programs, and unemployment compensation.

Emphatic order would also be a sensible choice with certain papers in which classification is featured. A paper focusing on the types of customers a store clerk faces during the Christmas season is a good example. People who come shopping without any gift ideas, for instance, are annoying; people who drag their exhausted children with them are more annoying; and people who change their minds after their purchases have been rung up are even more annoying. The people who complain the entire time they are in the store are the most annoying of all, however.

In this brief excerpt from his book *Here Is New York,* esteemed essayist E. B. White uses emphatic order to discuss the different ways New York City is viewed by those who come into contact with it:

> There are roughly three New Yorks. There is, first, the New York of the man or woman who was born here, who takes the city for granted and accepts its size and its turbulence as natural and inevitable. Second, there is the New York of the commuter — the city that is devoured by locusts each day and spat out each night. Third, there is the New York of the person who was born somewhere else and came to New York in the quest of something. Of these three trembling cities the greatest is the last — the city of final destination. It is this third city that accounts for New York's high-strung disposition, its poetical deportment, its dedication to the arts, and its incomparable achievements.

AN ANNOTATED EXAMPLE

Jonathan Walters

Throwing

Think of any of the ordinary things people do on a regular basis, and then think of how different people approach and perform the same task. That's essentially what sports enthusiast and writer Jonathan Walters does with this essay on the different ways people throw, which originally appeared in Sports Illustrated. *For his topic, Walters, who has also been a regular contributor on sports for* USA Weekend, *focuses on an action that is the fundamental element in a wide array of sports and other activities. He relies on division and classification to illustrate that while throwing may appear to be a simple act, it's one that many people perform many different ways for many different reasons.*

What elements of an action help to distinguish one method of performing it from another?

He uses his opening paragraph to outline his focus. (Note the humorous tone, too.)

You've got tosses, flips, flings, slings, lobs, heaves and Hail Marys. You can do it sidearm, underhand, overhand and behind the back. When you try a tough one and hit it, it can be one of the sweetest feelings in the world — or one of the worst. 1

He establishes three classes, and provides several examples for each class.

Throwing. Next to running it is probably the most natural athletic impulse we know. In a checkered career of chucking everything from dirt bombs to long bombs, I've come to know three basic types of tosses. 2

I unloaded a Type III one hot summer day at Crane's Beach in Ipswich, 3

Mass. My father was 100 feet away, beyond two softly swept sand dunes, and
moving. I heaved an ice cube. Threw
it as hard as I could. The ends of my
fingers hurt. My shoulder yelped. I
watched with growing disbelief as it
twirled and glinted toward its target,
catching bits of the afternoon sun in its
sweeping arc. It landed dead center on
my father's hair-free pate. I escaped personal injury only because he couldn't
believe I'd thrown it.

<u>Type III throws,</u> understand, are   4
the most dangerous. You try them because you figure you haven't a chance
in hell of making them. Not even a
presidential motorcade is off limits.

<u>My friend Paul recalls a Type III he</u>   5
let fly in his employer's parking lot. The
sun was setting on one of those rare
balmy February days in New England.
A co-worker was pulling out of the lot,
rolling open his sun roof as he went.
Paul packed a snowball, subconsciously
calculated trajectory and force, and
cranked it from about 40 yards away:
"All I remember," he recalls, "is seeing
the snowball explode all over the inside
of this poor guy's windshield. It must
have snuck in through about a six-inch
opening."

The distinguishing and unfortunate   6
feature of Type III throws is that you
have no defense to offer for your action.
True, you did mean to drop one through
that sun roof, but you never figured you
could do it. <u>This is the feature that sep-</u>
<u>arates a Type III toss from a Type II.</u>
Type II's are merely mistakes; you aimed
at one thing and hit another. Although

*He provides transition
and delineation
between classes.*

Type II's can make for unpleasant surprises, when confronted with the evidence you can — weakly — claim you were aiming at something else.

He uses multiple examples of Types II's, here and below.

Once my father and a friend were 7 tossing a balled-up jacket around the Greyhound bus station in Bridgeport, Conn. Between them was a flashing neon greyhound, its front and back paws churning for a finish line it would never reach. With one particularly hard throw, my father clipped the hound's back legs. In a spray of sparks and a wisp of smoke, the animal was crippled. My father and his friend sprinted past it and onto the bus. But they'd been spotted. A frantic porter leaped on after them, saw them hunkered down in their seats a few rows back and, pointing at my father, began yelling, "You killed the greyhound! You killed the greyhound!"

"I never was a natural athlete," my 8 father says.

The outcome of Type II throws 9 doesn't have to be bad. Another friend of mine was sitting at his desk one morning when a fellow employee threw him a cherry tomato, expecting him to catch it. The amazing thing wasn't that she was 30 feet away when she threw it, but that my friend was on the other side of a five-foot-high partition, completely out of view. As if guided there by Mission Control in Houston, the little red orb landed neatly in the breast pocket of his shirt.

He uses emphatic order — Type III to Type II to Type I. Note the transition, too.

As dazzling as a good Type II can 10 be, the most satisfying throws are Type I's. You want to make them, and you do. Hit your target with a Type I and you feel a surge of power and confidence that can turn your whole rotten week around.

He uses multiple examples, here and below.

A few years back, my friend <u>Bill was teaching high school English in Madison, Va. Being the liberal sort, he allowed gum chewing in class, but no bubble blowing.</u> One student in particular had been flouting the rule regularly — and loudly. "The kid was sitting in the center of the last row," Bill recalls. "I turned to write something on the blackboard and caught him out of the corner of my eye blowing another one — a big one. I picked up a piece of chalk, spun around and whipped it. Now, I can't throw. You know I can't throw. Well, the bubble just exploded all over this kid's face, and the class went bananas." 11

Although such Type I's may serve a valuable social purpose, <u>the most uplifting ones are undoubtedly those you unload just for fun.</u> A high school buddy of mine was on the second floor of the Smith College library peeling an orange in lieu of studying applied mathematics. The woman he was with leaned over, asked him for a piece of peel and said, "Watch this." With a neat sidearm flip, she sent the skin spinning the width of the library's central atrium toward a wastebasket one floor below. Bingo. She hit it. "And an orange peel isn't that aerodynamic an object, either," my pal points out. 12

A throw like that is positively therapeutic. It elevates you. For a second, you're Johnny Unitas, Cy Young and John Havlicek rolled into one. 13

He concludes his essay with his strongest example, good proof of his statement in the first paragraph: "one of the sweetest feelings in the world."

In the summer of 1972, I was working at a boatyard on a lake in New Hampshire, and one day I was fantasizing about my Celtics. I had a three-quarter-inch bolt in my hand. There were two seconds left in Game 7 of the world championship. Overtime. The Celtics were trailing 102–101. I twisted past one Philadelphia defender and looked to the basket. I fired. The bolt rolled out of my hand with a neat backspin. It twirled away in a hypnotic arc. The buzzer sounded. With a sharp "clang" and an unequivocal "plop," the bolt ricocheted off the I-beam backboard and into the rusty blue Maxwell House coffee can 50 feet away. I did a five-second victory dance: hands held high, a little workboot shuffle thrown in. As a fellow worker looked on bemused — and slightly amazed — I spun on my heel and headed out to the dock to pump a little gas.

14

Your Turn: Responding to the Subject

a. In this essay, Jonathan Walters takes the simple act of throwing and classifies the various ways people amuse themselves with it. For this assignment, consider other common activities that people perform (walking, singing, dancing, chewing, and so on), set up classes, and discuss them as Walters has.

b. Several of the examples in Walters's essay involve people throwing things when they were supposed to be doing work of some kind. For this assignment, classify the types of work-avoidance techniques you have seen people practice.

Judy Brady
I Want a Wife

More than twenty years after it first appeared in print, this essay by Judy Brady still raises consciousness about the roles of the sexes in marriage. A native San Franciscan, Brady received her B.F.A. in painting from the University of Iowa in 1962. Late in the 1960s, while married and raising two daughters, the then-Judy Syfers became active in the women's movement. She also worked as a freelance writer, publishing articles on political and social issues, including women's rights, education, and abortion. In addition, she is also the editor of 1 in 3: Women with Cancer Confront an Epidemic *(1991), a collection of essays and articles dealing with women and cancer. The article that follows was published in 1971 in the premier issue of* Ms. *magazine. Brady uses division and classification to point out that the division of labor in marriage is sometimes far from fair or equitable.*

Is it possible to work within a marriage to ensure that both partners carry an equal share of the duties and responsibilities?

I belong to that classification of people known as wives. I am A Wife. And, not altogether incidentally, I am a mother. 1

Not too long ago a male friend of mine appeared on the scene from the Midwest fresh from a recent divorce. He had one child, who is, of course, with his ex-wife. He is obviously looking for another wife. As I thought about him while I was ironing one evening, it suddenly occurred to me that I, too, would like to have a wife. Why do I want a wife? 2

I would like to go back to school so that I can become economically independent, support myself, and, if need be, support those dependent upon me. I want a wife who will work and send me to school. And while I am going to school I want a wife to take care of my children. I want a wife to keep track of the children's doctor and dentist appointments. And to keep track of mine, too. I want a wife to make sure my children eat properly and are kept clean. I want a wife who will wash the 3 children's clothes and keep them mended. I want a wife who is a good nurturant attendant to my children, arranges for their schooling, makes sure that they have an adequate social life with their peers, takes them to the park, the zoo, etc. I want a wife who takes care of the children when they are sick, a wife who arranges to be around when the children need special care, because, of course, I cannot miss classes at school. My wife must arrange to lose time at work and not lose the job. It may mean a small cut in my wife's income from time to time, but I guess I can tolerate that. Needless to say, my wife will arrange and pay for the care of the children while my wife is working.

I want a wife who will take care of *my* physical needs. I   4
want a wife who will keep my house clean. A wife who will pick up after my children, a wife who will pick up after me. I want a wife who will keep my clothes clean, ironed, mended, re-placed when need be, and who will see to it that my personal things are kept in their proper place so that I can find what I need the minute I need it. I want a wife who cooks the meals, a wife who is a *good* cook. I want a wife who will plan the menus, do the necessary grocery shopping, prepare the meals, serve them pleasantly, and then do the cleaning up while I do my studying. I want a wife who will care for me when I am sick and sympathize with my pain and loss of time from school. I want a wife to go along when our family takes a vacation so that someone can continue to care for me and my children when I need a rest and a change of scene.

I want a wife who will not bother me with rambling com-   5
plaints about a wife's duties. But I want a wife who will listen to me when I feel the need to explain a rather difficult point I have come across in my course of studies. And I want a wife who will type my papers for me when I have written them.

I want a wife who will take care of the details of my social   6
life. When my wife and I are invited out by my friends, I want a wife who will take care of the babysitting arrangements. When I meet people at school that I like and want to entertain, I want a wife who will have the house clean, will prepare a special meal, serve it to me and my friends, and not interrupt when I talk about the things that interest me and my friends. I want a wife who will have arranged that the children are fed and ready for bed before my guests arrive so that the children do not

bother us. I want a wife who takes care of the needs of my guests so that they feel comfortable, who makes sure that they have an ashtray, that they are passed the hors d'oeuvres, that they are offered a second helping of the food, that their wine glasses are replenished when necessary, that their coffee is served to them as they like it. And I want a wife who knows that sometimes I need a night out by myself.

I want a wife who is sensitive to my sexual needs, a wife   7
who makes love passionately and eagerly when I feel like it, a wife who makes sure that I am satisfied. And, of course, I want a wife who will not demand sexual attention when I am not in the mood for it. I want a wife who assumes the complete responsibility for birth control, because I do not want more children. I want a wife who will remain sexually faithful to me so that I do not have to clutter up my intellectual life with jealousies. And I want a wife who understands that my sexual needs may entail more than strict adherence to monogamy. I must, after all, be able to relate to people as fully as possible.

If, by chance, I find another person more suitable as a wife   8
than the wife I already have, I want the liberty to replace my present wife with another one. Naturally, I will expect a fresh, new life; my wife will take the children and be solely responsible for them so that I am left free.

When I am through with school and have acquired a job,   9
I want my wife to quit working and remain at home so that my wife can more fully and completely take care of a wife's duties.

My God, who *wouldn't* want a wife?   10

Understanding the Significance

1. In paragraph 3, Judy Brady outlines the various child-care tasks she would have her wife do. What then would remain for Brady to do relative to her children?
2. What are the classes of duties that Brady establishes in her essay?
3. In paragraph 5, Brady explains that although she doesn't want her wife to bother her with "rambling complaints about a wife's duties," she does want her wife to "listen

to me when I feel the need to explain a rather difficult point I have come across in my course of studies." What does this attitude tell you about the type of person Brady is describing?

4. In paragraph 8, Brady states that should she decide to start a new life with someone else, she should be free to do so. What point is she trying to make about fairness in this type of marriage?

Discovering the Writer's Purpose

1. In the second sentence of her essay, Brady capitalizes the words *A Wife*. What point do you think she is trying to make by emphasizing the phrase in this way?

2. In paragraph 2, Brady relates the story of a male friend who visits her, stating that he "is obviously looking for another wife." Why do you think she has used the word *obviously?* Is it significant that he is looking for another wife? Explain.

3. Brady initially captures her reader's attention with the unusual request for a wife. Then she holds that attention by spotlighting all the duties she would have her wife perform. In your judgment, would a paper on this subject be as effective if it discussed the duties without any mention of her desire for a person to perform them? Why or why not?

4. On the basis of the evidence presented here, do you feel it is possible to have a happy marriage in which one of the partners is solely responsible for the domestic duties? Why or why not?

Examining the Writer's Method

1. The first two paragraphs of Brady's essay serve as her introduction. How do these paragraphs prepare the reader for the rest of the essay?

2. Which of the categories of duties that Brady identifies has the most impact? Why?

3. Explain the method of arrangement that Brady uses to present her information.
4. One of the dominant features in Brady's essay is its tone. How would you describe this tone? In what way does this tone help Brady make her point?

Considering Style and Language

1. Brady uses the phrase "I want a wife" twenty-nine times in her essay. What effect does she create through this repetition?
2. In paragraph 9, Brady states that once she were through with school she would "want my wife to quit working and remain at home so that my wife can more fully and completely take care of a wife's duties." What point is she making by presenting this example last?
3. Brady closes her essay with a brief question. How does this conclusion help her reiterate her point?
4. What do the following words mean in the context of the writing? Nurturant (para. 3); rambling (para. 5); hors d'oeuvres, replenished (para. 6); passionately, clutter, entail, adherence, monogamy (para. 7).

Your Turn: Responding to the Subject

a. In this essay, Brady underscores the inequity in some relationships. For this assignment, focus on another relationship with potential for a lack of balance (for example, colleagues at work, study partners at school, co-owners of business, teammates, siblings, etc.) and discuss the kinds of duties that each member of the relationship might take on — or avoid.
b. Think of the career path you are following: what types of tasks or duties do you expect to face? For this assignment, discuss what you feel awaits you once you've finished school and started working in your profession.

Isabel Briggs Myers
Taking Type into Account in Education

Fascinated by the personality theory of Carl G. Jung, Isabel Briggs Myers, with some help from her mother Katharine Briggs, spent more than twenty years working to develop a practical application for Jung's theory. The result is the Myers–Briggs Type Indicator (MBTI), a personality profile. Now in its second version, this instrument classifies an individual as one of sixteen personality types, each with gifts and talents. Each year, more than a million individuals in business, industry, government, and education take the MBTI to help derive some insight about themselves and thus become more capable and productive. In this essay, Myers uses division and classification to show how failure to take personality type into account in the classroom makes for an unsatisfactory experience for all.

In what ways might your own personality type affect the way you manage your life?

Schools are being told that they are accountable for educating every child. They are required to teach the basic skills, so that every child grows up able to read, write and balance a checkbook. And they are required to plant various sorts of knowledge, deeply enough so that it will germinate, take root and bear fruit. 1

Both demands are better met if the schools take into account the type differences among children. These are not quantitative differences that can be expressed simply as a higher or lower degree of mental ability. They are qualitative differences, differences as to the kind of perception and the kind of judgment that the child prefers to use. It is his preferences that make his type. Children of different types have a different "mix" of abilities, different needs, interests and motivations, and different degrees of success in school. 2

The preference that has the most conspicuous conse-   *3*
quences in education is the choice between the two kinds of
perception, the choice between sensing and intuition. Sensing
focuses interest and attention upon the concrete reality that is
apparent to the five senses. Sensing children are more interested in doing something, almost anything, with almost any
tangible object, than in listening to what anyone is saying unless it has to do with action or adds something definite to
their picture of the physical world. In contrast, intuition focuses interest and attention upon the end results of one's
own unconscious processes, which include the translation of
symbols-words into meaning, and meaning into words. Intuitive children thus tend to take a positive interest in language,
spoken or written, and acquire a facility that is convenient in
class and in verbal ability tests and also enables them to state
clearly and usefully to themselves the relationships and possibilities suggested by their intuition.

It is therefore understandable that, as most schools are now   *4*
run, sensing children have less use for school than intuitive
children do (often no use at all), that on the average they make
lower grades and score lower on intelligence tests (though not
enough lower to account for their grades), and that they far
more frequently drop out.

If we are to have a system of universal education that does   *5*
justice to all the types, I think we must draw a sharp distinction between skills and knowledge. Knowledge spreads over a
tremendous variety of subjects, each of which may be interesting and useful to certain types and a waste of time to others.
But the basic skills are essential for all the types, and should be
taught in such a way as to give every child what he needs.

The usual first grade has a substantial majority of sensing   *6*
children and a smaller number of intuitives. The sensing children do not want to have to cope with anything unexplainable. The intuitives do not want to be bored by anything
tedious and dull. Except for an occasional child who may have
been let into the secret by an intuitive parent or have found it
out for himself, none of the children, sensing or intuitive,
know that letters stand for sounds.

In most first grades, nobody (for a long time) tells them this   *7*
one crucial fact that makes sense of the process of learning to

read. Reading thus consists of memorizing "sight words," recognizable only by their general shape. A new word is an insoluble mystery until teacher tells you what it is. Content is necessarily restricted to repetition of the few words thus far memorized. "Dick. See Dick. See Dick run." This method of teaching manages to frustrate both the sensing children and the intuitives. Reading, which ought to be a magical extension of one's own experience, is both unexplainable and dull.

To meet the needs of the sensing children who want things   8
to be explicit and the intuitive children who want unlimited possibilities, first grades should introduce intensive phonics at the very beginning, so that every child in the class knows that there is a perfectly good way to tell what new words are. He is going to be able to read, very soon, up to the limits of his speaking vocabulary. And removal of the artificial limits on vocabulary means that he can read vastly more interesting things. He can, in fact, attempt anything he cares to tackle.

From the standpoint of the child's success in school and his   9
development as a person, with ambition, initiative, and confidence in himself, the start of first grade marks a crucial fork in the road. That is the point at which he decides either that school makes sense or that it does not, that it is interesting or boring, that he can or cannot do these new things. If he cannot do the new things, his only defense against the humiliation of being "dumb" is to decide that such things are not worth doing.

The pitfall in the teaching of arithmetic skills is basically the   10
same as the pitfall in teaching reading. The children who try to cope with the symbols without recognizing the realities these stand for are doomed to frustration. They never win through to the beautiful certainties in the realm of numbers. They just memorize incantations. "7 and 5 is 12." "11 minus 4 is 7." "5 times 7 is 35." When the teacher gives you the first two numbers of an incantation, you have to remember the third. If you forget that third number, there is nothing you can do about it. And if you are given a problem and can't see what kind of incantation to use, there is nothing you can do about that.

The solution is to establish the reality of numbers first. The   11
symbols then can be understood as a way of talking about reality. There should be no operations with disembodied numerals, no incantations, no memorizing, no flash cards for "addition

facts" and "subtraction facts," no verbal drill, until the children are thoroughly familiar with manual operations with quantities. To many sensing children, things you can touch and move are real but words are not.

The form in which a question is put can change the whole   *12* spirit of the proceedings. "How much is 7 and 5?" implies that the child ought to know by this time and the teacher wants to find out whether he does or not. This is wrong side to.* The child is the one who should be doing the finding out. "Find out how much is 7 and 5!" is an invitation to action. Using number blocks, for instance, the child can take a block that is seven squares high and stand it against the number tower. Naturally it reaches to seven. Then he can take a block that is five squares high and stack it on top of the seven. Together they reach to twelve. Every time he does it they reach to twelve. In fact, he can see that they have to reach to twelve; the seven block is always three squares short of ten; the first three squares of the five block always get you to ten; the other two squares always stick up beyond ten and reach to twelve. A similar certainty has to exist in the case 17 and 5, 27 and 5, and so on up.

Consistent use of this approach gives the child a picture of   *13* the number system as a whole, the place of any given number in that system, and its relation to other numbers. When he starts doing operations with numerals instead of blocks, he knows the quantities they stand for and what he is doing with those quantities. And when he is given a problem, he has a decent chance of seeing what he must do to solve it.

Reading, writing and arithmetic are well-defined skills that   *14* every child needs to acquire. But knowledge, as distinguished from skills, is another matter. It has no limits. Schools must decide what tiny fraction they will try to teach. If we take it as axiomatic that a child should be taught things that are of lasting benefit to him, either by making him more effective or by otherwise enhancing his life, one brutal conclusion follows. There is no use in teaching a child things he intends to forget.

Nothing will stick in a child's mind long enough to do him   *15* any good unless it interests him, and here type plays a major role. The combination of a child's preferred kind of perception and his preferred kind of judgment tends to concentrate his in-

---

*This phrase is idiomatic for "backwards" or "inside out." — Editor.

terest in fields where these find scope. His remaining preferences influence the kind of work he will like to do in those
fields. Hence knowledge that is relevant, even illuminating, for
a person with a given set of preferences can be acutely boring
to a person with the opposite set. Aside from routine warnings
against common dangers, like carbon monoxide and the signing of documents unread, there is probably no body of knowledge that can profitably be "taught" to every child regardless.

Time and effort spent in trying to teach a child something   16
against his own will are worse than wasted. Real harm is done.
If a child is not interested in what he is supposed to be learning, he is bored. And the habit of being bored is disastrous for
children, because it destroys their native curiosity. Babies and
pre-schoolers have a great urge to make sense of the world.
They devote their energies happily to finding out one thing
after another, whatever fixes their curiosity at the moment.
They learn at a tremendous rate, and they remember what
they learn, because it becomes a part of their world as they
know it. Learning is high adventure, not a chore.

School should be a continuation of the adventure. Chil-   17
dren in all the grades should be given maximum opportunity
to learn the things that have meaning and interest for them in
terms of their own kind of perception and their own kind of
judgment. To the extent that they are given this opportunity,
they gain not only in interest but in application and intelligence as well. People of any age, from six to sixty, apply themselves with greater vigor to the task in hand when they are
interested. People of any age are more intelligent when they
are interested than when they are bored.

A child permitted to study what interests him learns more   18
and remembers it. The most valuable outcome, however, is the
effect upon the development of his perception and judgment.
A purposeful finding out about almost anything develops his
perception. And a self-imposed doing of whatever is necessary
to that end develops his judgment far more than would mere
obedience to a teacher's authority. The lifelong importance of
adequate development of perception and judgment is shown in
past and current studies with the Type Indicator. Good perception and judgment are associated with achievement, which is
reasonable because they make a person more effective in whatever he sets out to do. They are also associated with mental and

physical health, which again is reasonable because they enable a person to cope more competently with his problem and thus lessen or eliminate strain.

Ways of making room for individual interests and study can   *19* be worked out in any school where authority will accept the idea. In fact, they can be worked out independently by any teacher. A seminar approach can be taken, in which the class is given a bird's-eye view of the different aspects of the subject and then allowed to sign up to work on whichever aspect each finds most interesting. Or a list of individual projects can be designed to appeal to widely different types. Flexibility can be achieved by framing some exam questions for sensing types, others for intuitives, everyone being permitted to leave out the two he likes least. Or it may be announced in advance that everyone may formulate and answer one question of his own, substituting it for one not in his field. . . .

Children in lower grades can also practice using the differ-   *20* ent kinds of perception and judgment one at a time in appropriate ways. Exact observation will exercise sensing. Figuring out possible ways to solve a difficulty will exercise intuition. Thinking out all the unintended consequences that may result from an action will exercise thinking. Weighing how other people will feel about things will exercise feeling.

An early clue to a child's type may be obtainable from his   *21* response to these activities. The sensing child should find the sensing exercise easier and more fun than the intuitive exercise. The little thinker will prefer thinking about consequences to guessing about other people's feelings. And so on. An observant teacher may be able to draw useful inferences as to the way each child's mind works and what will help him most. Whether she does or not, the children will benefit directly from practice in these four different, important ways of using their minds.

Understanding the Significance

1. As Isabel Briggs Myers explains, what are the responsibilities that schools are expected to undertake?

2. In paragraphs 10–12 Briggs Myers discusses various ways a simple mathematics problem could be approached. How are the approaches different?
3. Briggs Myers says in paragraph 14 that there is "no use in teaching a child things he intends to forget." What point is she making about the information children face in school?
4. What approaches and techniques does Briggs Myers suggest to address differences in learning styles?

Discovering the Writer's Purpose

1. In the opening paragraph and again in paragraph 5, Briggs Myers draws the distinction between knowledge and basic skills. In your judgment, is she suggesting that one is superior or more important to a child's success?
2. Briggs Myers asserts in paragraph 9 that the beginning of first grade is a "crucial fork in the road" for children, that if school fails to stimulate them at this point, their education will greatly suffer. Do you agree? Why or why not?
3. In paragraph 19 Briggs Myers states, "Ways of making room for individual interests and study can be worked out in any school where authority will accept the idea." In your judgment, what point is she trying to make?
4. On the basis of the description of the learning types explained in paragraph 3, would you say you are more of a sensing or intuitive type? Explain how you reached your opinion.

Examining the Writer's Method

1. The first sentence of paragraph 2 is Briggs Myers's thesis: "Both demands are better met if the schools take into account the type differences among children." How does the information in the first paragraph make her thesis seem both practical and reasonable?

2. In paragraph 12, Briggs Myers provides a lengthy example of an alternative way of teaching a simple mathematical concept. Why do you feel she discusses the same scenario in so many different ways in the paragraph?
3. Briggs Myers's discussion of knowledge is far less specific than her discussion of basic skills. How do you account for the difference?
4. The final two paragraphs constitute Briggs Myers's conclusion. How do the ideas here relate back to the ideas expressed in the introduction?

Considering Style and Language

1. In paragraphs 1, 2, 10, 11, and 16, Briggs Myers uses figurative language — metaphors, analogies, and so forth — to describe such concepts or systems as knowledge, reading, and mathematics. How does expressing these ideas in this way help her explain the different ways people react to information?
2. In paragraph 7, Briggs Myers includes an example of a typical lesson in reading. Why does she include the actual passage rather than simply tell about the lesson?
3. Throughout the writing, Briggs Myers uses two-part division to discuss differences in interests and learning styles. How does this method of division make it easier for her reader to follow her discussion?
4. What do the following words mean in the context of the essay? Germinate (para. 1); quantitative, qualitative (para. 2); conspicuous, tangible, intuition (para. 3); universal (para. 5); tedious (para. 6); insoluble (para. 7); humiliation (para. 9); certainties, incantation (para. 10); disembodied (para. 11); axiomatic, enhancing (para. 14); relevant, illuminating (para. 15); native (para. 16); application, vigor (para. 17); cope (para. 18); formulate (para. 19); inferences (para. 21).

Your Turn: Responding to the Subject

a. In this excerpt, Briggs Myers points out the need for instructors to adapt their assignments and classroom presentations so that they will reach all their students. Think of a subject area you are interested in or a course that you are currently taking. Drawing from Myers's recommendations, suggest some different ways that a concept or lesson in the subject could be presented so that the needs of more students would be met.

b. It's not just in the classroom that the different types that Briggs Myers discusses must coexist and function. For this assignment, discuss how the types of people she discusses would handle the daily tasks faced by the typical person of your age in college, at home, or at work.

Diane Riva
Exposed Toes

Consider the old adage "clothes make the person," the implication being that what we wear defines us as people. In this essay, Diane Riva takes this old saying and narrows the focus a bit from clothes to just shoes. Riva describes herself this way: "I am a happily divorced, single parent with an eleven-year-old daughter, Leah, who takes my breath away. I try to express the thoughts in my head through various forms: writing, painting, and working with metals." Currently working for a jewelry design firm, Riva draws on her varied work and personal experiences and in her essay puts a different twist on the familiar axiom. She suggests that the different shoes we wear in the different aspects of our lives — as children, as spouses, as parents, as workers, and so on — reflect different aspects of us.

What do the shoes you choose to wear at any time say about you at that moment?

The shoes scattered throughout the house belong to me. I will find a pair under the dining room table, a pair in the parlor, or one or two pairs in the kitchen, and even a few in my bedroom. In my childhood memories, I can still hear my mother asking me to pick up my wayward shoes. Some habits are hard to break, and leaving my shoes wherever my feet release them is one I am still trying to overcome. When I look at my shoes, I see endless memories. They are part of my personality, and if they could talk, what colorful tales they would tell. 1

I own three pairs of black sneakers; they are my proud work shoes, and we spend the most time together. There are times when my feet melt when I enter them. My work as a bartender has enabled my sneakers to taste Guinness Irish stout, fine Russian vodkas, assorted hot coffee drinks, or whatever else I am rushing around the bar to make. They are the constant recipients of the over-filled glass of alcohol. 2

My black, tattered sneakers with tiny knots in the shoelaces have heard hours of endless stories from lonely travelers stop- 3 ping in the hotel lounge, guests pouring out tales of love, heartache, job stress, divorce, battles won, battles lost, and hundreds of irritating jokes. At the end of my shift, if we are fortunate and it has rained, I give the bottoms of my hard working sneakers a bath in a fresh puddle. It feels good to wash away work. When my feet arrive home, my sneakers are usually slipped off and left in the parlor to slumber. This is where they will quietly remain until I torture them for another eight hours of work.

Along with my sneakers, I own a pair of boat shoes. The tops are a reddish brown, the same color as an Irish Setter, and the soles are made of rubber. I have had these shoes for over six years, and still they do not age as I do. When I occasionally wear my boat shoes, I don't like the way they look on my wide feet, but they feel so good. They know me the least but struggle to be in my world. I will probably have these shoes for the rest of my life. They are like memories of past boyfriends: hard to get rid of.   4

When I open my closet door, my dress shoes lie dead in dusty boxes. About every four months, I will remove a pair and struggle into them. When I wear these high-heeled shoes, it is usually for a wedding, a Christmas party, or a night on the town. When I add one or two inches to my height, I end up having this pretty feeling, and my legs have a tendency to like the way they look. The sound of a high-heeled shoe on a polished marble floor at a posh restaurant, I will admit, has a certain appeal to me. I gather it is my whole look, from the top of my perfectly set hair to the ends of my smothered toes, that gives me this feeling of attractiveness.   5

But how I look forward to removing these falsely overstated dress shoes and returning them to their dusty coffins. Funny how these shoes never lounge around the house; they are always returned to their boxes. I would not want to insult the everyday, comfortable shoe with the high society heel.   6

Among my most treasured shoes is a pair of sandals. They can be worn throughout all the seasons, with or without socks. My huaraches are from Tiajuana, and on a hot day many years ago, I handpicked them myself from among many of their twins. The soles are made from black, recycled tires, and the upper portion consists of thick, tan leather strips that entwine to form an interesting open-toe design. They call my name   7 constantly, but unfortunately, they are the most inappropriate shoe for all occasions. As I picked up my paycheck from work one cold November day, my boss commented on my unusual footwear for this time of year. He could not help but notice my well-worn extra-wide huaraches and my thick woolen socks, so he stated that it seemed an unsuitable time of year for sandals. I tried to explain the comfort zone of these broken-in shoes, but he just looked at me with confusion. I don't think that he could relate to the love-hate affair that women have with their shoes. I have had the pleasure of spoiling my feet with these huaraches for over eight years. Each spring they take a trip to the cobbler for their yearly checkup. I think the cobbler looks forward to this annual visit and admires the workmanship in these weary old sandals.

I must admit my shoes of choice were given to me by my 8 parents, and I wear these constantly. Nothing has to be tied; they have no straps, no buckles, no leather between the toes, no heels. They are never too tight and always fit perfectly — my natural feet. Whenever possible, my feet are out of confinement, barefoot and happy. I love for my feet to touch and feel all the materials of life. They can be tickled, washed, counted, and colored. They hold all of my memories. They were on my honeymoon; they were at my daughter's birth; they feel spring and the ocean first; they have been bitten, cut, and bruised. I never have to look for them, they are always where I left them, and they never have to be put away.

As I search throughout my house and pick up my way- 9 ward shoes before my mother arrives for a visit, I look down at the bundle of leather and laces in my arms, and days of my past shout out to me. I know why these shoes are scattered about. They are my memories, and I do not want to put them away.

Understanding the Significance

1. In her essay, how does Diane Riva justify leaving her shoes scattered around her home?
2. Why do you think Riva describes the boxes in which she stores her dress shoes as coffins?

3. As Riva explains it, what is the "love-hate affair" women have with shoes?
4. In her conclusion, she mentions that habits are hard to break. What evidence in this paragraph indicates that breaking bad habits is nevertheless possible?

Discovering the Writer's Purpose

1. A second look at this essay shows that it is much more than a discussion about shoes. What do you think Riva's real purpose is in relating the various stories?
2. From her explanation, what sense do you get about Riva's attitude toward her job?
3. In the fifth and sixth paragraphs, what impression do you get of Riva's attitude about formal dress?
4. As her final category of shoes, Riva chooses feet. Do you agree with her reasoning that feet should be classified as a type of shoe? Explain.

Examining the Writer's Method

1. How does Riva use her introduction to set her reader up for the discussion to follow?
2. What titles would you give to the various categories of footwear that Riva discusses?
3. How would you describe Riva's method of arrangement? Has she followed emphatic order or set the paragraphs up in a more random fashion? Would her essay be more — or less — effective if she changed the order?
4. How does Riva's final paragraph serve as an effective conclusion?

Considering Style and Language

1. How would you describe the tone of Riva's essay?
2. In several spots, Riva provides wonderful sensory details. In your judgment, which use of detail is best? Why?

3. Throughout her essay, Riva uses personification to describe her footwear. What effect does she create by giving her shoes lives of their own?
4. What do the following words mean in the context of the writing? Wayward (para. 1); slumber (para. 3); posh (para. 5); overstated (para. 6); inappropriate, cobbler (para. 7); confinement (para. 8).

Your Turn: Responding to the Subject

a. In her essay, Diane Riva tells about the different kinds of shoes she owns and what they say about her. Like Riva, do you have several different types of shoes or other clothing items — jeans, ties, sweaters, and so on — each of which tells the world something specific about you? For this assignment, tell your reader what your bureau drawers or closet racks tell people about you.
b. To some degree, the ways people dress reflect the groups they belong to — or aspire to belong to. For this assignment, consider a place where large groups of people congregate — for example, your campus, a shopping mall, a nightclub, a sports stadium, or a concert hall — and write an essay in which you group people on the basis of common styles of dress.

Other Possibilities for Using Division and Classification

The following list contains subjects that could be developed into essays featuring division and classification. Some of these topics may lend themselves more easily to a focus on division, others on classification, and others on both. Feel free to adapt a subject in any way you think will enable you to develop an effective essay.

- types of postsecondary education
- ways to waste time
- the structure of a major corporation like AT&T or General Motors
- types of television shows currently on the air
- categories of popular music
- a successful play or concert
- kinds of commercials
- kinds of hobbies
- types of business careers
- a set of scuba diving equipment
- types of comedy
- your city or town
- people who ride roller coasters or other thrill rides
- a scientific theory
- a major appliance or device such as a computer, air conditioner, video camera

Practical Application:
Division and Classification

It has been a full year since you joined the management team at Fusion Heavy Metal Recovery Systems, Inc., a national hazardous waste recycling company, and you've certainly found it to be an exciting place to work. As a recent *Wall Street Journal* profile indicates, the company started up five years ago and experienced immediate and enormous success. The CEO, a native of your city, has made a serious commitment to give something back to his hometown that has given him so much. His company currently employs thirty-five city residents in well-paying, high technology positions, with plans for expansion both locally and in several other states.

The *Wall Street Journal* story also reports one of the more remarkable episodes in the company's history. The year before you joined the corporation, Fusion Heavy Metal Recovery Systems enjoyed a record year in terms of profits. To show his appreciation to the workers who made this success possible, the CEO decided to share the wealth in an unusual fashion: he surprised each of the thirty-five staffers, plus a guest of each person's choice, with a five-day cruise to the Caribbean with all expenses paid.

This afternoon, the CEO calls you into the office to tell you that history is about to repeat itself. Figures for the last six months indicate that profits are far ahead of the banner year two years ago, so once again he would like to reward his employees. This time, however, he wants to approach the situation a little differently, in part to counter some problems that he hadn't anticipated last time.

For example, he hadn't really considered that, to the government, such a vacation is considered income, meaning the so-called free vacation had actually increased tax burdens for the employees. Also, to some people, a vacation means getting away from the people they work with, no matter how good their relationship is. Furthermore, from a strictly business standpoint, a group vacation is not necessarily a great idea. What would happen if there were some terrible calamity? Would the company still be able to operate without key personnel? Would resulting litigation wipe out the company assets?

To avoid these and other potential problems, the CEO has decided to offer the employees a menu of at least five bonus possibilities (for example, a tax-sheltered college scholarship fund for a child, a voucher to buy company stock, etc.) from which to choose. As the CEO explains, $3,000 has been allotted for each employee. Your job is to do some brainstorming, develop that menu, and then submit a confidential *one-page memo* to him that details the possibilities. Once he reviews and approves of your selections, he will distribute the memo to the entire staff. To guide you in terms of *approach* and *format* he has given you a copy of the following memo prepared two years ago by Christine Baker, president of a local travel agency, that had helped the CEO settle on a Caribbean cruise in the first place.

North Shore Travel

158 Maple Road   Amesbury, MA 01913   (508) 976–3321

TO: M. Lars Oldengray, CEO, Fusion Heavy Metal Recovery
          Systems, Inc.

FROM: Christine Baker, President

DATE: November 12, 1997

RE: Group Vacation Possibilities

Thank you for inquiring about the vacation packages available through North Shore Travel. We want your employees to be thrilled with their vacations, so we have selected the most popular destinations of the year. In order to make things easy for you, we have tailored each trip to your specific requirements. Each package offers four nights and five days of travel, lodging, meals and activities for two people — for less than $1500. Spectacular sunsets are free! We take care of all details, so all you have to do is enjoy the trip.

Cruising in the   **$1428.00**
Caribbean

- Enjoy a deluxe ocean view
  cabin.
- Feast on your choice of cuisine.
- Gamble in a high-energy casino.
- Experience Las Vegas-style
  shows.
- Explore exotic ports of call.

Biking in Vermont $1499.00

- Ride diverse mountain trails.
- Learn from experienced guides.
- Dine on hearty gourmet meals.
- Play indoors in bad weather.
- Rest in our mountain-top lodge.

Exploring in $1490.00
Napa Valley

- Unwind in a garden view suite.
- Savor regional cuisine.
- Tour local wineries.
- Bike in the heart of Napa Valley.
- Relax with a whirlpool or
  massage.

Beaching in Florida $1475.00

- Enjoy beautiful sunsets each
  night.
- Lounge pool-side or on the sand.
- Shop in outposts & boutiques.
- Swim, sail and snorkel.
- Play golf, racquetball or tennis.

Prices shown include all ground travel, port charges and airfare from Boston (where applicable). Also, substantial discounts are available if one package trip is booked for all 75 people. There are no restrictions as to when you can travel, so trips may be booked any time during the year.

North Shore Travel offers the personal attention and outstanding service only a corporate travel specialist can provide. When you are ready to discuss your plans further, please contact us to schedule a convenient meeting time. If there is anything else we can do to assist you in this matter, please feel free to call.

11

Argument

The Approach: Understanding Argument

Writing that attempts to persuade a reader to accept a point of view is known as *argument*. Unlike the techniques discussed in the previous chapters, argument isn't a mode — it's an *aim*. Whenever you write, you fulfill an aim — to entertain, inform, or persuade — and with an argument paper, your primary goal is to persuade the reader to accept your point of view.

Some people draw a distinction between *argument* and *persuasion,* with argument specifically referring to writings that rationally and dispassionately attempt to convince the reader of the validity of a position and persuasion referring to writings that rely on additional appeals, including appeals to emotion, to sway the reader. For the most part, however, you need not be concerned about this distinction; when you take a stand on an issue, you will probably employ both approaches.

THE MODES IN COMBINATION

You fulfill the aim of an argument paper the same way you fulfill the aim of any paper — through an effective combination of modes. Consider a paper asserting that oil companies must be more responsible in both the quality of the ships they use to transport crude oil and the competence of the captains and crews piloting those ships.

You might begin the paper with some images of oil-soaked seals, sea otters, birds, and fish dying following the grounding of the tanker *Braer* off the coast of Scotland in early 1993 or the *Valdez* off the coast of Alaska a few years earlier. These images could then be followed by a brief retelling of the groundings, followed by an explanation of the oil companies' culpability in the disasters. The rest of the paper could be devoted to the changes that should be enacted to save our oceans.

In terms of modes, the images of sea creatures dead and dying in a fouled ocean would be description, the brief stories of the groundings would be narration, and the explanation of the companies' responsibility would be cause and effect. The remainder of the paper would also feature a combination of modes — for instance, process to explain how some companies have skirted current laws by registering their ships in countries with lax regulations, division and classification to categorize the variety of changes called for, and so on.

TYPES OF APPEALS

The ancient Greeks identified three types of *appeals* used to persuade someone to accept a line of reasoning: *ethos, pathos,* and *logos.* Writers still embrace these concepts, which today are explained respectively as appeals on the basis of *reputation, emotion,* and *logic.* As with the modes, these types of appeals generally appear in combination. An argument paper that appeals wholly to emotion or one that appeals wholly to logic would have some serious weaknesses.

An example of an essay appealing wholly to emotion would be a paper advocating that leaders of hate groups be imprisoned because their speeches are treatises on prejudice. Such a paper would no doubt inspire some cheers, but it would be flawed. Preserving freedom of speech for all of us means allowing people to express attitudes offensive to the majority. A better approach with this paper would be to incorporate an appeal to logic by suggesting that leaders of hate groups be prosecuted whenever their words violate the law and that efforts be expanded to raise the public's awareness of prejudice.

The Development of Your Paper

With an argument essay, your aim is always the same: to persuade the reader of the validity of your point of view. To fulfill this goal, you need to

- take *a clear stance on the issue;*
- develop *sufficient valid support;*
- recognize the importance of *tone;*
- avoid *errors in logic;* and
- provide *an effective arrangement* of the material.

A CLEAR STANCE ON THE ISSUE

With an argument paper, you must clarify where you stand on an issue to prepare your reader for the line of reasoning constituting your argument. Look at this introduction to an essay about the rights of adoptees and birth parents to unseal confidential adoption files. The final sentence, shown here underlined, makes it clear that the writer is in favor of allowing the files to be opened:

Today, many adopted children across the country are attempting to gain access to their sealed adoption files for information about their birth parents. Likewise, many individuals who had given their infant children up for adoption are also trying to have the files unsealed so that they can discover the whereabouts of the children they surrendered to others to raise. Meanwhile, the adoptive parents involved are caught in the middle, not wanting to deny their children the opportunity to learn about their roots but also fearing that they might somehow lose their children as a result. It's a gut-wrenching subject, one that has no easy answers. Regardless of the potential for pain, however, both adopted children and parents who surrendered their children for adoption should be able to read through their files and make contact with their biological relatives if they choose.

With this final sentence in place, the reader knows exactly where the writer stands and is therefore prepared for the line of reasoning to follow in the body of the essay.

SUFFICIENT VALID SUPPORT

There is no specific minimum — or maximum — amount of information needed to develop an effective line of reasoning. Think of a subject about which you are undecided; how much support for a position would you need to see before you would accept it? It's likely that you would require several solid supporting details and examples before you would be convinced; your reader demands the same of you.

As you develop these supporting details and examples, it's important to recognize the relationship between *fact* and *opinion*. By definition, a fact is a verifiable truth. Facts by themselves, while definitely informing a reader, allow no room for discussion. Opinion, however, is reasoning based on fact. Essentially, the line of reasoning underlying an argument is a fully developed opinion; for that opinion to be valid, it needs to be supported with relevant facts.

One way to help develop your argument is to make a list of points that support your position and a list of points that someone opposed to the argument might raise. The value of the first list is obvious: these are the points that will form the framework of your line of reasoning. But the second list is also important. You may be able to refute some of these points completely or somehow turn them to your advantage.

Imagine, for example, that you are interested in developing a paper in favor of banning all smoking in restaurants. Here is a list of reasons for and against the ban:

For:
- Smoke ruins the dining atmosphere for nonsmokers.
- Many smoking areas don't keep the smoke away from nonsmoking areas.
- The Surgeon General has declared the smoke from other people's cigarettes hazardous to nonsmokers.

Against:
- A total ban denies smokers an enjoyable night out on their own terms.

- It would be another case of the government intruding needlessly into personal lives.
- Smoking areas would work if businesses would install the proper ventilation systems.

The points in favor of the ban are valid, so you could feel comfortable including them in your essay. In addition, the first two points from the list against the ban could be adapted and used, too. Although banning smoking would inconvenience smokers, allowing smoking would clearly endanger nonsmoking patrons; the inconvenience is therefore justifiable, as are the government's actions to preserve the health of nonsmokers.

Incidentally, whenever you draw information from some document or individual to support your argument, you must indicate the source of this material for your reader. With brief, less formal writing situations, acknowledging the information you have used to support your ideas can often be as simple as this: "According to a recent item in *U.S. News & World Report,* the number of reported rapes on college campuses nationwide has risen dramatically." But with longer, more formal assignments, you need to provide more specific documentation, including such details as the title, date of publication, publisher, pages involved, and so on. In these cases, always ask which method of formal documentation your instructor prefers. The reference section of your college library will have guidelines for several different methods of documentation, including those of the Modern Language Association (MLA) and the American Psychological Association (APA).

TONE

Another aspect that will affect how your point of view is accepted is its *tone,* the attitude expressed about the subject. If your tone is sarcastic, superior, or patronizing, you may alienate a reader who might otherwise be persuaded to agree with your point of view. On the other hand, if your tone is sincere, concerned, or respectful, you'll increase the chance that your point of view will be favorably received.

Imagine an essay demanding that new gun control measures be imposed. With a volatile subject like gun control, it's easy to understand how a sentence such as this might appear in an early draft:

> A person would have to be stupid not to realize that an unlocked handgun is statistically far more likely to be stolen or to cause accidental injury than it is to be used to stop an intruder.

The message in the sentence is valid but the tone is insulting. Now consider this version of the sentence:

> Many people still don't realize that an unlocked handgun is statistically far more likely to be stolen or to cause accidental injury than it is to be used to stop an intruder.

The message is essentially unchanged, but the tone is clearly better. It no longer suggests that a person who hadn't come to this realization is somehow deficient. As a result, a reader who hadn't come to this realization may well be more receptive to the line of reasoning.

In some cases, you can adjust the tone of your writing by avoiding any absolute terms. It is better, for example, to say that patients with severe head injuries *rarely* emerge from deep extended comas to enjoy life as they once did than to say they *never* do, because it allows for the one-in-a-million, unexplainable recovery. Therefore, rather than use words such as *all, always, every,* and *never,* use words such as *most, frequently, many,* and *rarely.*

ERRORS IN LOGIC

To persuade a reader, an argument paper must have a logical line of reasoning leading to a valid conclusion. You establish this line of reasoning by engaging in one of two primary ways of thinking: *induction* and *deduction.* Although the goal of the two reasoning processes is the same, they involve coming at a subject from opposite directions.

With induction, you reason from a series of specific matters to a general conclusion. Physicians employ inductive reasoning when they conclude that a particular skin rash is a form of eczema because every other rash that they've examined like this one has proven to be eczema. An answer reached in this way is the result of what is called an *inductive leap,* which means that while this diagnosis is a reasonable conclusion, it isn't necessarily the only possible valid explanation. The rash might closely resemble the one resulting from eczema but might actually be the result of another condition that the physicians aren't aware of.

With deduction, you reason from a series of general statements to a specific conclusion. If flat, low-lying, inland areas are especially susceptible to tornadoes and you live in a flat, low-lying, inland area, then it is accurate to say that your area faces the threat of tornadoes.

Regardless of whether you use induction, deduction, or some combination of the two to make your point, it is important that you avoid the following common errors in logic, often referred to as *logical fallacies:*

- *Argument ad hominem* (Latin for "argument to the man") — objecting to the person making the argument, rather than that person's line of reasoning:
  "Film critic Jerry Cleaver has criticized the sex and violence in several of this year's movies, but he himself was once accused of assault and battery while he was in college."
- Bandwagon approach — urging acceptance of a point of view merely because other people accept it rather than because of compelling evidence:
  "Everybody is against the idea of allowing that historic house to be demolished."
- Begging the question — assuming as fact something that needs to be proven:
  "NASA's call for increased funding in these hard times is just another example that these scientists care about nothing except their own programs."

- Creating a red herring — purposely shifting from the main idea to some minor point to escape close scrutiny of the main point:

    "Congress is trying to indict the president over his involvement in the overthrow of two world leaders, but what do these legislators have to say about their own misuse of the congressional gymnasium?"

- Either/or reasoning — suggesting only two alternatives when many possibilities exist:

    "Unless we completely change the way we conduct presidential elections, we'll never attract good candidates."

- Hasty generalization — making an assumption on the basis of too little valid support:

    "Three friends of mine have had trouble with that brand of stereo equipment, so that company obviously doesn't make a very good product."

- *Non sequitur* (Latin for "it does not follow") — coming to an illogical or incorrect conclusion in relation to the evidence:

    "Because homeless people aren't working, it's clear that they aren't interested in helping themselves."

- Oversimplification — wrongfully reducing a complex subject by ignoring crucial information or factual inconsistencies:

    "Sex education classes will eliminate teenage promiscuity."

- *Post hoc, ergo prompter hoc* (Latin for "after this, therefore because of this") — assuming because one thing occurred before another that the first caused the second:

    "The killer had just completed an enormous meal at a fast-food place, so something in the food must have triggered his aggression."

AN EFFECTIVE ARRANGEMENT

Although it's not the only suitable way to arrange an argument paper, emphatic order is often an excellent choice. The idea is to use the initial points to spark your reader's interest and then to use the subsequent examples to feed that interest, thus cultivating acceptance of your point of view.

Look at this informal outline of an essay asserting that condoms should be made available in high-school restrooms:

Point 1: Many sexually active students are too self-conscious to obtain condoms otherwise.

Point 2: Students intent on having sex won't stop merely because condoms aren't available.

Point 3: The number of teenage pregnancies continues to climb at an alarming rate.

Point 4: Unprotected sex can lead to the transmission of HIV.

Arranged this way, the argument is indeed compelling. The initial example — that some students won't actively seek a condom because of embarrassment — is a strong example, adding credence to the stance that condoms should be freely available to high-school students for their own protection. The next two points add to the strength of the argument so that by the time the reader reaches the final point — that having condoms available may save some young people from the incurable disease of AIDS — the line of reasoning comes across as valid and reasonable.

AN ANNOTATED EXAMPLE

Arthur Ashe

Getting Serious about Academic Standards and Cutting Out Free Rides

Year after year, stories about them appear: former college athletes whose lives have hit bottom. They weren't quite good enough to make it to the pros, but they never received their college degrees, either. Some, we discover, can barely read and write. Once their four years of eligibility were used up and the colleges had milked the rewards of their athletic talents, these young men were left with nothing. It is this misuse of athletes, many of them African American, that the late Hall of Fame tennis player Arthur Ashe rails against. In this essay, which was syndicated to newspapers across the country, the former collegiate and professional tennis star and sports commentator supports a proposed tightening of academic requirements for athletic scholarships. His stance is indeed a controversial one, since a change in the regulations may mean that for some black youths the only avenue to college will be cut off.

What do colleges owe students to whom they grant athletic scholarships?

He uses the first four paragraphs to inform the reader about the controversy.

Georgetown University's basketball coach, John Thompson, is no longer boycotting his team's games to protest Proposition 42 — setting minimum academic standards for athletic scholarships — but the issue is far from decided. Shelved for now, the rule will be reconsidered by the National Collegiate Athletic Association next year. 1

Proposition 42 would deny major college athletic scholarships to high school students who fail to score a combined 700 (of a possible 1,600) on Scholastic Aptitude Tests, or 15 (of a possible 36) on the American College Test and fail to earn a 2.0 grade point average in 11 defined subjects. 2

Proposition 42 was a follow-up to Proposition 48, which was enacted in 1984, and under which, freshmen athletes who fail to meet those same standards are granted scholarships but forbidden to participate in varsity sports. They can regain athletic eligibility as sophomores by improving academic performance. 3

He notes some of the more prominent voices speaking against Proposition 42.

After one failed attempt, Proposition 42 passed by a vote of 163 to 154 — hardly a mandate. Protests swiftly followed. Mr. Thompson announced 4 his boycott. Harry Edwards, a sociologist at the University of California at Berkeley, called it "an elitist, racist travesty." John Chaney, Temple University's basketball coach, called it "racist and absurd." *Newsweek* said "There's got to be a better way."

He declares his stand on the issue.

Well, there may indeed be a better way. But so far we haven't found it. The rule still contains the most powerful inducement yet for high school athletes to abandon their cynical belief that they'll get a scholarship even if they don't bother to study.   5

He sets a pattern: first he presents a point held by those opposed to Proposition 42, and then he rebuts or debunks it.

It is conceivable that some college administrators see Proposition 42 as a convenient cover for a racist policy of reducing the numbers of black athletes who receive scholarships. But most probably see it as I do, as the only way to establish unequivocally the idea that a scholarship is a reward for academic as well as athletic skills and efforts, not an entitlement granted for athletic prowess alone.   6

Critics say that, intentionally or not, the rule discriminates against minority athletes. They point out that about 90 percent of its victims are black, and that the S.A.T.s and the A.C.T. are culturally biased. Maybe so. But just because the rule hurts some black athletes in the short run doesn't mean that it is wrong.   7

He spells out the cause of the problem and indicates who holds responsibility.

The critics talk about what colleges should do. They propose extending scholarship periods beyond four years, providing more and better academic counseling and limiting scholarships to schools with poor graduation rates. All address the deep-seated cynicism of   8 coddled, black public school athletes, many of whom are carried through school with inflated grades and peer group status that borders on deification. High school coaches need to be held accountable for the academic preparation of their would-be Michael Jordans.

He explains the basis for his theory.

The critics of Proposition 42 seriously underestimate the psychic value that black athletes place on their athletic success and how that could be used to motivate them academically. The screening process for superior athletes starts earlier — when they are 11 or 12 — and is more efficacious than for any other group of Americans. Social status is conferred at once. And they learn early that they don't get the idolatry, attention and, ultimately, Division I scholarships for their intellectual promise.

He suggests the effects of the imposition of Proposition 42.

Proposition 42 — or something like it — would motivate high school coaches and their best players to take education seriously. Most important, that dedication to academic concerns among athletes would set a tone in the schools that would very likely inspire nonathletes to study harder.

He concedes a potential problem, but then resumes the discussion by rebutting the point.

It is probably true that the immediate imposition of Proposition 42 would be unfair to high school juniors and seniors who haven't had a chance to adjust to the new standards. But the answer to that problem is simply to give fair warning of two years or so before enactment. That way, these streetwise 9th- and 10th-graders and their coaches would get the message that the free rides are over.

9

10

11

Are the standardized tests cultur- 12
ally biased? <u>Perhaps. They have been
shown to be poor predictors of college
success.</u> But a combined S.A.T. score of
700 is a low standard: it typically
places a student in the bottom 10th
percentile in the verbal portion and in
the bottom third percentile in math.

Is that too much to ask of athletes 13
who intend to attend a major university? After all, 85 percent of black freshmen athletes at Division I schools met
the Proposition 48 standards in 1988.
We need some sort of testing standard
like the S.A.T.s. Otherwise, the deadly
jump shot alone will virtually guaran-
tee the minimum 2.0 grade average.

He saves a powerful
specific example for
the end of his essay.

Finally, are we turning our backs on 14
athletes like <u>Notre Dame's quarterback,
Tony Rice, who scored 690 on the
S.A.T.s but subsequently earned his eligibility?</u> No. We should not be saying,
"See, Tony Rice got a 690, but counseling brought it up enough to quality."
Instead, we should be saying "Tony Rice
— and thousands like him — heard in
the ninth grade that if he didn't pay attention in class, he wouldn't get a scholarship, so he studied and succeeded."

He uses conclusion to
reaffirm his stand
and warn of the
consequences
otherwise.

It's no secret that 75 percent of black 15
football and basketball players fail to
graduate from college. With Proposition
42 tabled, that isn't likely to change. We
should either get serious about academic
standards or cut out the hypocrisy and
pay college athletes as professionals.

Black America stands to lose an- 16
other generation of our young men
unless they are helped to learn as well
as play ball.

Your Turn: Responding to the Subject

a. There is no mistaking Arthur Ashe's stance on Proposition 42 or any measure that would help drive home the point to talented high-school athletes that they must attend to their education. What's your view? For this assignment, take a stand on this issue. Should colleges tighten restrictions so that only those high-school athletes who are truly prepared for college-level work be awarded athletic scholarships?

b. Take the issue a step further by addressing whether stricter academic standards should be imposed in high schools — for example, should students be required to maintain a C average to be eligible for athletic teams, drama productions, band, or other extracurricular activities?

Frank Rich

The Sad Sitcom of TV Ratings

For a number of years, Frank Rich was the much respected theater critic for the New York Times *after earlier stints as editor and film critic at the* Times, *film critic at the* New York Post, *and cinema and television critic for* Time. *He has also contributed work to such periodicals as* Ms. *and* Esquire. *Several years ago, Rich made the move to the editorial page at the* New York Times, *where he now serves as one of the paper's featured columnists and writes on a broader array of subjects. He often focuses on news of the day or matters of popular culture, as in this piece dealing with the issue of rating television programming. In this essay, Rich explores the subject, arguing that the issue goes far beyond what type of rating system should be imposed.*

Who is — or should be — ultimately responsible for the quality of television programming?

It's always heartwarming to watch show-business executives,   *1* professional child advocates, congressmen and even the President fret over the television habits of America's youth. But after listening for a week now to the great and heated debate over the TV ratings that Jack Valenti is to hand down today with fanfare worthy of Moses and the Ten Commandments, it's clear that the nation's parents need more protection from fatuous reformers than their kids do from *Baywatch*.

The gist of the debate is as simplistic as it is beside the   *2* point. Valenti, the Hollywood lobbyist masterminding the ratings system, favors rating TV shows by age appropriateness, similar to the movie ratings he created 28 years ago. Everyone else wants ratings that label programing for its specific violent, sexual or four-letter content.

What no one will say is that even if content ratings prevail   *3* — which they should and eventually will — we'll still be almost back where we started. The ratings debate is not only in itself a fount of intellectually vacuous chat-show TV — how many politicians can dance on the head of a V-chip? — but is an escapist sideshow deflecting attention from any real discussion about the coarsening of our culture and the growing stranglehold of video in all its forms (including video games and the Internet's own junk programming) over the young, who watch 1,000 hours a year of television alone.

Parents do deserve all the information they can get in   4
helping to guide their children's viewing habits, and if more details are added by a ratings system, that will be a plus. But only a small plus. Such ratings will solely benefit parents who are already attentive to their children's TV diet, who already know much of the information they will convey.

Any parent who either doesn't yet know or care that the   5
prime-time hour starting at 8 p.m. is filled with sex-obsessed sitcoms — or that 10 p.m. shows like *N.Y.P.D. Blue* are not for children — or that pay-cable services like HBO and Showtime present unedited R-rated movies — is unlikely to heed detailed ratings now. And one need only look at those other ratings, the Nielsens, to see that these parents are in the vast majority.

Nor will that great push-button panacea, the V-chip, rescue   6
parents In either camp. For this Rube Goldberg invention to be effective, parents will have to replace every set in their household or equip every one with the device — a gesture that is not only costly but, again, will be carried out only by parents already on the case. Even those parents, however, may soon be in the market for family counseling. If they program their sets to block shows rated as inappropriate for 8-year-olds, they're going to have to answer to their angry teenagers. (This is assuming that a nation incapable of programming its VCRs will bother to activate the V-chip, once proudly installed, in the first place.)

Just as ratings and the V-chip are unlikely to change American TV habits (any more than movie ratings have elevated   7
moviegoing habits), so the debate about them has been a sea of red herrings. Much noise has been made about the fact that it's a "conflict of interest" for Hollywood to rate its own products, for instance, but what exactly is the alternative? Who will pay for and choose the ideological complexion of a huge bureaucracy that will have to be on 24-hour call to rate 2,000 hours of programming per day? No one has raised the more im-

portant issue of why commercials won't be rated — some are sexier than *Friends,* and sugary cereals can do more damage to kids than most TV — or why violent sports also get a free pass.

But these forgotten questions, too, pale against the big one of our national addiction to junk, and our refusal to take any personal responsibility for that behavior. It's adult consumers with spending power who drive the TV marketplace and set the example for the young; if adults were serious about eliminating coarse TV, they would turn off *Married . . . With Children* and refuse to subscribe to risqué cable channels. Sponsors would flee, cancellations would follow, channels would die. American children will never grow up in a healthier electronic environment unless their parents grow up first.

8

Understanding the Significance

1. Where does Frank Rich stand on the issue of providing ratings for television shows?
2. What is the difference between the two methods of rating television shows that Rich discusses?
3. Although Rich acknowledges that some type of rating system is probably necessary, what does he see as a more serious concern than identifying the proper method of rating shows?
4. In Rich's view, what is the obvious solution to the problem of objectionable television content?

Discovering the Writer's Purpose

1. Look again at the discussion of emphatic order on pp. 28–29. In your judgment, does Rich follow emphatic order in this essay? Explain your answer.
2. In paragraph 3, Rich mentions that the average young person watches 1,000 hours of television programming per year. What point is he making by citing this number?

3. In paragraph 6, Rich focuses on a number of potential problems related to the V-chip. Why do you think Rich discusses this aspect of the subject in such detail?
4. What point is Rich making in the final paragraph where he mentions personal responsibility?

Examining the Writer's Method

1. In the introduction to Rich's essay, what sense do you get about his attitude toward the debate over television ratings?
2. In his essay, Rich mentions four television shows by name. Why do you think he uses these shows as examples? Do you agree with his choices? Why or why not?
3. Rich devotes most of his attention in this essay to showing the flaws in the arguments of proponents of different rating systems. How does this approach help him to make his point about dealing with the content of various television shows?
4. What does Rich use his conclusion to emphasize?

Considering Style and Language

1. How would you describe Rich's tone in this essay?
2. In the third and sixth paragraphs, Rich discusses the V-chip. What is his attitude about the effectiveness of the V-chip? How can you tell?
3. Rich refers to the debate about television ratings as "a sea of red herrings." What is he suggesting?
4. What do the following words mean in the context of the writing? Advocate, fret, fanfare, fatuous (para. 1); gist, simplistic (para. 2); prevail, fount, vacuous (para. 3); convey (para. 4); heed (para. 5); ideological, bureaucracy (para. 7); risqué (para. 8).

Your Turn: Responding to the Subject

a. Today both movies and network television programming are subject to rating systems. For this assignment, consider one of these systems and then imagine that you have been asked to improve it. What changes would you make? Why? Then write an essay in which you present and defend your own rating system.

b. Early in his essay, Frank Rich laments what he calls "the coarsening of our culture," and in his conclusion he suggests that one reason for this increased crudeness is the unwillingness of people to exercise personal responsibility. Do you agree — is society in such a mess because people in general simply don't take personal responsibility for their actions? Or do you think such a view is too simplistic, that the types of changes in our society that Rich discusses are the result of a number of factors? For this assignment, take a stand on this issue.

Barbara Mujica
Bilingualism's Goal

An issue that is still hotly debated is how U.S. children who don't yet speak English should be educated. In response to dictates from state and federal officials, most school systems facing this problem have instituted some form of bilingual education through which students are taught in their native language while they are learning to read and write English. Proponents of such programs feel strongly that this type of classroom experience is clearly the best for bilingual students, who would otherwise feel inferior or left out in traditional classes. As Barbara Mujica's essay shows, however, not everyone agrees with this point of view. In this writing, which first appeared in the New York Times, *she advocates changing the way bilingual education is provided so that, although all cultures are embraced and validated, the emphasis is on ensuring that students enter the English-speaking mainstream as soon as possible.*

Is it the parents' or the schools' job to inculcate a student's cultural heritage?

Mine is a Spanish-speaking household. We use Spanish exclusively. I have made an effort not only to encourage use of the language but also to familiarize my children with Hispanic culture. I use books from Latin America to teach them to read and write, and I try to maintain close contacts with Spanish-speaking relatives. Instilling in my children a sense of family and ethnic identity is my role; it is not the role of the school system. 1

The public schools, supported by public funds, have the responsibility to teach skills needed in public life — among them the use of the English language. They also must inculcate an appreciation of all the cultures that have contributed to this country's complex social weave. To set one ethnic group apart as more worthy of attention than others is unjust, and might breed resentment against that group. 2

I differ with educators who advocate bilingual education 3
programs whose goal is to preserve the Spanish language and
culture among children of Hispanic families. These professionals argue that in an English-speaking environment, Spanish-
speaking children often feel alienated and that this causes them
to become withdrawn and hostile. To prevent this reaction,
they say, the home environment must be simulated at school.

Imagine how much more alienated these youngsters will 4
feel, however, if they are kept in special bilingual programs
separate from the general student body, semester after semester. How much more uncomfortable they will feel if they are
maintained in ghettos in the school. Youngsters feel a need to
conform. They imitate each other in dress and in habit. To iso-
late Spanish-speaking children from their English-speaking
peers may prove more psychologically damaging than hurling
them into an English-speaking environment with no transition courses at all.

The purpose of bilingual education must be to teach Eng- 5
lish to non-English-speaking youngsters so that they will be
able to function in regular classes.

The term "bilingual education" encompasses a huge vari- 6
ety of programs ranging from total immersion to special
classes for foreigners to curricula that offer courses in mathematics and history in the child's native language. The most effective bilingual education programs have as their goal the
gradual incorporation of non-English-speaking students into
regular programs in which English is used.

Not all children of Spanish-speaking parents need bilin- 7
gual education. Many Spanish-speaking parents oppose the
placement of their children in special programs; the wishes of
these parents should be respected. Furthermore, very young
children are able to learn a foreign language rapidly; bilingual
programs for the nursery, kindergarten and early primary
years should be kept to a minimum. Older children who have
done part of their schooling in a foreign country often need
to be eased into an English-speaking curriculum more gently.
For them, it is helpful to offer certain subjects in their native
tongues until they have learned English; otherwise, they may
feel so lost and frustrated that they will drop out of school.
High school dropouts have less chance than others of finding

satisfying careers and are more likely to find themselves in trouble and unemployed.

Hispanics are now the fastest-growing minority in the United States. According to the Population Reference Bureau, a private organization, Hispanics, counted at 14.6 million in the 1980 census, may well number 47 million by the year 2020. Yet, they are notoriously underrepresented in the arts, sciences, professions and politics. Economically, as a group, they tend to lag behind non-Hispanics. According to March 1983 Federal figures, the median income for Hispanics is $16,227; for non-Hispanics, $23,907. Certainly, part of the remedy is educational programs that give young people the preparation and confidence necessary to pursue satisfying careers. **8**

To get better jobs, young people must be fluent in English. Without English, they will be stuck in menial positions. Without English, they will be unable to acquire advanced degrees. Without English, they will be unable to protest to the proper authorities if they are abused. Non-English-speaking individuals are vulnerable to not only economic but also political exploitation. Too often, politicians who speak their language claim unjustly to represent their interests. **9**

The primary goal of bilingual education must be the mainstreaming of non-English-speaking children through the teaching of English. But while the schools teach my children English, I will continue to teach them Spanish at home, because Spanish is part of their heritage. Ethnic identity, like religion, is a family matter. **10**

Understanding the Significance

1. When it comes to educating students for whom English is a second language, what does Barbara Mujica feel that parents should do? What does she think schools should do?
2. Why does Mujica feel bilingual programs are not always appropriate for children?
3. Why in particular does Mujica feel that young children don't need bilingual programs?

4. According to Mujica, how will a reduction of the number of bilingual programs translate into better opportunities for the affected students?

Discovering the Writer's Purpose

1. How would you describe Mujica's tone in this essay?
2. Why do you think Mujica chooses to limit paragraph 5 to a single sentence?
3. In this essay, do you feel Mujica relies more on appeals to logic, emotion, reputation, or some combination? Explain.
4. Clearly Mujica's essay persuades, but does it also inform and entertain? Explain your answer.

Examining the Writer's Method

1. What impression do you feel Mujica makes by arranging her introduction so that she first lists the various ways she teaches her children about their culture and then presents her stand on the issue?
2. Mujica relies on a number of modes in combination to make her point. Which mode do you feel provides the strongest support? Explain.
3. Why do you feel Mujica saves the statistics that support her case until paragraph 8?
4. In this essay, Mujica both advocates her own position and rebuts opposing arguments. Do you feel she is more successful when she supports her own view or when she refutes the opposing points? Why?

Considering Style and Language

1. Mujica makes references several times to her own experiences. How does this use of firsthand experiences help her make her point?

2. Mujica does not completely dismiss the need for bilingual programs. What advantage does she gain in proceeding this way?
3. How does the final image of Mujica's essay help reiterate her main point?
4. What do the following words mean in the context of the essay? Exclusively, familiarize, Hispanic, instilling (para. 1); inculcate, breed (para. 2); alienated, simulated (para. 3); ghettos, transition (para. 4); encompasses, incorporation (para. 6); notoriously, median (para. 8); menial, vulnerable, exploitation (para. 9).

Your Turn: Responding to the Subject

a. In this essay, Mujica is clearly opposed to any bilingual education program that doesn't have as its goal the mainstreaming students into classrooms where English is spoken. She also feels that parents should have a big say concerning how such classes are conducted. How do you feel about these issues? Do you think classes should be taught in the student's native language or in English? Explain and support your opinion.
b. Regardless of the subject, how much power should parents have to influence what is taught in schools? For example, should parents be able to dictate whether sex education is presented in schools, whether controversial books are available or taught, whether subjects such as homosexuality and euthanasia are discussed, and so on? For this assignment, take a stand on one of these issues.

Thomas Sowell
Ability and Biology

Thomas Sowell, whose newspaper column is syndicated in over 150 newspapers across the United States, is currently the Rose and Milton Friedman Senior Fellow in Public Policy at the Hoover Institute. He is also the author of a number of books, including several on economics, social policy, the history of ideas, and cultural history. He holds degrees in economics from Harvard University and Columbia University, as well as a Ph.D. in economics from the University of Chicago, and he has worked as an economist and researcher in the fields of government and business. In addition, he has taught economics at a number of leading colleges and universities, including Cornell, Amherst, Rutgers, and UCLA. This piece originally appeared as a "My Turn" essay in Newsweek; *Sowell, considered by some to be among the most influential and scholarly black conservatives in the United States, suggests that the concept of racial or ethnic groups automatically possessing innate abilities in certain fields is little more than a stereotype. He argues instead that any ability is the result of a person's heredity rather than the individual's ethnic or racial origin and that environment affects the development of any ability.*

Are members of a particular racial or ethnic group more similar to each other than to members of society in general, or are all of us truly unique individuals regardless of ethnic or racial heritage?

Mathematical ability and musical ability may not seem on the surface to be connected, but people who have researched the subject — and studied the brain — say that they are. Research for my book "Late-Talking Children" drove home the point to me. Three quarters of the bright but speech-delayed children in the group I studied had a close relative who was an engineer, mathematician or scientist — and four fifths had a close relative who played a musical instrument. The children themselves usually took readily to math and other analytical subjects — and to music.

1

Black, white and Asian children in this group show the   2
same patterns. However, looking at the larger world around us,
it is clear that blacks have been greatly overrepresented in the
development of American popular music and greatly underrepresented in such fields as mathematics, science and engineering.

If the abilities required in analytical fields and in music are   3
so closely related, how can there be this great disparity? One
reason is that the development of mathematical and other such
abilities requires years of formal schooling, while certain musical talents can be developed with little or no formal training, as
has happened with a number of well-known black musicians.

It is precisely in those kinds of music where one can ac-   4
quire great skill without formal training that blacks have excelled — popular music rather than classical music, piano
rather than violin, blues rather than opera. This is readily understandable, given that most blacks, for most of American
history, have not had either the money or the leisure for long
years of formal study in music.

Blacks have not merely held their own in American popular   5
music. They have played a disproportionately large role in the
development of jazz, both traditional and modern. A long string
of names comes to mind — Duke Ellington, Scott Joplin, W. C.
Handy, Louis Armstrong, Charlie Parker . . . and on and on.

None of this presupposes any special innate ability of blacks   6
in music. On the contrary, it is perfectly consistent with blacks'
having no more such inborn ability than anyone else, but
being limited to being able to express such ability in narrower
channels than others who have had the money, the time and
the formal education to spread out over a wider range of music,
as well as into mathematics, science and engineering.

There is no way of knowing whether Duke Ellington would   7
have become a mathematician or scientist under other circumstances. What is clearer is that most blacks have not had
such alternatives available until very recently, as history is measured. Moreover, now that cultural traditions have been established, even those blacks who have such alternatives available
today, and who have the inborn abilities to pursue them, may
nevertheless continue for some time to follow well-worn paths.

In these supersensitive times, merely suggesting that there is   8
such a thing as inborn ability is taboo. Yet the evidence is over-

whelming that mental abilities run in families, even when the families are broken up when the children are young and siblings are raised separately and in complete isolation from one another.

When it comes to the role of heredity and environment, a   *9* key sentence written all in italics has nevertheless been one of the most ignored sentences in one of the most widely discussed books of our time: *That a trait is genetically transmitted in individuals does not mean that group differences in that trait are also genetic in origin.* This sentence is from "The Bell Curve," a book routinely accused of being racist, especially by those who have not read it.

What this italicized sentence is saying, in effect, is that en-   *10* vironmental differences between two groups may be much greater than environmental differences between two individuals chosen at random from the general population. Since tests measure developed capabilities, rather than inborn potential, you would expect groups from very different environments to differ in particular capabilities, even if most differences among individuals are due to heredity.

That makes sense when you stop and think about it. What   *11* is remarkable is how few people have stopped to think about it before going ballistic. Mention genetics and it will be taken as a code word for race. But, within every race, there are genetic differences among individuals and families.

There are important biological differences that are not ge-   *12* netic. Recent research has indicated that the brain's physical development is promoted by an environment in which there is much interaction with a baby during the brain's early formative years.

If even half of what has been said about the old-fashioned   *13* "Jewish mother" is true, then her busy, talkative attentiveness to her children may have given major lifelong advantages to the very children who later complained about how smothered they felt.

Contrast that with other cultural groups and social classes   *14* who pay little attention to small children, replying to their questions with impatient short answers or even telling them to shut up. More than a quarter of a century ago, Edward Banfield's classic study of urban life, "The Unheavenly City," said that this unresponsive reaction to children's questions and comments was characteristic of a lower-class lifestyle and pointed out how stunted the development of such children might be. Now brain research backs him up.

Those who argue that there is no innate difference in the 15 mental abilities of different racial and ethnic groups often conclude that different social results must therefore reflect discrimination by "society." But equal innate potential at the moment of conception does not necessarily mean equal mental capacity even at the moment of birth, given the many prenatal influences at work, such as the mother's use of alcohol or drugs.

Add differences in child-rearing practices and the culture 16 of the home and the street, and there can be very large differences among children from different backgrounds before they ever reach the first employer or otherwise encounter the larger society.

Understanding the Significance

1. In the opening of his essay, Thomas Sowell first discusses research findings that indicate a link between musical and mathematical abilities. Then he points out the disproportionately small number of African Americans in mathematics-related fields versus the large number of blacks who have achieved success in popular music in the United States. According to Sowell, what explains this discrepancy?
2. What explanation does Sowell offer for why so many blacks have excelled in American popular music?
3. What does the research indicate about heredity and mental abilities?
4. What does research suggest about the connection between environment and mental ability?

Discovering the Writer's Purpose

1. Why do you think that Sowell opens his essay by citing research findings that indicate that abilities needed for mastery of music and mathematics exist across racial and ethnic boundaries?

2. In the fifth paragraph, Sowell lists a number of blacks who are giants of American jazz. He then says in the sixth paragraph that their success is not the result of any innate ability enjoyed by African Americans. What is he saying about aptitude?

3. In paragraph 7, Sowell notes that as a result of "cultural traditions," some African Americans who enjoy both innate abilities and greater opportunities to develop them still may "follow well-worn paths." What point is he making?

4. By contrasting the parenting associated with the stereotype of an "old-fashioned 'Jewish mother'" (paragraph 13) with the parenting of people who demonstrate the "characteristic of a lower-class lifestyle" (paragraph 14), what is Sowell suggesting about child rearing?

Examining the Writer's Method

1. How do the statistics to which Sowell refers in his introductory paragraphs help him set up his argument?

2. The subject that Sowell addresses in his essay is one that causes many people to go, as Sowell puts it in paragraph 11, "ballistic." In your view, how does Sowell manage to make his point without resorting to or calling for a highly emotional reaction?

3. Which point provided by Sowell does the best job supporting his point? Why do you think this point is so strong?

4. How does Sowell's final paragraph serve as an effective conclusion for his essay?

Considering Style and Language

1. How would you describe the tone in Sowell's essay?

2. In the ninth paragraph, Sowell refers to *The Bell Curve,* the much debated, highly controversial text about race and IQ, as "a book routinely accused of being racist, especially by those who have not read it." By referring to *The Bell Curve* in this way, what is Sowell suggesting about the entire debate about ability and race or ethnicity?

3. Sowell takes issue in paragraph 15 with those who argue that no innate differences between racial groups exist and conclude that the differences in achievement between groups are the result of prejudice. How does putting the word *society* within quotation marks help him to indicate that he disagrees?

4. What do the following words mean in the context of the writing? Analytical (para. 1); overrepresented, underrepresented (para. 2); disparity (para. 3); presupposes, innate (para. 6), taboo (para. 8); trait, genetic (para. 9); environmental, random (para. 10); ballistic (para. 11); formative (para. 12); attentiveness, smothered (para. 13); stunted (para. 14); prenatal (para. 15).

Your Turn: Responding to the Subject

a. Sowell's essay deals in part with the issue of child rearing. For example, the research he cites about aptitude indicates that regardless of ethnicity or race, children need both opportunity and attention to develop their innate abilities fully. For this assignment, focus on this subject and write an essay which answers the following question: What is the single most important factor in raising a child?

b. Because there is no way to ensure that all children enjoy the same supportive environment at home, perhaps the answer is to change our educational system. For this assignment, explain how you would modify our public schools so they would do a better job meeting the needs of all children.

Other Possibilities for Argument Essays

The following is a list of topics that are suitable for argument papers. As they stand, however, these topics are merely starting points. After choosing and adapting one so that it reflects the issue as you'd like to address it, you must decide whether to take a stand for or against the issue and then develop a sufficient number of details and examples to support that stance.

- forced "outings" of prominent homosexuals
- English as the national language of the United States
- a limit on any classroom discussion that is not "politically correct"
- changes in the way prepared-food products are labeled in terms of ingredients
- the legalization of assisted suicide for terminally ill patients
- a ban on television advertisements for beer and other alcoholic beverages
- use of alternative sentencing such as home confinement, boot camps, or extended community service for some lawbreakers
- laws requiring the use of automobile seat belts or motorcycle helmets
- mandatory recycling of paper, glass, and plastic products
- warning labels or other restrictions on music and music videos
- use of fetal tissue for treatment of medical conditions such as Parkinson's disease
- the elimination of the F grade
- the practice of harvesting human kidneys from live donors in third-world countries by U.S. "organ brokers"
- the imposition of dress codes in public schools
- the elimination or modification of tenure in education

Practical Application: Argument

Tacked to the bulletin board above your desk is an article from last week's local newspaper. It details the plans of a local demolition firm, Aloysius Brothers, Inc., to construct what company officials are calling a trash–recycling transfer station on a ten-acre site bordering your neighborhood. The firm plans to truck solid waste to the site, where recyclables will be removed and the rest stored for transfer to the city's landfill at a later time. Right now, the area is zoned for residential and light business use only, and a trash–recycling transfer station doesn't fit this designation. Therefore, the demolition firm is seeking a zoning variance from the city planning board.

You have saved the clipping because you oppose the project, and you are sure that if people had a fuller understanding of the ramifications of such a plan, they would definitely join you in opposition and urge their elected officials to reject the Aloysius Brothers' request. To give people a fuller understanding, you have decided to take advantage of the opportunity your area newspaper provides and prepare a guest editorial on the subject.

To prepare to write the editorial, you quickly jot down some reasons that the plan should be rejected, including the following:

- The city already has a full-scale, active landfill in the east end of town. For years, this area has been plagued with problems associated with the landfill, including foul odors, groundwater pollution from rain running off the mountain of trash, and dust and trash remnants blowing about. One landfill is bad enough. Why add a second potential problem?
- The site contains several areas that appear to be wetlands, home to unique plant and animal species. Draining and filling these areas will permanently destroy their habitat.
- Such a project has the potential of lowering property values for people who own homes in the surrounding area. When these people built or bought their homes, they had every

expectation that the zoning would remain constant. Now they face the prospect of grave financial consequences.

- Once a zoning change is made for the trash–recycling transfer station, no additional variance will be needed if the owners decide to convert the site to an actual full-scale landfill.
- Instead of building a trash–recycling transfer station, Aloysius Brothers could donate the land to the city in the form of a land trust. The company would realize a tax advantage of several million dollars and the city could convert the land into a nature trail.
- The plans call for as many as fify eighteen-wheeler dump trucks to bring trash to the site each day. The only safe access to the area is by an elementary school and then through a closely settled residential neighborhood. (This point is a particular concern to you, since your home is on the road leading to the site.) This factor will translate into a dramatic increase in traffic and danger, especially to the neighborhood children.
- The site borders Watuppa Pond, a small body of water that feeds the city's water supply. Although the company claims to have a plan to keep any run-off from the trash–recycling transfer station from reaching the water, officials have offered no concrete proof that the company can actually do so.
- The property need not be turned into a trash–recycling transfer station to make it profitable to Aloysius Brothers. Over 1,000 feet of the land is on the shore of Watuppa Pond, making the property highly attractive to people who would like to build homes with a water view. The rest of the land slopes upward, providing great views of both the pond and the north end of the city.

Now choose the strongest reasons to reject the request for a zoning change and write an editorial of *five hundred to eight hundred words*. If additional strong ideas occur to you as you are developing your editorial, feel free to include them. Use the following guest editorial entitled "If You Truly Care about Your Pets," written by Therese C. MacKinnon of the Potter League for Animals on the need to have pets spayed or neutered as a guide in terms of *approach* and *format*.

If You Truly Care about Your Pets . . .

When I was seven, I saw a neighborhood girl carrying a cardboard box. The children surrounding her were squealing with delight. There in the box were 4 adorable black and white kittens. The girl's cat had had babies and they couldn't keep them. Would I like one, she asked? I was elated as I skipped home with my furry bundle, announcing that we had a new kitten. My mother reluctantly agreed to keep her, and we named her White Socks.

Seven short months later, White Socks had her own litter of five beautiful kittens. This was all so exciting for my siblings and me. But one morning, a man in a uniform came to the door. He examined each kitten, telling my mother which were the males and which the females. Slowly I realized that he was there to take them away.

Mom picked out one male kitten to keep. Over my sobbing and pleading, she tried to explain that we couldn't keep them all. Her words fell on the deaf ears of a broken-hearted seven-year-old. All I knew was that I was losing my beloved Socks and her babies.

The real sadness of White Socks' story is not that a little girl lost her pet. The tragedy is that Socks and her kittens probably lost their lives that day. It's likely that the soft-spoken man from the city pound picked up several more litters of puppies and kittens that day. It's probable that, much as they tried, the people at the pound were unable to find new homes for most of them. There were just too many animals then and, although the numbers have declined, there are still too many now.

Pet overpopulation has been a recognized problem in America since the 1920s when, in New York City alone, in 1928, 287,000 surplus cats and dogs were destroyed. Had pet sterilization been an option then, there would have been no excuse for such a tragedy. Now that it is so routine, one would think that such tragedies no longer occur. But we are still not controlling the breeding.

Many of the reasons why people don't alter their animals are based on myths and misconceptions. One excuse is the expense. The fact is, breeding a pet is far more expensive in the long run. Think of the food and supplies required for 4 to 10 puppies or kittens and a nursing mom for 2 to 4 months.

Then there are veterinary visits for worming, first vaccinations and exams. Medical complications are possible before, during and after birth. And think of the tax dollars spent on the thousands of surplus animals brought to shelters every year.

Licensing fees are often higher for unaltered pets than for sterilized animals. And unaltered animals have far more health problems throughout their lives than those altered. Financially, spaying and neutering is just good sense.

Another belief is that neutering changes a pet's personality. This is true, in a way. Altered pets become more relaxed, playful and content and more interested in their human family and home.

Altered males in particular are much less aggressive toward other animals and people. The overwhelming desires to wander, to mark their territory and to fight for mates are eliminated. Females no longer go into heat. These urges undeniably help wild animals to survive, but they are not desirable traits in a domestic pet. Simply put, an altered animal makes a more pleasing pet.

Another common myth is that a female should have one litter before she is spayed. Medically speaking, giving birth does nothing beneficial for a pet. In fact, spaying is a more complicated and expensive operation after a birth has occurred.

Overall, the health benefits associated with spaying and neutering are tremendous! Unspayed dogs and cats are highly at risk for breast tumors, breast inflammations, uterus infections, ovarian cysts and cancers.

Unneutered animals are equally at risk of developing enlarged prostates and testicular and prostate cancers. In general, the life expectancies of spayed and neutered animals are double those of unaltered pets.

In 1996, authorities conservatively estimated that about 4.2 million surplus dogs and cats were euthanized in America the previous year. Thousands more were abandoned roadside, in wooded areas and in dumpsters by people who found themselves with too many pets. These animals spent their brief lives searching for food, coping with disease and the elements, and defending themselves against wild animals.

Such facts are astonishing when the solution is so simple. All we need to do is stop the breeding! And the simplest way to do that is to spay and neuter our companion animals. The very best reason for spaying and neutering is that it is the responsible thing to do.

Glossary

Abstract language refers to concepts, ideas, qualities, and other intangibles — for example, freedom, creativity, and greed — as opposed to concrete language, which refers to tangible items, individuals, and locales.

Active reading is the process of critically examining the context, structure, and key ideas of a writing.

Active voice is a way of arranging a sentence so that the subject is doing the action — "Jacqueline reviewed the movie" — as opposed to passive voice, in which the subject is acted upon — "The movie was reviewed by Jacqueline." An active-voice sentence is generally shorter and more direct than a passive-voice sentence.

Aim — see **Purpose**.

Allusion is a reference to a work of literature, real or fictional individuals, events, places, and so on. For instance, "These accusations suggest a cover-up of Watergate proportions," is an allusion to the political scandal that eventually led to the resignation of President Richard Nixon in 1974. For an allusion to be effective, it must refer to something the reader could easily recognize.

Alternating method involves arranging the elements of a comparison and contrast analysis so that you switch back and forth between subjects as you discuss the elements or features under discussion. In the block method, you discuss all the elements or features in relation to one subject and then all the same elements in relation to the second subject. In a paper arranged in the alternating method about competing fast-food restaurants, you would discuss restaurant A then restaurant B on the basis of the variety of food available, then restaurant A on quality of service and restaurant B on quality of service, and so on. With the same paper arranged in the block method, you would first discuss all the features in terms of restaurant A and then discuss all the features in terms of restaurant B. With the mixed method, you use a combination of both types.

Ambiguity is a lack of clarity leading to the possibility of multiple interpretations of words, phrases, or sentences rather than the one meaning intended.

Amplifying means providing numerous specific details, illustrations, and explanations to communicate full meaning to a reader.

Analogy is an extended comparison of two dissimilar things used as illustration — for instance, the suggestion that shoveling out after the fourth snowstorm in five days is like fighting a war.

Anecdote is a short, often humorous story about a person's experience, intended to illustrate or support some point.

Appeals on the basis of emotions, logic, and reputation are the three methods used to persuade a reader. An appeal to emotions, from the Greek *pathos,* involves attempting to convince the reader through details, claims, or statements that stir the reader's feelings. An appeal to logic, from the Greek *logos,* involves a massing of factual evidence to convince the reader. An appeal to reputation, from the Greek *ethos,* involves relying on the writer's good standing, esteem, or name to sway the reader.

Approach refers to the combination of techniques used to fulfill the purpose in a piece of writing.

Argument refers to writings whose primary aim is to persuade the reader to accept a point of view as valid.

Argument ad hominem is a logical fallacy. A writer makes this error by attacking the individual holding a position rather than attacking the position itself: "Since he didn't rank in the upper ten percent of his medical school graduating class, why pay any attention to Dr. Peter Neville's views on health care reform?"

Audience is the reader or group of readers to whom you direct your writing. To write effectively, you must always identify and address the needs of your audience.

Awkwardness refers to parts of a writing that, although not grammatically incorrect, don't effectively or efficiently communicate the writer's ideas.

Bandwagon approach is a logical fallacy that results when the writer urges acceptance of a point of view solely because others hold that view: "Nobody is interested in endangered species anymore."

Begging the question is a logical fallacy. This mistake in reasoning occurs when the writer expresses as fact something that is actually an opinion. To state, "Wearing seat belts does not reduce the risk of serious injury, so seat belt laws should be abolished," is to beg the question, because no evidence has been presented that seat belts don't reduce the risk of injury.

Block method — see **Alternating method.**

Body in an essay is the series of paragraphs that provide support for the thesis.

Brainstorming — see **Prewriting.**

Branching — see **Prewriting.**

Cause and effect is a rhetorical mode used to examine what leads to or has led to something (cause) and what will occur or has occurred as a result (effect). In some cases, the focus in an essay is on cause, sometimes on effect, and sometimes on both.

Chronological order is the arrangement of events in the order that they actually occurred. Sometimes chronological order is altered for some effect through the use of a flashback, an event deliberately presented out of sequence.

Classification is a rhetorical mode through which items, concepts, individuals, and so on are grouped to make them easier to understand. It is generally discussed along with division, the rhetorical mode through which a single subject is separated into its component parts in order to make it easier to understand.

Clichés are tired, overused expressions, such as "like looking for a needle in a haystack" or "the bottom line," that should be avoided in writing because they add no freshness or originality.

Clustering — see **Prewriting.**

Coherence is achieved in writing when all the elements are effectively and logically presented. A coherent essay follows a set order with appropriate paragraphs and transitions so that the reader can easily follow the ideas expressed.

Command — see **Imperative mood.**

Comma splice is a serious sentence error in which a comma is used between two sentences rather than a period or semicolon. To correct a comma splice, either (1) change the comma to a period or other appropriate mark of end punctuation, (2) change it to a semicolon, or (3) insert a conjunction after the comma.

Comparison and contrast is a rhetorical mode used to examine similarities (comparison) and differences (contrast). Three methods are available for arranging an essay featuring comparison and contrast: the alternating method, the block method, and the mixed method.

Composing is the stage of the writing process during which you develop the ideas from the prewriting stage into sentences, which are then arranged in paragraphs to create a draft version of the final writing.

Conclusion is the final section of a writing that brings it to a logical, appropriate, or pleasing close. With an essay, a conclusion is often a single paragraph. A common concluding technique is to restate the thesis and the ideas supporting or illustrating it. Additional techniques include closing with a relevant quotation, relating an anecdote, and raising a question.

Concrete language — see **Abstract language.**

Connotation is an additional subjective meaning attached to or inspired by a word, whereas the denotation is the exact, literal dictionary definition of a word. The denotation of the term *immature,* for example, is to be not fully grown or developed, yet the connotations include to be childish, irresponsible, and inexperienced. Therefore, to ensure that the reader understands your point as you intend to make it, you must carefully consider the denotations and connotations of the words you use.

Content refers to the various examples, ideas, and details used in a piece of writing.

Context means the overall setting or circumstances of an event or situation. When you read critically, you must identify the context of the selection in order to understand the writer's motives and approach.

Contrast — see **Comparison and contrast.**

Critical reading skills are those steps — including identifying the writer's purpose, reading actively, and focusing on the writer's technique — that enable you to understand a writing more fully.

Dangling modifier is an error in which there is no appropriate object in a sentence for a modifying word or phrase to modify: "Sailing down the river, the improvements in water quality were evident." To correct this error, restate the sentence so that *Sailing down the river* modifies an appropriate word: "Sailing down the river, Christa could see that water quality had improved."

Deduction is a type of reasoning that involves moving from general statements to a specific conclusion, as opposed to induction, which involves moving from specific instances to a general conclusion. When you conclude that a muscular woman must be a bodybuilder because bodybuilders are muscular, you have used deductive reasoning.

Definition is a rhetorical mode through which the characteristics of an item, individual, concept, and so on are delineated. In some cases, you'll use a limited definition, a one- or two-sentence explanation, and in other cases you'll prepare an extended definition, a multiparagraph discussion.

Denotation — see **Connotation.**

Description is a rhetorical mode through which specific, vivid details and examples, expressed objectively or subjectively, are used to recreate a situation, capture a scene, recall an individual, or explain a concept or feeling. (See also **Objective description.**)

Dialect is dialogue that is presented and spelled to represent the particular sound of a geographical area, social class, and ethnic or racial group — for example, *gonna* rather than *going to, wunst* rather than *once,* and *cain't* rather than *can't.*

Dialogue consists of the conversation of two or more people, recorded as it was expressed and presented within quotation marks.

Diction is the writer's choice and use of words. Depending on the writer's aim and the needs of the reader, the diction of a writing may range from formal to conversational or colloquial, occasionally including uses of slang.

Division is a rhetorical mode through which a single subject is separated into its component parts in order to make that subject easier to understand. It is often discussed along with classification, the rhetorical mode through which items, concepts, individuals, and so on are grouped to make them easier to understand.

Editing is the step in the revising stage of writing during which you polish what you have already developed. It consists of two parts: tightening and proofreading.

Effect — see **Cause and effect.**

Either/or reasoning is a logical fallacy which results when the writer suggests that only two possibilities or solutions exist: "If you want to succeed in business, you must be an outstanding public speaker."

Ellipsis is a series of three spaced periods used to indicate an omission from a quotation.

Emphatic order, also occasionally called "dramatic order" or "least-to-most-significant" order, is a method of arrangement in which you present the supporting examples and details from strong to stronger saving the strongest support for the end. (See also **Order**.)

Essay is a relatively short multiparagraph nonfiction writing in which a thesis is specified and then developed, explained, or illustrated. It consists of three parts: an introduction, body, and conclusion.

Ethos — see **Appeals**.

Etymology is the origin or derivation of a word.

Euphemism is a word or phrase used in place of another because the original word was considered offensive, inflammatory, or objectionable in some way — for instance, *revenue enhancement* rather than *taxes* and *passing away* rather than *dying*.

Example is a rhetorical mode through which you provide a series of circumstances, instances, conditions, locales, concepts, or individuals to illustrate some point. In a more general sense, example also refers to any circumstances, instances, conditions, and so on used to help you make your point.

Extended definition refers to a multi-paragraph presentation that delineates in detail the characteristics of a subject.

Fact is a verifiable truth as opposed to an opinion, which is a reasoning based on fact. It's a fact that driving on icy roads is dangerous because it can be proven that more accidents occur when roads are icy. It's an opinion to say that your city didn't do an adequate job treating icy roads last week because there were numerous accidents: those accidents may have been caused by other factors such as excessive speed, mechanical failure, inexperienced drivers, and so on.

Figurative language refers to expression that is symbolic rather than literal, the purpose being to achieve some effect. Common figures of speech include the following:

- metaphor — implied comparison between two dissimilar subjects: "Their evening together was a dream."
- simile — explicit comparison between two dissimilar subjects: "This course is like a mystery movie."

- personification — the granting of human qualities to an inanimate object: "The wind whispered through the trees surrounding the first-time campers."
- analogy — extended comparison between dissimilar subjects, generally intended to make the first subject easier to understand: "Self-esteem is like the foundation for a building. If the foundation is weak, even a small structure will fall, but if the foundation is strong enough, a skyscraper can be erected."
- hyperbole — overstatement for effect: "All you could see in the dorm room was dirty laundry and empty pizza boxes."
- understatement — undercutting for effect: "Being pulled over in front of my mother's office while I was driving her car was a little embarrassing."

Flashback — see **Chronological order.**

Form refers to surface elements of writing such as spelling, usage, punctuation, and so on.

Format involves the physical arrangement of a document.

Fragment — see **Sentence fragment.**

Freewriting — see **Prewriting.**

General language — see **Specific language.**

Hasty generalization is a logical fallacy that results when a claim is based on too little proof or on proof that isn't representative: "Last year's extremely cold winter shows that the Gulf Stream has now shifted." Actually, many years of consistently lower temperatures would have to be observed and documented before meteorologists would make such a claim.

Homonyms are words that sound the same but are spelled differently and have different meanings. Troublesome homonyms include *it's/its, they're/there/their, to/too/two, who's/whose,* and *you're/your.*

Homophones—see **Homonyms**

How-to writing, also called a set of instructions, refers to a type of process writing that involves explaining how to do something.

Hyperbole — see **Figurative language.**

Illustration refers to those details, cases, and instances that you use to make some point clear for the reader. (See also **Example.**)

Image is capturing in words a vivid moment or experience. An image can be either literal or figurative. (See also **Figurative language.**)

Imperative mood, also called command, refers to a sentence construction in which the reader is addressed directly, with the subject implied or understood rather than directly stated: "Connect the printer to the computer on the left." In this case, the subject is the individual who is being told to connect the printer.

Induction is a type of reasoning that involves moving from specific instances to a general conclusion, as opposed to deduction, which involves moving from general statements to a specific conclusion. When you decide that damage to your lawn has been caused by skunks digging for insects, because skunks are known to dig under turf for bugs, you have used inductive reasoning. With induction, reaching a conclusion involves an inductive leap; that is, although the specific instances suggest the finding, the conclusion is still a leap into possibility rather than an established fact.

Introduction is the opening section of a writing, which introduces the thesis, directing and engaging the reader. With an essay, the introduction is often a single paragraph. Common introductory techniques include using an anecdote, providing relevant statistics or facts, including a famous saying or quotation, and asking a leading question.

Irony refers to a situation or experience that is contrary to logic or to what might normally be expected. In writing it is the use of language to express a meaning different from and often opposite of the literal meaning of those words. A statement such as, "And then she fired me — the perfect end to a perfect day," is ironic, since the day was anything but perfect. Sarcasm, which is especially bitter humor, is a form of irony.

Jargon is language peculiar to a profession or to a field of interest or study. Because most people are unfamiliar with such specialized, technical words, use jargon sparingly and include a brief definition unless the meaning is clear through the context of the passage.

Journal is a record of impressions and reactions. In its most general sense, a journal is an idea book, a private place for a writer to explore ideas and practice expressing them.

Key ideas in writing are those contained in the various topic sentences, as well any specific names, dates, amounts, and ideas emphasized by the writer through such cue words as *important, vital,* and *crucial.*

Linear order is the arrangement of steps of some activity or operation in the order that the steps occurred, happened, or must be performed.

Logical fallacies are common errors in reasoning that weaken your ability to sustain a point of view. Common logical fallacies include

- *argument ad hominem*
- bandwagon approach
- begging the question
- the red-herring fallacy
- either/or reasoning
- hasty generalization
- *non sequitur*
- oversimplification
- *post hoc, ergo prompter hoc*

Logos — see **Appeals.**

Metaphor — see **Figurative language.**

Misplaced modifier is an error in which a modifying word or phrase is not placed next to the word it actually modifies: "As a high school student, my grandfather taught me to drive." To correct this error, restate the sentence or move the modifier so that it is next to the word it modifies: "As a high school student, I learned to drive due to my grandfather."

Mixed method — see **Alternating method.**

Modes — see **Rhetorical Modes.**

Narration is a rhetorical mode through which the events constituting an experience are recalled. For the most part, the experience is presented in chronological order, although sometimes the sequence is purposely broken for effect through the use of a flashback.

Negation is a technique used in definition in which a subject is explained in terms of what it isn't rather than what it is.

Non sequitur, a Latin phrase meaning "it does not follow," is a logical fallacy that involves a conclusion that doesn't make sense in relation to the evidence used to reach it: "If more people took up swimming, heart attacks would be more common."

Objective description is writing that presents sensory details and experiences without any reaction or emotional response, as opposed to subjective description, which is writing that records the impact or impressions of such details and experiences.

Opinion — see **Fact.**

Order is the way you structure or arrange a writing. Depending on your needs, you may follow chronological order, linear order, spatial order, or emphatic order.

Organization — see **Order.**

Oversimplification is a logical fallacy that results when a writer incorrectly reduces a complex subject by ignoring or overlooking crucial information or factual inconsistencies: "That student developed cancer because his family lives near high tension lines." Other factors, including the health of others living in the same home, personal and family medical history, and so on, must also be considered.

Paragraph is a group of related sentences, set off by indentation, consisting of an idea presented in one sentence that is then supported or illustrated by the other sentences. In an essay, each paragraph serves in some way to support or illustrate the thesis.

Parallelism is the arrangement of related words, phrases, or clauses in a similar form, as the underlined sections in the following example show: "Peter enjoys writing <u>in the early morning,</u> <u>before supper,</u> or <u>after midnight.</u>"

Paraphrase is a rewording of a text or passage in different words to simplify or clarify it, as opposed to a summary, which is the trimming down of the original to its main points.

Passive voice — see **Active voice.**

Pathos — see **Appeals.**

Patterns of development — see **Rhetorical modes.**

Person refers to the point of view from which a writing is presented. First person means writer as speaker, featuring first-person pronouns such as *I, me,* and *mine.* Second person means the reader is directly addressed through the use of the imperative mood, featuring the second-person pronouns *you* and *your.* Third person means the writer as observer, featuring third-person pronouns such as *she, they, it, him,* and so on.

Personification — see **Figurative Language.**

Persuasion — see **Argument.**

Point of view — see **Person.**

Post hoc, ergo prompter hoc, a Latin term meaning "after this, therefore because of this," is a logical fallacy. With this error, one thing is mistakenly thought to have caused another simply because it came before the other: "The decision two months ago to change to a new math curriculum led to a decline in standardized test scores reported today." Chances are that conditions existing *before* the change in curriculum — perhaps the problems that originally led to the decision to change the way mathematics was taught — are responsible for the decline in scores.

Prewriting is the initial stage of writing, during which you focus on a subject and begin generating and developing ideas to support or illustrate that subject. Prewriting techniques include brainstorming, branching, clustering, and freewriting.

Process is a rhetorical mode that presents in linear order how to do something or how something was done or occurred.

There are three general types of process writing: sets of instructions, which detail how to do something; process analysis, which explains how something operates, occurs, develops, and so on; and process narrative, which explains how the writer completes something.

Process analysis is a type of process writing that involves explaining how a condition or activity occurred.

Process narrative refers to a type of process writing that involves explaining how some task or action was carried out.

Pronoun/antecedent agreement refers to the relationship in number, person, and gender between pronouns and the words they replace or refer to.

Proofreading is the final part of the editing step in the revising stage of writing. When you proofread, you concentrate on eliminating all awkwardness, ambiguity, faulty parallelism, and sentence errors (comma splices, fragments, run-on sentences), as well as mistakes in spelling, tense, and agreement.

Purpose in writing is the writer's aim or goal: to entertain, to inform, and to persuade. Many writings will fulfill more than one purpose, although one purpose will likely predominate.

Qualifying words are used to avoid making unsupportable statements with absolute terms. For instance, the qualifying term *rarely* should be used rather than *never, frequently* rather than *always, many* rather than *all,* and so forth.

Reader — see **Audience.**

Reader-centered material is writing that is expressed in terms that a reader will understand.

Reassessing is a step in the revising stage of writing. After allowing some time to pass, you reassess by objectively reexamining what you have written, noting what parts are effective and which aspects need additional attention or development. The feedback of another reader can be especially valuable during reassessing.

Red-herring fallacy is a logical fallacy in which the discussion is deliberately shifted from the main idea to some minor point in order to divert attention from the main idea: "Critics accuse the tobacco industry of using sleazy advertising techniques to attract young smokers, yet they make no complaint about the widespread use of sexual images to sell any number of products."

Redrafting is a step in the revising stage of writing during which you generate and develop new information to address the remaining problem spots identified during reassessing.

Relevancy is the condition of being related to the matter at hand. In writing, relevant details and examples are those that are directly related to the main idea.

Revising is the stage of writing during which you reexamine and improve the writing developed in the prewriting and composing stages. Revising involves three steps: reassessing, redrafting, and editing.

Rhetorical modes are the following patterns, techniques, or strategies of development, all with their own characteristics, that you use to fulfill the aim of your writing: cause and effect, comparison and contrast, description, definition, division and classification, example, narration, and process.

Rhetorical question is a question to which no answer is expected or required because the answer is obvious or implied in the question itself. Such a question is designed to begin or stimulate discussion.

Run-on sentence is a serious sentence error in which two sentences are run together rather than being properly connected by a conjunction or a semicolon or properly separated by a period or other appropriate mark of end punctuation. To correct a run-on sentence, either (1) insert a period or other appropriate mark of end punctuation between the two sentences, (2) insert a semicolon between the two sentences, or (3) insert a comma and a conjunction.

Sarcasm — see **Irony**.

Satire is writing that pokes fun at a subject in order to make a more serious point.

Second person — see **Person.**

Sensory details are those words, phrases, and passages that are drawn from hearing, sight, smell, taste, and touch.

Sentence fragment is a serious sentence error that occurs when you set a portion of a sentence off as a complete sentence. To eliminate a fragment, you must either (1) add to the incorrect section to make it a complete sentence or (2) add the fragment to a related sentence.

Set of instructions — see **Process.**

Sexist language is terminology that inappropriately designates gender and should be avoided. Words such as *foreman, salesman,* and *mailman* are examples of sexist language because the terms themselves imply that managing a department or operation, making sales, or delivering the mail are jobs intended for a man. Contrast these terms with these nonsexist versions, words that mean the same thing but that don't designate sex: *supervisor, sales representative,* and *mail carrier.* In addition, the masculine pronouns *he, him,* and *his* should no longer be used to mean both males and females, as in the sentence, "Every student should bring his book to class." Instead, use both masculine and feminine pronouns: "Every student should bring his or her book to class." Or, better still, change the words to plural forms: "All students should bring their books to class."

Simile — see **Figurative language.**

Slang refers to words and expressions that tend to be short-lived and are not widely understood outside the group that uses them. For these reasons, you should avoid using slang except when you are quoting someone directly or when you are attempting to create some effect. (See also **Diction.**)

Spatial order is the arrangement of a discussion on the basis of where the elements are in relation to each other: for instance, the contents of a room from left to right, from front to back, or from top to bottom. (See also **Order.**)

Specific language refers to words, phrases, details, and examples that designate particular, definite, or precise individuals, locales, and items (for instance, Eric Clapton, Disney World, Levi's Dockers) versus general language — words, phrases, details, and examples that note broad, common, or universal persons, places, and things (for instance, a rock guitarist, a vacation resort, a pair of pants). In writing, the more specific the language is, then the greater the chance that the reader will understand the point the writer is making.

Squinting modifier is an error in which it is unclear whether a modifying word or phrase describes something before it or after it: "Evonne hadn't realized for two weeks her husband had been depressed." To correct this error, restate part of the sentence to eliminate any ambiguity: "Evonne hadn't realized her husband had been depressed for two weeks."

Structure — see **Order.**

Style is the way a writer presents, develops, and supports an idea. One's style is a unique combination of diction, tone, and voice.

Subjective description — see **Objective description.**

Subject/verb agreement refers to the relationship in number between subjects and verbs. Singular subjects call for present tense verbs ending in *-s* or *-es,* and plural subjects call for present tense verbs without the *-s* or *-es* endings.

Summary — see **Paraphrase.**

Synonym is a word that means the same or nearly the same as another word.

Tense refers to the form of a verb as it reflects time in the past, present, or future.

Thesis is the main idea of an essay expressed in sentence form. An effective thesis provides a clear direction for the reader and establishes the reader's expectations for the support, explanation, and illustration that follows in the rest of the paper.

Third person — see **Person.**

Tightening is part of the editing step in the revising stage of writing. When you tighten, you concentrate on eliminating all unnecessary use of the passive voice and all deadwood —

needless qualifiers and indirect expressions such as *due to the fact that* and *a large number,* which can easily be replaced by the more succinct words *because* and *many.*

Tone is the writer's attitude towards the subject and audience, as made evident through such elements as diction, level of formality, use of figurative language, and so on. The tone of a writing can range from serious to silly, from angry to sympathetic, from ironic to instructive.

Topic sentence is the main sentence in a paragraph.

Transition refers to elements that provide connection within a writing and thus maintain coherence. Common methods of transition include repeating key words (or their synonyms or appropriate pronouns), phrases, or ideas, and using common transitional expressions such as *also, for instance, however,* and *then.*

Understatement — see **Figurative language.**

Understood subject — see **Imperative mood.**

Unity is achieved when all the elements in a writing directly support, illustrate, or explain the thesis.

Voice is the writer's distinctive sound, impression, or sense of personality that comes across in a writing. (See also **Style** and **Tone.**)

Writer-centered material is writing that makes sense to the writer but that doesn't necessarily communicate fully to a reader.

Credits

Index of Authors and Titles